CALL
of the
DOLPHINS

Lana Miller

Rainbow Bridge Publishing
Portland, Oregon

Rainbow Bridge Publishing.
P.O. Box 19730-616
Portland, Oregon 97219
Phone:

First printing: October 1989
Second printing: April 1990

Cover art: Marie Neufeld
Cover design: Georgia Peterson
Editorial Assistance: Claud Sutcliffe
Final Editing: Steve Sinovic

Library of Congress Catalog Number 89-92125

Miller, Lana
    Call of the dolphins.

    Bibliography

    1. Metaphysics 2. Mysticism
    2. Evolution 4. Animal Behavior

ISBN 0-9623970-0-8

Overall distribution by:
Knoll Publishing
831 Washington St.
Ft. Wayne, Indiana 46802
Phone: 1-800-637-6053

For my daughters.
DAWN and LAURALEE
Who inspired me to liberate
the dolphin spirit inside
so I could be
free fluid and flowing.

"Three things we should do in our lives:
Have a child, plant a tree and write a book."

The Talmud

For information on

swimming with wild dolphins,

send S.A.S.E. to

Rainbow Bridge Publishing
P.O. Box 19730-616
Portland, Oregon 97219

Acknowledgements

A heartfelt thanks to all my teachers, living and dead, and to Ascended Masters St. Germain, Merlin, El Morya and the dolphin spirit guides who made their presence known to me. Special thanks to Claud and Bonnie Sutcliffe for their loving support and assistance and to all those who contributed by granting written permission to share their personal journeys, as well as those who acted as invisible mid-wives assisting with the birth of the book. Thank you as well to those people who read the book and provided feedback, to Marie Neufeld for the cover art, Steve Sinovic for final editing and Georgia Peterson for cover design.

The author acknowledges the following authors and publishers for permission to excerpt material: Excerpt(s) from THE POWER OF MYTH by Joseph Campbell and Bill Moyer, copyright (c) 1988 by Apostrophe S Productions, Inc. and Bill Moyers and Alfred Van der Marck Editions, Inc. for itself and the estate of Joseph Campbell. Used by permission of Doubleday, a division of Bantam, Doubleday, Dell Publishing Group, Inc. Excerpt from TALES OF THE NIGHT RAINBOW by Koko Willis and Pali Lee copyright 1984. Used by permission of Pali Lee, Night Rainbow Publishing. Excerpt from THE KUNDALINI EXPERIENCE by Lee Sannella, M.D. copyright 1987. Used by permission of Lee Sannella, M.D., Integral Publishing. Excerpt from ANO ANO, THE SEED by Kristin Zambucka copyright 1978. Permission granted by Kristin Zambucka, Mana Publishing. Excerpt from THE CETACEAN MYSTERY Sherie Stark copyright 1987. Used by permission of Sherie Stark, author and publisher of UFO magazine. Excerpt from from KAHUNA POWER by Timothy Beckley copyright 1987. Used by permission of Timothy Beckley.

And last, but not least—-Thank you Joe and Rosie, wherever you are.

Contents

Introduction

THE DOLPHINS BEGAN to call at Uxmal, a classic Mayan ruin in the center of the Yucatan Peninsula. I was too asleep to hear. For four years I'd been exploring and participating in numerous personal growth and metaphysical processes, searching for ways to break free of addictive behavior patterns. Innocently, I became a student of Egyptian Huna and The Mysteries (secret teachings of ancient adepts, masters and kahunas encoded in the Bible and other records that reveal our godlike powers). During a third-level training seminar I learned to embody the power of ancient deities and made an inner journey to connect with Saraswati, Goddess of Illumined Knowledge and Brahma, the Creator, in the Hindu tradition.

Being very grounded and pragmatic I sensed an opportunity to simplify the process of collecting research material for some writing projects I had planned and naively asked Saraswati and Brahma to enlighten every cell in my body. That same weekend I found myself impulsively signing up for a spiritual tour to visit the major Mayan ruins. I had no previous interest in either the Mayan culture or dolphins. Everything I knew about dolphins came from watching the Flipper TV series years earlier and Egyptian Huna and The Mysteries were still a mystery to me. I was intrigued by the guided visualizations and initiations but had yet to integrate any real knowledge or understanding of my experiences. Mystics, masters, ancient records, extra-terrestrials and other dimensions of reality were only concepts in my mind when I arrived in the Yucatan.

Three days into the tour I began to suffer from culture shock, confusion and exhaustion. It was in this state that I attended the Spanish version of the Light Show at Uxmal. While listening to the sounds of drumming and the Legend of Chac the Rain God, I slipped into an altered state and found myself fighting the urge to spend the night alone in the ruins.

I'd never spent a night alone outside anywhere in my entire life, let alone in spooky ruins or a foreign country whose language I couldn't speak. Years earlier, my tour guides, veterans of Third World travel, had camped in ruins overnight. They didn't consider my request unusual. And so it came to pass that I found myself trapped on the top of the information center, under a full moon, overlooking the temple of the Magi and the shadowy nunnery complex, home of the Mayan priestesses. I fearfully contemplated my predicament while two armed guards snored peacefully in the courtyard below, unaware of my presence.

That night the dolphins came to me, flashing images of themselves frolicking in the open ocean, while the huge black hulks of whales lurked in the background. I'd come to the Yucatan hoping to learn what it was I was supposed to do with the rest of my life. Jane, a close friend and co-worker had died of cancer a year earlier. I'd been in a state of limbo, hiding out ever since. Her death triggered issues around powerlessness and abandonment stemming from childhood. We had both experienced the death and loss of several parents and caretakers while young. I knew it was time for me to make myself known in the world again, but part of me was in resistance and didn't want to come out of hiding. I had to find a way to come to terms with the past, move beyond suffering and pain and to free the invisible inner child. At an early age she had adapted to my father's violent behavior by freezing in a corner of the room to protect herself. As an adult, that paralysis crippled me emotionally in times of crises and prevented me from becoming known as the kind of writer I wanted to be.

Earlier in the afternoon I'd found a page torn from a magazine that depicted the devastation of the Brazilian rain forest. Somehow, that night under the full moon, my mind linked cetaceans and rain forest together and concluded that I was to do something concerning the environment pertaining to dolphins and whales. At Uxmal, I crossed a threshold into another dimension of reality. The ancient, lingering energy of the ruins stirred something at the cellular level and I awakened to the call of the dolphins.

Several weeks after returning from the Yucatan I connected once more with Saraswati and Brahma and this time asked them to make me a storehouse for all the wisdom and knowledge in the Universe. I reasoned that if a *little* knowledge could take the struggle out of the writing process, *all* the knowledge in the Universe could only make it easy, graceful and effortless. Unwittingly, I opened myself to a raging torrent of information, experiences and adventures that led me on a merry chase from one end of the continent to the other, from the middle of Baja to the Canadian border and from the Virgin Islands to Hawaii and back. While camping atop Mt. Shasta I met a mystic who channeled St. Germain. A few days later, Merlin the Magician made his presence known to me as a Master Teacher from the Pleiades. While the dolphins acted as the lure, leading me from person to person and place to place with the hope of connecting with them in captivity and in the wild, St. Germain and Merlin acted as compelling forces of inner guidance. They led me to make an in-depth exploration of the mystery of the dolphins appearance in mass consciousness and to learn about the spiritual evolution of the planet.

In R. J. Stewart's "The Prophetic Vision of Merlin," I discovered that Merlin comes into awareness as an archetype at the end of a solar cycle to seed human consciousness with the wisdom and knowledge needed to begin a New Age or era. He symbolizes the dark goddess energy of the Earth. St. Germain is an Ascended Master who some people feel may be a reincarnation of Jesus Christ. According to the channeled works of Mark L. and Elizabeth Prophet, and others, he is known as a freedom fighter and commander of the lightbearers who has incarnated under many guises. He represents the masculine principle or the "father." It is his invisible helping hand that is said to be responsible for the designing of the plan for the New Age which was embedded in collective consciousness through the Shakespearean plays. St. Germain was a guiding force behind the Freemasons and the Rosicrucians during the 17th century. A majority of America's founding fathers were Freemasons, responsible for guaranteeing personal and religious freedom through the creation of the Constitution and Bill of Rights. St. Germain's vision was to reunite the 12 lost tribes of Israel, the sons and daughters of God from fallen Atlantis, in a land where people could exercise free will and return to the spiritual path.

As we ride the cusp between Pisces and Aquarius, civilized humanity finds itself threatened with extinction, just as Atlantis and the Mayans once were. Pollution, AIDS, overpopulation, war, famine, addictions of every sort and nuclear disaster pose major threats to our survival as a species. We are today facing the choice of changing our behavior and raising our level of consciousness or enduring planetary disaster. Which path will we choose—materialism or spiritualism? This is the critical and as yet undecided question confronting the masses.

Merlin and St. Germain, appearing simultaneously as archetypes, indicates we are being given an opportunity to integrate the masculine and feminine principles, to marry the light and dark forces in the human psyche and bring ourselves and the world into balance. Merlin represents, as well, the path of the intellect—one who gains wisdom through the mind but fails to apply it to his/her actions in the world. St. Germain represents the path of the heart—where wisdom and knowledge are tempered by compassion and integrated and acted upon in daily life.

It was the dolphins and whales and their accelerating appearance in human awareness, however, that intrigued me and led me to explore the role they are playing in personal and planetary evolution. I sold and gave away nearly everything I owned to pursue the mystery. It has been a journey into the unknown, filled with surprising twists and uncanny encounters—a spontaneous and still unfolding story of people who are in the process or who have already answered The Call Of The Dolphins.

1 *Dolphins in the Desert*

THE LEAST LIKELY place I would expect to connect with dolphins is in the desert. Yet dolphins were the first thing I heard about when I arrived in Sedona, Arizona on a spiritual odyssey the winter following my journey to the Yucatan. For nine months after my return, dolphins danced around the fringes of my mind. I thought I might connect with them along the coast of California during my drive south in Freedom, my motor home. Some compelling inner voice, however, urged me to bypass the coastline and head directly to Sedona.

Sedona is the metaphysical melting pot of the country, a mecca for seekers and initiates of the New Age. The city spreads out like the tentacles of an octopus along the bottom of Oak Creek Canyon, embracing the sculptured red rock formations that surround the valley like sentinels guarding the most sacred of sites. These are no ordinary rock formations. They are temples of transformation and change…mystical cathedrals of the soul that trigger remembrances of lost civilizations and forgotten realms of existence.

Many of the pilgrims who travel to Sedona are devout disciples of Ramtha and Mafu or whoever the new channel on the block happens to be. Others unknowingly stray in from the highway and get trapped in the energy field. Some are guided to Sedona by an amorphous urge they can't explain and don't understand. Amidst the highly charged vibration field of Sedona, earthly goals of wealth and status are replaced by desires for higher consciousness. Sedona is a leaping off place, a place of endings and beginnings where people come to graduate and embark on the path of higher truth. Here they awaken to their true selves, to the spirit within…to the one true essence.

The people I met were in the process of letting go…of materialistic life-styles, careers, families, friends…as well as most of their possessions. They were living on IRA money, savings, inheritances and nest eggs of one sort or another. Most weren't sure why they were there. They only knew they'd been called…many said "by the dolphins."

In Sedona, one of the primary lessons is about learning to trust in the unknown…learning to trust that when you are a seeker of truth and enlight-enment in quest of the Holy Grail, all your needs are taken care of. That is, as long as you practice the universal laws of manifestation and listen to the voice of inner guidance or higher self or whoever that nagging voice inside your head belongs to. A rather sizable colony of elitist, yet transient New Agers, call Sedona home.

I had only a vague sense of why I was going there or what I would encounter. All I knew was that I'd drawn the card of the Initiate in a Tarot reading at Palenque, another of the Mayan ruins, and the word kept pop-ping up again and again in the months that followed.

The day before I left home I learned that Jackie, a woman I knew, had moved to Sedona several months earlier. I got her phone number from a mutual friend and when I arrived in town two days before Thanksgiving, I called her hoping she'd invite me to dinner. I was told, "She's on her way home from the Dolphins-in-the-Desert open house at Carefree."

"The what?" I said, not believing I'd heard what I heard. The voice on the other end repeated itself.

"I'll call her in the morning" I replied. I'd been warned about Sedona.

The next several minutes were equally disorienting. I walked into The New Age Aquarian bookstore next door to the phone booth and there, laid out boldly on the desk where I couldn't miss seeing it, was a flier advertising an evening of channeling with Merlin the Magician by a woman who lived in Sedona. It seemed obvious to me they were awaiting my arrival in town to launch their premiere performance.

When I saw the flier I said to myself, Okay, Merlin, you got me here, now what?

Lying on the same desk was a copy of a small booklet entitled "The Sedona Vortex Experience" by Gayle Johansen. It was a self-help guide on how to handle the overpowering energy of the vortexes around Sedona and how to be a vortex (vortex being a Latin word which means to turn or whirl.) Around Sedona being a vortex is like standing in a giant psychic wind tun-nel. The energy passes through you rather than around you. You sense it rather than feel it directly. When you're unconscious about its effects, it can turn you into a whirling dervish inside, totally disorienting you while it shifts you into other levels of reality. Long-forgotten memories suddenly awaken, people burst into tears, hug the rocks and kiss the ground as if they have returned home after a long, long journey, according to Gayle.

A thought passed casually through my mind that it might be interesting to meet her, and then it was gone. Sedona is synonymous with synchronicity. Instant manifestation of one's thoughts and desires is commonplace. The next morning when I walked into The Eye-Of-The-Vortex bookstore, Gayle Johansen just happened to be volunteering her half day a week behind the counter. Before I could ask her about her book, however, Vic, the bookstore manager and closet healer, clasped the wrist of my right arm and began reading my palm. The lines told him, "You are a powerful teacher, healer and communicator." I nodded agreeably, having been told the same message at least a dozen times before by an assortment of seers. It was a destiny I'd been resisting. The frozen child in me stubbornly refused to become visible in the world and continually sabotaged my own and other people's efforts to lure it out of hiding.

Later that day I reached Jackie on the phone and she invited me not only for Thanksgiving dinner, but for as long as I wanted to stay. She and her housemates had created an informal metaphysical retreat center out of their beautiful rented house overlooking the stunning red rock canyons and the Sierra pine-covered hills. They welcomed a steady influx of people from all over the country and world.

Over dinner that night, Jackie told me about the Dolphins-In-The-Desert project, the vision of a woman named Mary Caroline who said she cured her multiple sclerosis, cancer and heart disease using alternative methods of healing and then committed her life to promoting them. Mary Caroline's plan is to create a rejuvenation and birthing center where women can give birth to their babies underwater with dolphins present. As Jackie talked, I could feel chills running up and down my spine, a sure sign that some kind of psychic connection or cellular memory had been triggered.

Since I was already involved in a rejuvenation center of sorts and felt my assignment there was nearly complete, my first thought was that I was sent to the desert to become involved in this project. Despite my impulsiveness at Uxmal, I'm usually thought of as being very grounded and earthbound. But, as I thought more about the Dolphins-In-The-Desert project over the next day or so, it seemed too far out and weird for me. I gave up the idea of becoming involved.

On a sunny afternoon several days after my arrival I climbed close to the top of Bell Rock, one of the more notorious of the vortex sites where many people claim to have made contact with extraterrestrials. When I sat down to rest and looked out across the canyons to the rimrocks in the north,

I began to see hazy images darting around. There, swimming in the ethers were dozens of dolphins and whales. I rubbed my eyes to see if they'd disappear. Instead they became more vivid.

Sitting on Bell Rock watching them swim and frolic about, the idea of dolphins in the desert seemed suddenly credible. Persistently the dolphin and whale spirits made their presence known to me. "Well", I sputtered to myself, "this must have been the bottom of the ocean at one time and the energy is still here." I sat on the warm red sandstone rock for a long time that afternoon contemplating what I'd seen and felt.

The only other time in my life that I'd seen energy like this was out on the ocean during a sailboat trip. It was Memorial Day weekend and the seasick captain of our vessel had just told me that his son had been killed in a traffic accident three years earlier while they were taking the boat up north. At that moment my daughters were headed north in my car to drop it off for me. I began to feel anxious. The last thing I needed was someone else close to me dying.

"Dear God," I begged, "not my children." I'd reached my limit, coped with more than my share of death and loss, learned all the lessons I was willing to learn. I called forth guidance and protection for them.

What happened after that I can't explain. The yacht was surfing on the crest of the waves, nudged north by a following wind. The sound of the waves had a peaceful, calming effect on me as I sat at the helm. I looked up to see two luminescent shapes, one larger than the other, floating in the ethers ahead of the foredeck. Between the struts themselves appeared a pale, rainbow-hued membrane shimmering in the late afternoon sunlight. I turned my head to the side, looked all around behind me, thinking something was going on with my eyesight. I couldn't see the luminescent shapes anywhere but in front of the sailboat. Finally, I concluded the mysterious translucent spheres were letting me know that I'd been heard. Some form of ethereal essence had appeared in response to my call of distress. I wonder now if they weren't dolphin spirits. Legends abound about dolphins making their presence known to humans in distress on the open ocean. And we were in distress. Both the captain and his first mate were suffering from severe seasickness and hypothermia.

A few days after my experience with dolphins in the ethers on Bell Rock, I drove to the Grand Canyon with a friend. We took a hike with one of the park rangers and as he turned and looked out over the expanse of canyon before us, he swept his arm over the view and said, "By the way, this used to be the home of the dolphins and whales." The proof that the Southwest was once ocean had been established in archaeological findings. Maybe dolphins-in-the-desert isn't crazy after all, I thought.

Back in Sedona, I dropped in to see Vic at The Eye-Of-The-Vortex. We chatted briefly and as I turned to leave, I saw, tacked to the doorjamb, a flier advertising a dolphin seminar due to happen in two weeks. Again it was placed in a spot that I couldn't help but notice. I planned to drive to Santa Fe and spend time exploring there. Attending the dolphin seminar required a shift. By this time there was no doubt in my mind that I'd been sent to Sedona and the Southwest to connect with dolphin energy. The question now was, why?

DOLPHIN PEOPLE IN THE DESERT

I'd been hearing about the MacCarthys and Joan Ocean and Jean Luc Bozzoli from Jackie. The MacCarthys lived just up the street from her in Sedona. She'd been telling me, "You've got to meet them." The opportunity came through the dolphin seminar the four of them co-facilitated. Twenty-four people showed up the first evening of the workshop. We got to know each other by sharing stories of our connection to the dolphin energy.

Joan was working as a psychologist in the field of women's issues and child abuse when a friend introduced her to Jean Luc, an artist. He was on his way to British Columbia to participate with a small group of people engaged in a research project that involved communicating musically with Orca whales, the largest species of dolphin. One of the regular participants dropped out at the last minute and Jean Luc invited Joan to join them.

Says Joan: "We kayaked for eight hours in a cold wet mist to arrive at the island and did not see any whales." She stood shivering on the beach wondering what she was doing there when, "Suddenly, I noticed an unusual movement in the distant waters." She watched in amazement as the great mammoth hulk of a gray whale moved through the water toward her. "It rolled once and then stopped at an odd angle—an angle that left one of its gentle moist eyes gazing intently at me. I stared back, and in that moment a great flood of well-being and acceptance swept over me. I was suddenly filled with a love so strong and so deep that I felt my body would disintegrate from an inability to contain it." Joan added, "What I was experiencing was the love for humanity and all living things that is the energy field of the whale." That trip formed the foundation of a collaboration between Jean Luc and Joan.

Jean Luc was a free spirit who'd been living in the South Seas and Australia on the beach and in a Chinese junk he was restoring. One morning before sunrise as he was working on the boat, a dolphin visited him. The same dolphin returned morning after morning for 10 days. Shortly after those visits Jean Luc began to paint and is now known around the world as a mystical artist. His images are a blend of matter and spirit; a lush tropical beach dotted with palm trees and dolphins swimming in the ethers, an undersea temple with dolphins swimming around a spaceship, an embryonic human, circled by speckled pink dolphins.

Joan and Jean Luc share the essence of their experiences together through a multi-media presentation that integrates high-technology and the world of spirit. It has gained them acceptance and renown around the world. While Jean Luc focuses on artistic expression, Joan expresses herself through the channeling that comes to her from dolphin and whale spirits.

"After the planners of a tourist center on the Great Barrier Reef in Australia saw Jean Luc's artwork, he was asked to design the building," said Joan. "Oceania is to be a temple of transformation featuring a crystal-topped central pyramid, three submerged domes and an underwater walkway in which people can observe the life on the reef, dolphins and other sea life in their natural environment."

Joan and Jean Luc came to the desert, to Carefree, to spend the winter and take a rest from the lecture circuit. When they connected with the Mac-Carthys the four of them gave birth to a joint seminar. Alon and Lydia Mac-Carthy's romance began when they were both led to Sedona by the dolphins. Lydia had been working as a volunteer at Dolphins Research Center in the Florida Keys as an interspecies behaviorist for nearly two years when the dolphins made it apparent to her it was time to leave. "I loved my job," she said, "and didn't want to go." When she resisted their telepathic messages to her, they tried another approach and made such shrill sounds in the water when she entered the tank to be with them that she had to get out. Her ears hurt too much. Finally she relented, packed up her belongings and headed for Sedona.

Alon, an industrialist from Connecticut, had been involved in Transcendental Meditation for many years. He was given an image of dolphins during a meditation and told to find Sedona. He sold his business and admits, "I didn't even know where Sedona was. I just climbed in my car one morning and headed out." Some weeks later he found himself in Sedona, climbing Courthouse Rock. As fate would have it, he encountered Lydia and said to her, "I think I was a dolphin in a past life." The two of them fell in love and got married and are now part of the dolphin seminar circuit.

As the other participants began to share their stories I grew curious about how they'd been drawn to the desert. At the tea break later, I asked many of them privately, "What attracted   you to Sedona? Without hesitation they replied, "The dolphins called me."

One woman felt our affinity with dolphins stemmed from being seeded on the planet at the same time. Another told a mythical tale about our evolution from humans into dolphins. Both Joan and Lydia shared some channeling that had come through them from the dolphins. Joan's contact began in 1984, the same year she made a visit to the pyramids in Egypt. What came through Joan was a direct message for all humanity about the evolutionary changes now occurring and what role the dolphins and whales play in it.

MESSAGE TO HUMANITY

Joan was told:

"As you experience the changes on your planet, call on us for explanations and understanding. We are aware of the order of the occurrences on your planet and we offer you the assurance that you are evolving into Beauty and Right Action. At this time your planet is experiencing vibrational changes that have never occurred in this intensity before. All who dwell on your planet are being affected. Be assured that these changes are ultimately Good and all is in proper Order. As you change, we are here to assist and guide you. We add our balancing energies to those being transmitted to the planet by other star systems. You can feel the joy in your heart as you acknowledge the Legions of the Stars who support you with their Love and healing Light now.

As dolphins and whales, we are physically available as reminders and catalysts for all you can Be and Are. Utilize our Light and our presence in your waters. Meet with us, talk of us, share the dolphin knowledge. Interact with us in every way you can. As you do, we are able to fill your open heart with our wisdom. This is your wisdom too. It is knowledge already within you. Contact with us evokes the memories of who you are, and allows humans to express the fullness of their nature. There are positive and negative fields being received by your planet now. We are the balancers. We are here to sustain and protect you. Use our example to remove encumbrances from your life. Swim free and simply in the oceans of your world. Use our information to remind you of the nature of your world...a planet of Love. Use our energy field to heal your mind and body. We only radiate to you as you call to us. Open yourself to our emissions.

We Bless you for your work, and strengthen you with the Loving vibrations of harmony."

UNDERSEA JOURNEY

Later the next day Lydia guided us on a visual journey that was given to her by the dolphins in 1987.

"And now we are going to take you home," she said, "to the stars. To the dolphins. Home to the sea, to Sedona, City of Light. Where our journey begins. Leave your bodies now and join us in the Temple of Attunement at the top of Courthouse Rock. You're standing alone in the center of a circular crystal floor, silently guiding the glow of the rising full moon to bathe the crystal-domed sanctuary with its powerful light. The Temple comes aglow with sparkling beams of moonlight. The moment is at hand. The chants begin to rise from below. The vibration also rises. You turn and begin your descent. Hundreds of stone steps spiral down the white mountain, from the temple to the sea below. Along the way triads of beings chant sacred tones in a language of antiquity. Listen! And Remember!

Finally your foot touches the sand and the silent sea caresses your toes in the moonlight. The chanting stops. The moment of anticipation. Are they coming? Suddenly the sea surges with power and song. The priests and soldiers of Sirius rise in unison from the sea. Hundreds and hundreds of stately dolphin sentinels merge into columns of embodied light. As one being they focus their sonic vibrations on one spot in the shallow water at your feet. The sea seems to ripple backward, a golden beam shoots down from the night sky and slowly a glowing blue sphere rises from the sea before you. It is about 10 feet in diameter and it pulses and glows in the surf.

Two huge sleek dolphins come forward to greet you. You are invited to enter the flashing blue womb. You enter, and instantly the orb guided by the two dolphins, sinks swiftly into the sea. You fly through the sea at hypersonic speed. You are traveling through a tunnel of sound waves created by the dolphins. You descend through layers of colors and sounds and you realize to your wonderment that the sea is formed from a spectrum of hues and vibrations that are more felt than seen.

You speed forward to the mouth of a huge grotto and stop. Your dolphins urge you to leave the orb. You do and find that the vibrations inside the sphere have ionized your blood and cells to an accelerated rate that allows you to function and breathe perfectly under the sea. Smiling with their large eyes, your guides direct your attention to a giant blue dolphin waiting for you. He is stunning in his beauty. It's not just his giant size, but his color. He is blue, aqua, sapphire, turquoise, and green. He flashes with blue color. His dorsal flukes and fins are ruffled and tinged in gold. Your two guide dolphins lift their flukes in salute and disappear. You grasp the golden dorsal offered by this huge blue dolphin and together you enter the grotto. You spiral down, down, down deeper into the center of the sea. Finally you're at the mouth of a cavern that glows with blue light. Inside you see an ancient temple, its frieze carved with archaic symbols. You don't quite remember how to read them, but some of the symbols look like whales. You sense friendly beings watching you from behind temple columns.

Anu, the Blue Dolphin, directs your gaze to the back of the room. From behind the pillar steps a glorious being. Her name is Alita and she is high priestess and guardian of this Temple of the Sea. She is humanoid in form from the waist up. Her hair is dark, her eyes green and filmy rainbow gills ruffle on her arms and back. On her head she wears a crown fashioned like a golden starfish with a grand red amber stone in its center.

From the waist down she has a soft green tail coiled in the proud stance of the Sea Horse. She tells you of her race, the webbed people, seeded into this planet with the dolphins from her home star system, Sirius. Their job is to lift and cleanse the vibration of the emerald star, Earth, from inside and under its sea. She tells you that the dolphins are some of the teachers from Venus. They shared their cosmic truths with the initiates of Lemuria, Atlantis and the Crystal Cities. These truths were given to them by great souls from Sirius who were inspired by Illumined beings from more advanced galaxies.

She turns now and you follow her to the inner sanctum, where a small altar glows with the light of two tiny golden pyramids. Their capstones flash with rays of pink light. These are your gifts from the sea, she says, to be used on the surface in your home, your City of Lights.

The pyramid placed in your left hand is coded with the secrets of the Sacred Science of Sonics. Use it to raise Earth's vibrations. The pyramid in your right hand is coded with the secrets of Joy. Use it to bring the true understanding of love to your planet.

Now the three of you, dolphin, mermaid, and human, starseeds all, merge your beings in a moment of golden harmony. You separate, she remains in her world and you return to yours, riding back with your blue brother. Up, up, around and around, spiraling through the colors and hues, the sounds of the sea, Anu brings you back to the mouth of the sea cave, where your two dolphin guides wait for you.

Now, between these two, one hand on each dorsal fin, you three become one as you spin and spin and spin and finally with a great twist of their powerful tails, you burst from the sea in a rainbow of bubbling froth and fly into the sky. Higher and higher, in a graceful arc, you fly, and become embodied joy and you KNOW it. Down now, back to the surf, back to the soft sands and gentle sea that laps at the foot of the mountain in the City of Light.

Thousands of dolphins wait in the soft glow of the fading moonlight as you slide from the backs of your friends. As you say farewell, one of them gives you yet another gift. A tool, a tiny sphere of blue light, to remind you of your blue sun, your star of origin. Take them now, your gifts from the sea and return to your own temple of sound, your precious body. Say goodbye to the dolphins, to Anu, to Alita, to the Crystal Temple of Attunement and Sound. Slowly, slowly, slowly feel your body…"

Several people that day said they'd had earlier visions of a mermaid like Alita. Many came to the seminar curious to know more about dolphins and to understand why they had been appearing in their dreams and visions in recent months. One man connected with dolphins while out at sea on a Navy patrol boat and felt a great kinship with them. Each person seemed to hold some key to a mystery that was unfolding in our midst.

I sensed we were being drawn together for a purpose. What that purpose was I had not a clue, although it seemed that it had to do with telepathic communication with extraterrestrials and our own evolution. I felt ignorant and uninformed yet totally intrigued by the concept of dolphins acting as intermediaries with other dimensions and went home that night wondering if anything had been written about the connection between dolphins and extraterrestrials.

CETACEAN HISTORY

The next morning when I arrived at the seminar I walked to the literature table. The first item that attracted my attention was an article from UFO magazine written by Sherie Stark. Sherie had interviewed Toni Lilly, wife of John Lilly, before her death a few years earlier. Toni, after years of work with dolphins, felt that they were meant to teach us more about ourselves, and give us a different view of our culture than we might have otherwise. She felt dolphins provided a "training ground" for humans to develop compassion for alien intelligences that would open a door in our minds and hearts and enable us to communicate with these beings in the future.

Sherie had also talked with Aldo Aulicino, a researcher in charge of an international multidisciplinary project called Kyklos. Aulicino explained that dolphins have had the same brain for 65 million years...cetaceans have what he refers to as "communal, cumulative, collective consciousness." This giant communal brain enables them to communicate telepathically around the world.

Under laboratory test conditions, Aulicino related, "A mated pair of dolphins were split, with one in Miami and one in New Zealand and the one in Miami was put into an artificial distress mode. The mate in New Zealand would go bananas at that split second and want to jump out of the aquarium to go and help his mate."

As another example, he explained that when whales find a wealth of food, other whales from 500 miles around make an instant U-turn to join them. "Nothing short of satellite radio transmissions works that fast," he says.

According to Aulicino, cetaceans are the most intelligent creatures on Earth. He believes their intelligence factor exceeds that of humans by at least 100 to 1. Kyklos anthropological studies have revealed that cetaceans descended from "Protoceti," an animal that resembled a short squat horse and had hands with opposable thumbs with which to grasp objects. Nearly 65 million years ago they built a technologically advanced civilization in the northern hemisphere. The civilization was wiped out by an environmental catastrophe. According to Aulicino "Some went into the water to survive and became the first true marine mammals 50 million years ago."

Because they no longer had a need to construct or build, they had no need to pass on information. Their communal consciousness became their memory. Aulicino believes they developed in other ways. "Cetacean communication is a communication of overwhelming feeling of experience."

Kyklos researchers uncovered historical data that leads them to believe that cetaceans influenced humans in progressing toward civilization and knowledge. Going back to the legends of Babylonia, Mesopotamia and Sumeria, the Kyklos project uncovered tales relating the idea that "civilization was given to man by whales."

Root words from ancient languages support this idea. A word that branched off from the Aryan language for instance means both wheel and whale. Whales taught us about the cyclical concept of existence. Kalpa, a Hindu offshoot of the same word, means recurring cycle.

What Aulicino feels is most important is not the technical, analytical knowledge we might learn from them, but their holistic communication of feeling, emotion and understanding. Dolphins demonstrate a propensity for picking up feelings of distress not only among their own kind but among all species of life.

Sherie also talked with Neville Rowe, a channel for a group of six dolphins. Known as Kajuba, the dolphins who speak through him say they communicate with incorporeal entities from other planets. Kajuba says that dolphins are far more able to communicate with off-planet consciousnesses than humans. They act as a relay station between humans and other dimensions.

According to Kajuba, there are other beings who would like to destroy planet Earth because they fear us. If we were to destroy the Earth through a nuclear disaster it would affect all aspects of the space/time continuum. To protect the planet, friendly entities from the Pleiades, Sirius and Arcturus have wrapped us in a "blanket of invisibility."

Some of those entities are now on Earth among us as visible and invisible beings. Because we humans have a difficult time believing in anything that we can't see, the entities have created metal spacecraft to prove their existence to us, though they do not need to travel in that way. To further protect us, only limited contact is being made with humans. Kajuba tells us that as we develop higher consciousness, connections with entities or energies from other planets will become more common.

During the course of the weekend seminar in Sedona, Jean Luc shared the images of his artwork in a slide presentation. One appeared to me to be a giant brain of sorts with dolphins swimming in and around the skeletal structure. Considering Aulicino's theory on the collective consciousness of the dolphin and whale being one large entity, it's possible that the dolphins' way of communicating this to Jean Luc was through the image he was given to paint.

At the end of the seminar I told Joan Ocean, "I think I'm supposed to write a book entitled "The Call of the Dolphins."

"That's interesting," she told me, "I just received a letter from a woman in Hollywood who said she was writing a screenplay by the same title."

Laurie Clark was her name. I got her phone number a few days later and called her. I told her I was writing a book entitled "The Call Of The Dolphins." Her first reaction was, "We have a problem." I assured her it wasn't time to worry over the shared title.

My first question was, "What's your screenplay about?"

She said, "It's about a Pleiadian who comes to Earth as a man and connects with a young girl under unusual circumstances and teaches her about the spiritual evolution of the planet through the dolphins."

"What's your book about?" she asked in return.

"It's a non-fiction version of your play or something very similar," I told her and added, "It seems like the dolphins want to teach us how to communicate with extraterrestrials." We agreed to meet on my trip north. Laurie was blown away to think we were both being given the message to write about the call of the dolphins at the same time. Our conversation convinced me that there was definitely something going on around dolphins and that I was hot on the pursuit of some great cosmic mystery.

2 *Oceans in the Desert*

A FEW DAYS after the seminar ended Jean Luc flew off to France to spend Christmas with his parents. Joan stayed in the house outside Carefree. She planned to spend her time answering fan mail that had been piling up for several months and to have some quiet space alone. The letters were from people all over the world who were curious about what was going on with the dolphins and what their psychic connections with them were about. After the seminar, I was ready to leave Sedona and cold weather behind and seek some warm air and sunshine. Joan told me I'd be welcome to park at her place near Carefree for a while. I arrived a few days later. We took long walks in the desert almost every afternoon and discovered we shared a great many commonalities. Both of us were Librans, born a year apart. "As a child", Joan told me, "I spent long hours alone playing amongst the roots of giant trees dreaming my own vision."

I remembered escaping from our family dramas by hiding out in the tall rye grass behind the ice house on my grandparents' farm. I watched piles of cumulus clouds tumbling across the sky and dreamt that one day the world would be a better place to live. We shared a strong connection to the Earth and to nature and understood the importance of being caretakers of the planet. Both Joan and I had forsaken the Great American Dream, gotten divorced and left our children in the well-qualified care of their fathers in search of a different way of life. Curious, I asked her, "Did you ever wonder why you couldn't just lead a normal life and be happy?"

"Oh, yeah!" she replied, "Years ago I used to ask myself, but you can't ever go back. I wouldn't want to, if I could."

I remembered saying that same thing to my best friend a year before I got divorced. I had started down the path of awareness and there was no way to turn around and go back.

Joan volunteered, "I had an out-of-body experience in a group I was attending and it totally changed my life. My spirit left my body and I remember being out there in the Universe swept on the wind, feeling so free, so much apart of the birds and trees and flowers, like all the weight of my physical body had been taken off me."

She paused briefly. "It was such total freedom that I didn't want to come back. I could hear people calling, 'Come on back now Joan, we're going to break for lunch.' They were really concerned for me. I knew I had the choice to stay out there or return. Eventually I choose to come back and the experience changed my whole life. My husband and I were very much in love and my leaving was very painful for him. But I knew I had to."

I admired her for doing what was best for herself, but wondered where she found the strength to leave someone who loved her so much. I stayed too long out of compassion and killed the love that was there before I could leave. Joan answered my thoughts. "I had enough strength and love after that experience that no matter what happened I knew I would choose to be free. I knew though that I had to make my leaving as gentle as possible."

So here we were out in the world, alone in the desert the day before Christmas having embraced our inner dragons, ready to face whatever the future held. The dolphins had brought us together. We felt certain our paths would cross more than once. Above all we shared a common destiny…a common connection to Atlantis and to Egypt, though neither of us could explain or remember it.

One afternoon as we came to a crossroads in the desert and were undecided about which path to take, we simultaneously looked toward the huge pile of sand-colored boulders to the east. They formed a gateway at the entrance to Carefree. Intrigued, we decided to climb them. For nearly a half hour we climbed up and around them awkwardly, only to find the path blocked. We had to descend before we could go up. Soon we were leaping and hopping up the rocks like a pair of fearless mountain goats, ascending rapidly toward the peak. From a distance, the boulders seemed smooth like sandstone. Up close they were coarse and brittle, almost like coral.

When we reached the top we discovered, to our surprise, a bench and a lighted landscaped path. It led easily to the golf resort below. We laughed and realized that we loved the adventure of climbing the uncharted path and the mystery of not knowing what was ahead. Our experience that afternoon was a fitting metaphor for our personal lives. We had forsaken our comfortable materialistic lifestyles in favor of the spiritual quest. We took the easy way down, pondering the hugeness of the boulders and the casual way they were piled on top of one another, some in precarious positions.

"Maybe Goliath was here," I joked. What seemed more probable, however, was that they had slid around and tumbled into their present formation during a polar shift.

As we walked out the gate of the resort, I asked, "Wouldn't it be amazing if there was an ocean just over the rise?"

"It feels so much like being at the ocean here," Joan agreed. The smell of the sea was in the air, in the ethers just like the images of the dolphins and whales.

The desert was full of metaphors. On another afternoon walk, we followed a wash for a long way, then headed back into the sagebrush and cactus. The desert floor was coming alive, watered by a recent winter storm. Beneath each bush was a cushion of green-velvet grass. It surprised me to see it growing there. I didn't know the desert was so fertile. All it took was a smidgen of water for the life force trapped in the grass seeds to come to life. All it took for people to come to life, to begin growing, were a few teardrops, a release of pent-up feelings…like the life force released when a seed sprouts.

Water and emotions are synonymous I'd discovered on my first night out on the open ocean. Listening to the rhythm of the waves as the following seas nudged the boat north, watching the phosphorescence wink at me from the depths of the dark swirling sea, sensing the undercurrents of the tides changing, the sense of being cradled and soothed by the movement of the water…I felt so at one with it and so peaceful and safe that the ensuing drama of the captain and his wife no longer made a difference.

I felt that same oneness and peacefulness in the desert. It didn't matter what drama might be unfolding in the world. It didn't matter that in Sedona and in metaphysical circles everywhere I'd been in recent months, all people were talking about were polar shifts, war in the heavens, prophecies of doom and darkness, California dropping off into the ocean, the economy collapsing, food shortages, drought, AIDS epidemics and on and on. They were saying we'd go through a period of intense darkness and death and panic before we entered the Age of Aguarius…the Golden Age of Enlightenment.

None of it mattered. I'd made a decision to be content, to have my life be easy and graceful even in the midst of chaos. I felt I'd made my peace with my shadow side…with the dark forces in the world. All I had to do now was keep reminding myself and them that I chose the light and they'd disappear. No more dark nights of the soul for me. Faithfully, I wore a dragon necklace I'd been guided to buy at Mt. Shasta for protection, from what I wasn't sure.

Seeing all the holes in the desert floor created by prairie dogs, rabbits, snakes and insects, I said to Joan, "There's a lot of life teeming beneath the surface." They reminded me that we can't always see the whole of our reality. If we never peer into the dark recesses of the Earth, of our minds...if we base our beliefs, decisions and actions only on what we can see on the surface...we miss much of the depth and beauty of nature, of life, of people, and the events around us. I hadn't expanded my vision to include the whole of the Universe yet.

A little later, Joan said to me, "It's time for people to start putting their spirituality to work. There are enough of us awake now who could create peace. We just have to get down to work rather than talking about what it was like in Atlantis and Lemuria and going back and exploring past lives. We've done enough of that."

I reminded her gently that some of us are very new at this metaphysical stuff and it takes a certain amount of time to sift through it all, decide what we are going to keep or throw away before we can create our reality the way we want it.

"Give us another three to five years," I urged.

"Let's hope it happens before that, the energy is moving so fast now," she said.

I agreed it could happen a lot quicker.

"So many people are writing now, such beautiful letters, asking us how they can work with the dolphins, willing to volunteer their time and not get paid if they can just play with them and be around them," Joan told me. "Lloyd Borguss at Dolphins Plus has people coming there all the time wanting to volunteer to work and the first thing he asks them is 'What do you want to do?' 'Work with the dolphins' they say. 'I have more than enough people to work with the dolphins,' he tells them. 'I need people who want to do paperwork, take care of business, give talks, take care of details,'" Joan added.

It sounded to me like the people who write Joan and Jean Luc and show up at Lloyd's doorstep want to learn to be more like the dolphins and less like us humans. I certainly couldn't argue with that. Leaping around in the water, soaring through the air, playing with one another and being sensual sounded like a lot more fun than doing paperwork and giving talks.

As far as I was concerned, we needed more visionaries like Mary Caroline who are willing to stick their necks out and risk their lives and reputations to create places where more of us could connect with dolphins. Bringing them to tanks in the desert may not be the way to go, yet I didn't have a better location in mind, given the amount of dolphin and ocean energy there seems to be around Carefree.

Joan disagreed. Her opinion is that, "It's time for human beings to stop shaping the beauty of the world into their limited reality, and time for them to start listening to the wisdom of nature and the other animals."

A strong opposition force was brewing in Carefree, I told Joan. Earlier in the week, I walked into a small gift shop and was immediately smitten with the Peruvian harp music playing in the background. I asked the clerk about the tape, then felt inspired to ask her if she had any dolphins. She laughed and said, you should connect with the man over in the corner, he's looking for dolphins too." He wanted a dolphin gift for his secretary.

The next thing I knew we were talking about the dolphin project and the clerk asked with an incredulous tone to her voice, "You're in favor of it?"

"Why, of course." I hadn't taken the time to ponder another viewpoint, to even consider that some people might not be in favor of it.

"But the dolphins don't belong in the desert in a tank, they'll commit suicide," she insisted vehemently.

"The dolphins are already here in the ethers," I insisted "and they're calling people to join them."

"If God had wanted dolphins in the desert he would have put them here," she retorted adamantly.

"God did put them in the desert. Millions of years ago this part of the world was the bottom of the ocean. The dolphins are just returning home."

She interrupted me before I could say more. "Well, I know a lot of people here who are going to fight this project. We're not going to let it happen."

It came to me then, that maybe we were all in for one of those infamous dolphin lessons I'd been hearing about. Maybe the project will never materialize. It could be an issue that attracts lots of media attention, bringing into the public eye greater awareness of the dolphins' connection with healing and planetary evolution and maybe even alien intelligences.

I had to have the last word with the clerk and reminded her that, "The dolphins have been around for 65 million years and they are much more intelligent than we humans. If they don't want to be brought to the desert, they won't be here." I ended by saying, "The dolphins are here to serve."

Neither of us would budge from our opinions so we graciously extended season's greetings and parted on a friendly note.

Mary Caroline certainly has her work cut out for her, I thought. She might have to call upon some dolphin humor to assist her if she expected to win those Carefree hearts.

Joan and I laughed over the names of the streets of Carefree. There was plenty of dolphin humor around already. Someone had gleefully named them...Tranquility Way, Never Mind, Ho Hum, Languid, Easy Street.....

3 *Dolphin Mystery Deepens*

I LEFT CAREFREE to pursue dolphins in the flesh, hoping to communicate with them in person. The day I arrived in San Diego was a school holiday and the petting tank at Sea World was crowded with spectators attempting to entice the dolphins to them with dead fish. The dolphins ignored all but a few of the smaller children in favor of playing among themselves. Chasing tails, splashing onlookers and swimming inside out and upside-down, round and round the pool, they relieved their boredom. They were not leaping joyously about as we see them frolicking in the wild.

Occasionally a dolphin swam lazily to the edge of the pool, opened its rostrum and allowed a spectator to plop a limp fish into its mouth. The lifeless fish would lay in the dolphin's mouth for a few minutes before sliding into the water untouched. Attempting to communicate meaningfully with dolphins in this setting, I saw, was hopeless. My telepathic commands failed. I gave up and sent out a message from the heart, which simply said, "I love you." An instant later, a dolphin jumped out of the water in front of me and soaked me as it splashed down. Apparently it had gotten the message.

Spending time watching a dozen or more dolphins and small whales swimming frenetically round and round their tank, I began to understand the fevered opposition to the Dolphins-In-The-Desert project. Honoring my own desire for freedom, I felt the need to honor theirs as well.

Human and dolphin brains I was to learn later, from a booklet entitled "Dolphins" (published by the Marine Mammal Fund), are similar in size, but it appears that the foldings in the dolphin cortex are more highly developed. While humans must have light to see, dolphins use echo-location or sonar. They emit sounds which bounce off objects and reflect back telling them where objects are and what direction they are moving. Using sonar, dolphins are able to find food, communicate and maneuver through murky waters. With sonar, a dolphin is able to hear a single buckshot dropped into water 100 feet away and get an accurate range and bearing on it. So acutely developed is their sonar, that they can determine the difference between brass and aluminum or two kinds of fish equal in size.

Echo-location is performed through a series of sonar clicks sent out in two narrow beams focused by the dish-shaped frontal melon on the skull. The dolphin receives the returning signal on many parts of the head and gets a three-dimensional echo or aural picture of the object to determine size and shape. The second part of the click provides internal information about the characteristics of an object (i.e. pulse rate, heart beat, tissue condition, blockages, spinal alignment, pregnancy and even tumors). Dolphins have demonstrated their ability to determine whether a fish has been freshly killed or has been dead for one and a half days. Their sonar is effective up to a quarter of a mile and its beams are directed by the snout. When examining something, the dolphin's snout moves up and down and side to side in a circular fashion. Sonar works as well above water as below, enabling a dolphin to gently tug on a trainer's hair, or snatch a fish or small object from someone's hand without injury to them. While experiments have shown that dolphins are capable of understanding basic sentences and are sensitive to sentence structure and semantics, it is their ability to transmit holographic images telepathically that is most intriguing. I would learn much more about this in the months to come.

A few days after my visit to the dolphin tank, I picked up a friend at the airport and we headed south into Baja seeking a connection with dolphins and whales in the wild. During our 10-day pursuit we seemed always to be one flipper behind them. Whenever I asked someone about dolphins along the Sea of Cortez I'd hear 'Oh, yeah, they were just here yesterday.' I gave up and headed north again, determined to pursue the mystery of their appearance in human consciousness further.

By then I was beginning to wonder if I had been led into the Baja not to connect with dolphins and whales in person, but to experience firsthand, the devastation of the environment. Litter lined the highways from one end of Baja to the other and huge tracts of virgin desert had been demolished to make way for corporate farming that required the use of pesticides and herbicides which polluted both water and air. Suffering once more from culture shock, I was thankful when we crossed the border to return home.

After dropping my friend off at the airport, I drove to Hollywood to talk with Laurie Clark, the young woman who said she was writing a screenplay entitled "The Call Of The Dolphins." I poured out the story of meeting a mystic on Mt. Shasta who channeled St. Germain, encountering Merlin in my meditations and the dolphins in Sedona, as well as the extra-terrestrial tales I'd been hearing. She grew particularly intrigued when I started talking about initiation. In her meditations she'd been told to include an initiation in her screenplay and to use the symbolism of the dolphins. She was confused and didn't know anything about initiation rites or dolphin symbols. I told her what little I knew at the time and she thanked me for giving her information she felt was valuable in writing her screenplay.

ENVIRONMENTALIST ANSWERS CALL

From Southern California, I drifted slowly north to visit my friend Meredith, the woman who organized the first Healing Connection groups in Califor-nia. The minute I said dolphins, she said, "Oh, you've got to meet John. He's really tuned into them."

We met over breakfast the next day. John is a career environmentalist who'd been employed in state and city government for about 20 years. He'd been lured to California two years earlier by a job offer. About 14 months after his arrival dolphins and whales began to enter his dreams and medita-tions. "My first encounter with them was in a powerful and beautiful dream in April of 1987, two months after the birth of our child. A week or so later I decided I was going to quit my job and open myself up to the light...my light." He resigned his position to spend sometime in retreat, clearing his energy field so that he would be receptive to "new impulses that are coming in."

Soon after he journeyed to the Yucatan with his wife. "We spent three weeks visiting ancient ruins of the Mayan civilization. The Yucatan trip was inspired by the Edgar Cayce books in general and "Edgar Cayce on Atlantis," in particular." At Chichenitza, John said, "I nearly died. I got very sick. It felt like a cleansing with past life energies and karma."

When Meredith called and told him I'd like to meet him, he was eager. "Whenever anything comes in relating to dolphins, I listen," he told me, "sort of with a third ear. When this first started happening to me, a flood of channeling of Pleiadian and Sirius and dolphin information came through. I like to deal with big pictures, so I treated it like a mystery and tried to solve it." It seemed our minds operated on the same wavelength.

"I started connecting with people like Joan Ocean," he said, "and decided to coordinate a retreat for people connected to the dolphins and whales. I picked Halloween weekend."

When he said "Halloween," my third ear tuned in for more details. A psychic friend told him Halloween was the perfect date. "It's when the Earth and celestial energies are most aligned...the last time man communed openly with dolphins and other species was during the fall of Atlantis ...on Halloween."

Halloween and All Saints' Day held great symbolic significance in my own psychic death and rebirth process.

"I was raised a Catholic," he told me. "At first I thought 'This is crazy...weird.'"

He had a reading with a psychic on Palm Sunday, 1987 and she told him he'd had a loving, powerful encounter with Christ in a past life. His next reading with her occurred on All Saints' Day. He began to sense some connection and asked the woman what it was about. She told him, "What you are trying to do is marry the forces of darkness and light. It's like they both cease to exist and you transcend them...bring them into balance and they disappear...that's the symbology behind Halloween and All Saints' Day." We discovered over the course of several hours of talking that we were reading the same books, tuning into the same energies and the same people.

He'd become so involved with listening to the dolphins that he began to bring marine biologists and dolphin and whale channels together over Sunday brunch about once every other month. Several of these people had swam with dolphins in the Caribbean and reported being zapped by their sonar. One felt that the dolphins projected their essence out of their bodies into human bodies as a way of aligning us and making us more open.

"Whenever I go to the coast, the dolphins show up," John said. He was told by someone who channeled dolphin energy that he'd been present in the Yucatan in an earlier life when ancient records were stored and that he would be one of the people who would rediscover these archives or hall of records—which were stored in crystalline structures under the land and under the sea.

"You'll be led to them by the dolphins," he was assured.

The dolphin and whale channeling led him to believe that within the next three to five years he will be responsible for creating a foundation to protect the waters of the world. While his background as an environmentalist qualifies him for this role his left brain insists, "This is weird. How do you do stuff like this? Then I think, 'Oh, well, it will happen if it's meant to happen. Just listen and see what happens and watch if things start to lead you in that direction.'"

John told me he'd been into extraterrestrials since he was a kid. "I just knew there was life out there and I went on this crusade to tell other people." Finally he gave up. "I started having out-of-body experiences. I'd be flying through space, doing somersaults, thinking I can do anything. In my dreams, I'd see UFOs approaching while I was flipping around in space and I'd say, 'Oh, those are UFOs' and go on about my business."

He simply accepted that they existed and it no longer mattered whether other people believed in them.

John invited me to an upcoming Sunday brunch to meet more dolphin people. Part of me longed to stay but my more practical, grounded part insisted on heading home to take care of business.

PURSUING THE MYSTERY

I arrived home, in the northwest, in a rainstorm, and convinced myself it was time to find a warmer, sunnier, drier climate to move to. The only thing that sparked my interest in living the remainder of that rainy winter was exploring the mystery of the dolphins and our mystical connection to them. For the first few weeks after my return no one I talked with seemed to have any pieces to add to the puzzle. Then, at a Sunday gathering, I met Dana, a woman friend who did toning work and guided meditation classes. She told me she had first connected with dolphins in her visualizations while she lived in Santa Cruz. In her visions, she was shown that dolphins were once human beings who went to live underwater just before the Fall of Atlantis. They were given the option of remaining in human form or incarnating as dolphins. They chose dolphinhood. Their purpose was to hold the high vibratory rate of Atlantis until those of us who died in the Fall reincarnated and awakened to our lost identity. Is it possible the dolphins are calling us to recreate Atlantis, I wondered?

As Dana meandered away, I turned and nearly bumped into the director of the underwater birthing association. "What do you know about dolphins?" I asked him.

"Not much," he said pausing "but I just read an article by Timothy Wyllie on waterbirthing. I'll send it to you." Timothy wrote a book entitled "Dolphins, Extraterrestrials and Angels." On the phone later, the director and I talked about dolphins coming into people's consciousness and directing them. "I have a hard time believing dolphins can control our minds," he said.

HOMO DELPHINUS

I learned from the article that Timothy had attended the second International Homo Delphinus Conference in New Zealand, sponsored by the Rainbow Bridge Dolphin Center and its director, Estelle Myers. The purpose of the conference was to educate people about underwater birthing. A few weeks before the gathering the Maori heard about it and invited Estelle to hold the conference at their Marae, the tribal meeting hall and ceremonial center. It was a rare invitation. The Maori are very intrigued with the idea of underwater birthing with dolphins present.

What came out of the group consciousness after four days of sharing and meditating together was the possibility of an entirely new physical being evolving on the planet...a cross between humans and dolphins...a mutated species that can adapt to life both in the water and in air.

In 1980 in Florida, Timothy connected with a pod of three wild dolphins that communicated to him their desire to "see created on the planet a new physical form—a phylum that would include the finest features of several of the leading species." He feels dolphins are a race of skilled "bioacoustical surgeons" capable of using sound waves to engineer or alter DNA structures.

Later in the Bahamas, he was given the vision of an interspecies environment where artists, scientists and other people interested in non-verbal communication could co-habitate. He envisioned, as well, a center where couples could come and give birth to their babies underwater with dolphins present. Says Timothy, "And this was well before I'd heard of Igor Charkovsky and his work with dolphins in the Black Sea."

Charkovsky is considered to be the pioneer of waterbirthing with dolphins. Dr. Judyth Reichenberg-Ullman in Spiritual Women's Times wrote about Charkovsky's work with "Underwater Birthing." In 1962, struggling with the birth of his own premature daughter who was critically underweight and near death, Charkovsky kept her alive in a shallow tub of warm water. She began to thrive. Intrigued by the results he experimented with an assortment of land animals and found they became stronger and more intelligent than their non-swimming cousins. Their lifespans increased, as well. He found that the need for oxygen decreases by 60 to 70 percent in water births, creating extra energy for healing and development. Unlearning the fear of water, he believes, is the key to the mental and physical development of the human race. Charkovsky is credited with assisting in well over 400 water births to date. In 1979, he assisted in the first underwater birth with dolphins present. He found that newborns would peacefully sleep in the sea with dolphins swimming around them. On one occasion, the dolphins sensed that an infant needed air and shoved him aside to push the baby to the water's surface.

Ancient Greek, Egyptian and Mexican women, according to Sondra Ray, a former nurse and now leader in the rebirthing and waterbaby movements, gave birth to their babies in the sea. The water soothes and calms the nervous system, lowers the body temperature and slows the heart rate. According to Charkovsky, water also "drastically reduces blood loss."

The babies themselves thrive in a water environment after birth as well. Speaking about year-old waterbabies, Jacques Mayol, the French skin diver famous for diving to 100-meter depths without equipment, says "God, they're beating records. These kids will some day settle the ocean." They are pictures of radiant health, have stronger immune systems and rarely become ill. They sit up, speak and walk earlier than their counterparts. Swimming stimulates their nervous system, blood vessels and respiratory systems. By the age of four months, they are able to swim several kilometers and hold their breath two or three minutes underwater. Mayol's record is four minutes.

Mayol was present at the Maori conference when Timothy channeled information about the new physical being or phylum that might evolve: "This might come through the womb of a woman or it might come through the womb of a dolphin." When Jacques seemed shaken by what he was hearing Timothy added that he was not suggesting interbreeding between species, "Rather, that it might be an entity born to both species."

Cetaceans and humans share many similarities. If we were willing to make a few adaptations such as streamlining our bodies, telescoping our necks, shortening our arms, growing skin between our fingers, losing our hair and slicing our external ears off, we could pass for dolphins. In ancient times, whales had four legs and a pelvis. Adult whales today have five bones hidden in their flippers and embryo whales upon examination during various stages of development are found to have rudimentary fingers, hair on their heads and tiny ear flaps.

Timothy talked about the synchronistic group-mindedness that occurred at the Maori center. "Although I've been present at much smaller group-mind experiments, certainly I have not participated in as intense a coming together as was heaving over this gathering's horizon. The mechanics may well lie beyond our conscious understanding, but it became a unified experience with our group of about 200 in all...visitors and Maori hosts alike."

Returning to what Aldo Aulicino said about cetaceans having a "communal, cumulative, collective consciousness," it seems that part of what the dolphins are attempting to teach us is to act as one mind as a way of preserving the human species...opening ourselves up to commune with group minds from other dimensions and other species.

Igor Charkovsky couldn't attend the conference in person, but he sent a taped message suggesting that the group meditate on our "extraterrestrial brethren" and "our invisible friends."

John, the environmentalist, had reminded me that the Age of Aquarius has to do with water initiation. Charkovsky's work and the waterbaby movement seem to symbolize gaining entry into the new Golden Age by embracing our fear of water and becoming one with it. Is it possible they are also telling us, "If you want to survive the evolutionary changes, you had better tune into what is happening in the waterbaby movement, learn to swim, dive deep and hold your breath underwater for several minutes?"

4 *Swimming With Captive Dolphins*

BETWEEN THE AGES of seven and eleven I lived in the outdoor swimming pool near our home. I was there every day—from the time it opened in the spring until it closed in the fall. Sickly and anemic from eating too much candy and white flour food, I was prone to chronic ear and throat infections. I didn't swim at all again after my mother died until I was married and moved to the tropics. Swimming in the ocean caused the chronic ear infections to reappear creating a hole in my eardrum. It caused me so much pain I had to give up swimming underwater. Years later I had the ear repaired but still avoided swimming underwater out of fear.

To fulfill the urge to be around water I took up sailing and sailboat racing and met Art, owner of a 40-foot sailboat. It was one of those relationships that have people scratching their heads in wonder and asking, "What do they see in each other?" I am very intellectual and he is extremely kinesthetic and intuitive. The last thing he'd do for entertainment is read or enter into a philosophical discussion. Art, however, has a wonderful capacity for listening and creating safe space for people like me to express their feelings. Spending so much time around Art and around water was an unconscious way of cleansing my emotional wounds and healing them.

In my 20s, I'd fallen off a runaway horse and landed on my sacrum. Years later, X-rays revealed a degenerating disc that was aggravated by hours and hours of sitting to write, then doing heavy yardwork. Despite all the releasing I did with Art, in growth seminars and in bodywork sessions, I suffered from low back tension that caused chronic pain around the disc that now has a spur on it. The root chakra area at the base of the spine is also supposedly where we store our survival issues.

Over a period of 10 years I had spent thousands of dollars on osteopathic, chiropractic and naturopathic manipulations, physical therapy, neurological tests, and traction, not to mention thousands more on psychotherapy, healing seminars, personal growth workshops and bodywork. I got very little relief. Deep bodywork, hot tubing and lying in the float tanks released some of the tension temporarily but I wanted to be free of the pain.

After hearing about the dolphins' ability to zap people with high frequency ultrasound, realign their backs, identify tumors, measure pulse rates and in general tune them up, I was anxious to swim with them. In late February, Art came by early one morning for coffee and told me he was going to the Virgin Islands to check out the possibility of sailing his boat there to do charter work. He invited me along. I agreed to go the Virgin Islands with him if he'd go swimming with the dolphins in the Florida Keys with me. It didn't take much to convince him.

I'd heard that you had to swim underwater with the dolphins to get the full effect of their sonar or sound radiation. Fearful of further bouts of ear infections and uncomfortable about swimming underwater, I was nevertheless determined to receive the full benefit of swimming with them. I bought a snorkel and flippers and Art taught me to dive. I had only a few days to break through the fear and adapt to being a fish...an awkward one at best.

We left home during a downpour. My back pained me all the way across country during the plane ride. I could only tolerate sitting for half an hour. Several times, I got up and stretched and paced up and down the aisles, trying to keep it loosened up.

Two weeks before leaving for the Keys, I'd been lucky enough to make two appointments to swim with dolphins, one at Theatre-of-the-Sea at Islamorada, the other at Dolphins Plus at Key Largo. By the time we jumped into the lagoon to swim with the dolphins at Theatre-of-the Sea the next afternoon, I'd forgotten all about my back. As long as I moved around, it didn't hurt.

Half our 30-minute swim with the dolphins was directed by the trainer. Initially, she gave us a few minutes to get acquainted, to pet them and talk to them. While we were interacting they surveyed us carefully with their penetrating eyes. We swam across the lagoon and they towed us back to the dock three times. Then, two at a time, we held up bars for them to jump over and they stood upright on their tails in the water so we could hold their fins and dance with them a few seconds. During the 15 minute free swim, Art, who is totally comfortable underwater, attracted the dolphins to him by blowing bubbles beneath the surface. They circled round and round him while the remaining five of us labored to get a minute of their attention. I did manage to dive underwater long enough to hear a series of clicking sounds. I can imagine they were making fun of a bunch of floundering humans poorly imitating fish.

The trainer signaled us to swim back to the dock. As we were hanging on the edge of the dock waiting to say last goodbyes I was stroking one of them and talking to her in a soothing voice, telling her how beautiful she was. A few seconds later she dove beneath the surface and circled me, gently nudging my low back with her rostrum right at the point of my degenerating disc. She then moved to my left side and nudged me in the hip joint where I held a lot of tension that created sciatic pain and numbness in my left leg and foot. I didn't feel any sensations and so didn't give it much thought until later. Feeling totally refreshed and exhilarated by the swim with the dolphins, we drove back to our hotel.

A few hours later I developed a high fever and chills that turned rapidly into an ear and throat infection. Only once or twice in my adult life have I felt so sick. Around the age of 10 the chronic ear and throat infections caused me to be hospitalized for a mastoid operation. When the doctor discovered how malnourished I was he cancelled the operation and ordered a total blood transfusion instead. Though family violence and trauma had been going on for several years, it culminated and intensified during this period. Unknown to my mother, my father molested me. A year later my parents divorced and a few months afterward my mother had my father thrown in prison for non-support to keep him from harassing her. She died the following year and my brother, sister and I were split up. If I felt at all, it was superficially. I had to stuff emotions to survive. When the dolphin nudged me, zapping me with her high frequency sonar, she apparently released old blocked emotions I was holding in my back and hips from that traumatic time period. My back felt better. A lot of the tension was released, but now wave after wave of grief and sadness unfolded.

The day after we arrived in the Virgin Islands, I thought I was going to die. An intense pain emerged around my heart and crept down into my left arm. It felt like I was about to have a heart attack and I seriously considered going to the hospital in the middle of the night. Instead, I stayed in bed in the hotel room and allowed the pain to sink into my awareness. By morning, it had dissipated. When you release tension in one section of the spine, it affects other areas as well. Whenever I sit to write, especially about the past, a tight muscle glitch appears next to my left shoulder blade, directly behind my heart, the area where we tend to store unexpressed grief.

The healing crisis lasted nearly a month. Back home, I sank into a despair so deep I didn't want to be touched and stayed curled up in bed wallowing in my sadness for days. Art did his best to reconnect me with the world. Like the dolphin friend he is, he stood by and waited patiently for me to move through whatever was happening. For the first time in my life, I gave the wounded child in me full permission to grieve for as long as it took to release the pain. As the weeks turned into a month, however, I knew I was stuck at the child level and needed help. Having participated in dozens and dozens of traditional and non-traditional therapies and bodywork over the previous six years, I had become jaded about anyone else's ability to heal me. The real healing, I knew, had to come from within and I was not about to allow someone else tell me how I must do it or lay a trip on me about being in resistance. Too many healers I'd come to know weren't willing to deal with their own blocked emotions and projected their issues onto their clients. I seemed to be a mobile mirror for people who didn't want to look at their shadow sides, particularly at issues of grief and sadness.

It was a time of transition. I was dying once more to my old way of being in the world and surrendering my life even more deeply to Divine Will. Shortly after my return home, I had signed an agreement to sell the building I owned so that I could pursue the mystery of the dolphins' appearance in human consciousness. The sale of my property would provide me with enough money to move to a sunnier, drier climate to avoid the winter blahs and take time out to write this book. But I was in resistance to letting go of important relationships and sources of emotional support that would leave me feeling even more alone than I already was. I needed some dynamic process or confrontation to propel me out into the world in a big way and energize me to action. Hiding out had become too comfortable.

After a month of standing by and comforting me Art brought me a flier. It was promoting a free introductory evening for a seminar that promised to revolutionize your mind and break through your deepest fears. I had sworn off seminars, but I decided to go just to get myself out of a rut. The next thing I knew I had signed up for a two-week intensive training. It proved to be exactly what I needed to rocket launch me into a new life. In addition to learning how to change states and move in and out of grief at will, I climbed a 40-foot pole blindfolded and leaped off into the unknown, calling on Merlin and St. Germain for help in catching a trapeze swing suspended in mid-air. "If you're ever going to let me know you're present," I told them as I stood at the bottom of the pole, "do it now." Catching the trapeze swing while blindfolded was a major breakthrough, a graduation, if you will, to yet a higher level of trust in the unknown.

Two days later, without any transportation, money, credit cards or identification, the seminar facilitator sent 500 or more participants out into the world at midnight. We were told to go at least 70 miles away before returning by 6 o'clock the following evening. Over a dozen strangers whom my partner and I encountered during our odyssey provided food, transportation and money, showing me once again what an abundant universe we live in when we are willing to take the risk and trust. I felt so high and so alive, I decided to skydive for the second time in a week, this time blindfolded, with the help of a jumpmaster. We were securely linked together, my back to his front. I'd been wanting to skydive since I was 18 and had given up hope of doing it because I didn't want to risk injuring my spine further. The jumpmaster, however, controlled the landing and was able to soften it. "Next time," I told him, "we both jump blindfolded." He awarded me a special certificate, but declined the challenge. In the wee hours of the following morning, I strolled across 42 feet of hot coals in a world-record firewalk.

One of the side benefits of the two-week intensive training was that I had survived the high energy, all day into late night sessions, feeling physically fit and good. I had resigned my position with a college of massage therapy three years earlier, at the time of Jane's dying, due to stress and hadn't worked at a routine job since, believing my body needed lots of rest and quiet every day just to survive. Coping with so much death and loss had taken its toll on me physically and emotionally. I was suffering from Delayed Stress Syndrome. Thanks to the challenges of the seminar, however, jumping off into a new life, into the unknown, would now seem like a cakewalk. It prepared the way for the dolphins to lead me on a merry chase from one side of the continent to the other, from the Canadian border to Baja and finally to Hawaii.

VISIT TO ATLANTIS

The pursuit began on the East Coast—in Virginia Beach— supposedly once part of Atlantis. I flew there to visit my daughter and son-in-law. It just happened to be the home of the Edgar Cayce Library. Edgar Cayce is the world's best known clairvoyant healer and psychic reader. A majority of the channeling or psychic readings Cayce did over the years reveal connections to Atlantis. Among the circulating files I found reference to temples that are storehouses of ancient records. The readings suggested these will be opened at some point in the future during the times of change—by initiates of the knowledge of the One God. The readings spoke about temples that will rise again and openings of the Hall of Records in Egypt as well as records that were stored in the heart of the Atlantean land. The Cayce readings positioned Atlantis between the Gulf of Mexico and the Mediterranean. He said evidences of the lost civilization are found in the Pyrenees and Morocco, as well as British Honduras (now Belize), the Yucatan and America. According to Cayce's readings it was warring between the Sons of God and the Sons of Belial that brought about the destruction of Atlantis. The Sons of God believed in Oneness, the Sons of Belial in materialism.

One afternoon as I was reading the Edgar Cayce on Atlantis book I idly asked my son-in-law who feels a strong connection to dolphins and whales if he ever had the feeling he was from Atlantis.

"Yeah. I had a dream where I was half fish and half human and I could breathe underwater."

"What does that have to do with Atlantis?" I asked.

"Well, some of us are workers. We're here to rebuild Atlantis. We're just waiting to be picked up and taken to Atlantis to rebuild it."

"Who's they?" I asked.

"The guys in the spaceships."

"When are they coming?" I wondered.

"When the vibration level is right," he answered.

"Amazing," I said. "You haven't even read anything, have you?"

"No," he said.

"And yet you're totally tuned into the same things other people have been telling me. Is this why you're so tuned into Greenpeace and the dolphins and whales?"

"Yeah," he said.

"Whales are adaptor compensators. They compensate the vibration rate of the Earth after we humans mess it up."

"Like mining uranium from sacred sites and screwing up the magnetic field...."

"You should check the effects of the whales' migration according to the seasons and where the Earth is rotating or how far off it is from its polar axis..."

Brilliant, why didn't I think of that. "What else do you know?"

"Nothing," he said. "That's all I've been given."

"Where are you from? The Pleiades, Orion or Sirius?"

"Sirius," he said. "Seriously."

My son-in-law is 21 years old. He's never been involved with metaphysics. His parents are fundamentalist Christians. He's not a reader but he is very attuned to nature...to the Earth and apparently to the stars as well.

I learned, too late, the day I was leaving Virginia Beach that the dolphins swam close to shore just across the road from the Cayce Library almost every day. Someday I might get my timing down.

CONTAMINATING THE OCEAN

Norfolk and Virginia Beach are part of the East Coast stretch of shoreline where 300 dolphins had reportedly washed ashore due to a disease that caused lesions on their snouts and in their mouths. According to a report from the Marine Mammal Stranding Center, the dolphins showed fluid in their bodies and badly infected lungs. Most of them appeared to have died quickly. Scientists who studied the bodies found a bacteria called Vibrio which is common in marine mammals but should not have been killing the dolphins unless they had a breakdown of their immune systems. The lesions were believed to be the result of a dolphin pox virus which created openings for the bacteria to enter their bodies. Vibrio, like other bacteria, thrives on decaying matter. That same summer, humans reported having lung problems after swimming along this same stretch of coastline.

Although the deaths cannot be directly attributed to the pollution of the oceans, a high incidence of them occurred following the "accidental" spillage of sewage and hospital wastes into the water off the Jersey shore. Three billion gallons of partially treated sewage was dumped into the Delaware River during the month of July. There were also reports (as yet unfounded) that chemicals had been dumped overboard by outlaw barges that wanted to avoid paying fees or traveling long distances to dumping areas.

The Sea Shepherd Conservation Society in one of its newsletters stated that, "Every day the oceans serve as a garbage dump for over five million containers discarded by merchant ships. The Center for Environmental Education estimates that at least 450,000 of them are plastic, 4.8 million of metal, and 300,000 of glass. Moreover, about 50 million pounds of packaging or gear is cast off daily by commercial fishing vessels, and another 100,000 pounds is added by recreational boaters. Some of this stuff takes 450 years to decay."

The Cousteau Society says, "Reefs that teemed with life only 10 years ago are now almost barren!"

How can humans expect to survive on the food that comes out of the ocean, if dolphins and sea life can't exist there? I began to wonder.

5 *Awakening Through Art*

BACK HOME AGAIN, I learned that Marie Neufeld, a Huna sister and visual artist, had begun channeling dolphin and whale energy. Marie had recently returned from her second journey to the Southwest where she spent a great deal of time around Sedona, Ship Rock and other powerful vortex areas. Following her first journey, she had returned home and began painting a series of images that had come through to her of sacred power places; beautiful rock formations, overlaid with geometric forms, classic Egyptian symbols and fields of light that created a context of these sacred places as "temples of the earth." For Marie, the vortex areas stirred memories of Atlantis and Lemuria. Shortly after she completed the first series of paintings I invited her to give a presentation as part of the Harmonic Convergence information evenings I was sponsoring.

I didn't see much of her after that evening until I returned from Sedona the following winter. By then we were both living life in a state of complete trust, not knowing where we'd be led to next or what might unfold. Marie knew only that the images were part of series of teachings she was meant to share in the future. Hearing that she was now channeling dolphin and whale energy, I was anxious to talk with her. On a hot summer day, we sat around her dining room table sipping lemonade and talking about the accelerated changes that had occurred in our lives over the past year.

I asked her when she had begun to receive her connection with the dolphin and whale energies. "Fairly recently," she said. "I've been working on a painting of a nebula spiraling outward from a center point of light and within this nebula came a whale image made of the stars. I was experiencing the whale song as I created this work and it began to emanate in light patterns—as if I were creating visual patterns of its song. Shortly after that experience I received a message in my meditations from an aspect of my guidance called Astra."

Marie opened her journal and read some of the channeling.

Astra informed her that she would be receiving awarenesses at many levels through what was called the "O-binary oceanic wave of bilateral expression" or sound frequencies transmitted into the "psi bank membrane" of the ocean by the dolphins and whales. Astra informed Marie "They are carrying this message in their sonar equations; sound waves amplified over the oceans of the world transformed into light waves which carry their encoded message out into the galaxy. These transmissions are picked up in the Earth's crust. They are embedded into the plates which then relay the sound-light recording into the crystalline structures of the Earth which then amplify their wave. As these amplifications solidify, thoughtforms of a harmonious nature are created within the human membrane. This exo-vehicular expression can be seen in Tellard's radionics work and also in the reinforcing chromowave amplifier. You will begin to make connection with this work in the future."

Marie told me, "When this message came through I was puzzled by some of the terminology. Later, when I read some of Jose Arguelles' work in 'Earth Ascending,' which talks about the various energy fields as membranes, it made more sense."

She continued with the channeling. "You are now going to be instrumental in radionics amplification of sound and light. Dolphins are extraterrestrial in their origins. They came into being in this century as an outward expression of guidance to re-establish man's link with the guardianship of the oceans. You can establish a new link with them by being aware of their internal structures of light and sound."

Marie said, "As I was receiving this I experienced dolphins and whales visually as energy forms and had a sense of this process of creating light patterns from sound."

Returning to her journal, she read, "This sense of the conversion of sound into light waves can be most helpful to the new pioneers of scientific exploration to bring this into visual form. Your painting of the whale as Sound/Light Galaxy is the fecund issuance. It will encapsulate the tonal coordinates of resonance in the psi issuance..."

"Here I was starting to rebel—wait a minute—what are you saying? Please make it easier to understand!" Marie said.

"You mean, you wouldn't normally speak this way," I asked her, jokingly.

"No...No.."

"I just wanted to be clear on that," I teased.

"I said, 'All right, let's hear it in English.'"

Astra continued, "The tones of the whale are sufficient to soothe the feelings of children and the mentally/emotionally disturbed. Played in this context, their amplified harmonic brings into resonance the internal messages of cooperation and intunement with life. Going outward, the whale as a visual symbol expresses this unity of purpose and harmony with the atmospheric pulsations that amplify energy. In other words, it's the transference of a signal in visual—your eyes see the image and transform it into the thoughtform creating an image of a whale. The brain sees it, recognizes it, translates it and then it's translated at a subconscious level."

"So, in other words," Marie said, "When you see a T-shirt with a dolphin or a whale on it, you have that feeling of 'Oh, Yeah—harmony and quiet.' It's one way we can transfer that harmonious message they carry."

"The whale painting of your galaxy is your next inter-dimensional contact," Astra continued. "Journey with the whale to enliven this psi phenomena. To receive its message of transmogrified awareness, go into the entire cre system...."

Marie asked, "'What is the cre system?'"

Astra told her, "It's the system of creating thoughtforms from cellular impulses. Receiving the verbal visual message, transmogrified into the living enactment of the coded reception. Dolphins have established themselves all over the Earth to engage in the intergalactic sound network. Your affiliation with this interchange is just beginning. To increase your awareness of this link up you should become increasingly aware of the binary code of dolphins. This is expressed in their issuance of light amplifications. Flashes which engender their link up to the paranormal outside relativity. They are the ones who translate the encoded receptions into the human psi link up. Their encoded messages interface with humans who are their transcribers. Their vital data is encapsulated into human potential by thoughts and creations artistically and musically through sound and light. These encoded messages issued at irregular intervals will precede the work which will begin shortly—the enactment of brain wave interface, direct intercommunication with the outer world."

Marie commented, "In my understanding, we are now receiving inter-dimensional contact on many levels. This includes contact with what is experienced as outer space beings—time/space blending experiences—the whole spectrum. Science is making headway into being able to directly make communication possible on the physical plane as a manifestation of this inter-dimensional interaction."

"I know they are working on it, I don't know how much success they've had using traditional means. It seems to be a matter of perception. We don't have the technological capability yet to fully grasp and understand the capabilities of the dolphins and whales. They surpass our understanding," I said. "Sounds like what you're doing, Marie, is transcribing information that could potentially help science understand the mind of the dolphin and whale."

"I think maybe that's true on some level," she said. "I also had that sense when I was doing the painting as I listened to whale songs and directly allowed that sound to enter my body, go through the cells, and to come out my arm and work on the painting as a light pattern. It was like turning the sound painting into light—into visual form. This work hasn't really gotten going yet. I feel like I will be transcribing that kind of thing into light patterning which people will see and they'll get the message. This is indeed an ongoing communication. It is visual, telepathic and sound but in a language that we don't normally understand through logic. I seem to experience it and then receive verbal messages to help me understand it intellectually."

Marie stopped for a few moments to refill our glasses and said, "I'm beginning to understand through my personal work that channeling is tuning into other frequencies that seem to be other entities or energies, but which because in truth 'we are one' are really another part of ourselves. There are times when I receive guidance which feels very 'close to home' and other times it feels more distant. It is really all a part of this evolutionary adventure we are all participating in. For us to come in tune with these higher frequencies and become blended with them is what it's all about. Ken Carey's work with the Bird Tribes is a beautiful example of that blending of spirit and matter. When I receive the emanations of the energy I call Astra it is tuning into a certain frequency where that specific ray can activate."

She turned to another page in her journal to read.

"This is Astra," Marie read. "Yes, my voice is lower. I come in through your pineal. I have come to deliver teachings which will be regulated by the flow of your worship. It is time to understand the sacred trust we have bestowed upon this work at this time. You have up until now shared all. It is time to bestow understanding of the nature of the work on stardust—the oldest known substance. It takes you back into the eons before the Earth was created into the planet of pure creation of the essence of fire. It is a gaseous state culminating in the absolute dissemination of stardust throughout the nebula. I speak literally of the one nebula from which Earth sprang. There are many. This nebula acts as one atom; as a microcosm. As one nebula it enacted a force field to distinguish the particles of stardust. These particles encapsulated a tiny segment of the whole creative conceptualization. Each one reacts to its log (carrier). Log means 'to carry out.' This log is the impulse to bring out this segment of truth into the collective mind. These segments are being lit by thousands of people now and the knowledge is recreated in the psi bank. It is with this input that you are charged.

It is no longer just a theory that we create our reality. It is spun out from the center of thought. There are many circles. Central thought became form eons past and each thought created new thoughtforms. They lived and created new thought forms. This extension is at its maximized peak and is spinning.

Your work with whale is going to be a new song in your life. The whale has the power to overcome negative forces in your life.

It also has the power to create harmonious spirals which amplify this energy. The whale song is the reduced vibratory issuance of this harmony which is carried into the Earth. Play the whale song and now you will begin to efface with its inner code. You will create light patterns. They will teach you what you need to communicate in this next series. The energies you received during the super nova include the issuance on the psi bank on whale and dolphin. It was with this issuance that the input to illustrate this phenomena will be happening."

"Why is it that I am doing this work?" Marie asked Astra.

"You were chosen only because you have established link up with the Atlantean connection. Your source of light is one of Astra. Astra is the vibration of the dog star Sirius. She is unveiled in a ray of your regenerative force. You were given the ray, which included Astra, in the time when the super nova elicited its energies to earth. New information was encoded in the link-up. (Telhard's radionics is before or pre-super nova. It was the link-up to precede.) Now the super nova input is issuing in all its channels. Astra is a clear light. You can recognize this vibration by the sound you associate as voice. It is with Astra that you will begin to associate light with whale sound patterns. These light patterns will infuse your paintings to encode messages for distribution over the Earth. These messages are encodements of harmonious light emanations and affect the cre system in each individual who sees the image."

"I asked for an explanation," Marie said.

"The cre system is the innate creator within. It is encoded into the cells, the etheric messenger of light, it acts as an overseer of thought form wave amplification which imbues the directive to divine principle. It carries the code into the brain to receive specific vibrations which are needed to recreate the next increment of spiritual or divine ascendancy."

Marie said, "I asked for an example to illustrate that."

Astra replied, "An apple receives light emanations and knows through its DNA encodement how to react with the organic sub-structure to create its form. When that form is interrupted by viral or other intrusions, the form is recreated in a varied form or mutates."

Marie put the journal down. "What these emanations do is to take a message into the light body to return to divine pattern. These emanations carry holographic images of light in its perfected pattern to realign the light-body. Light forms are living symbols which can be used to open ourselves to new levels of being."

"So it's like returning to a state of perfection," I said.

"Yeah! That's what all this is about. That's what the dolphin art is about also, returning to divine pattern or principle," Marie concurred.

My mind suddenly caught fire, "Minus the disease, the viruses and all that—what the dolphins and whales are emanating are the divine pattern." Amazing, I thought, everywhere we turn one of these days we'll be zapped with the perfection images.

Marie continued, "In the present work I'm doing with the Southwest paintings it works much the same way. Each painting contains the energies of its place and an overlay of symbols expressing the encodements for its energetic function. In the seminars I give, we use these images as visual forms that illustrate the meditations and inner processes. For example:

In one of these meditations we bring ancient symbols which express 'the return to divine pattern bringing it into physical form.' Taking this message, we create a living light form containing these symbols and bring it in through the third eye and down into the body. It is like reprogramming the body to return to divine pattern. The symbols can be used generally like nutrients or sent to specific parts of the body for healing. They can also realign the experience that created the problem or energy blockage in the first place. By each person bringing about their return to divine pattern, we bring about that perfection to the whole. It's really exciting to work on ourselves at this level! This kind of work is being done in many areas through many cultural traditions today. It's taking the roots of the ancient mysteries and bringing them into a new context. The work that will be coming forth from this whale and dolphin connection really excites me. I guess because it feels like another step! I can't begin to conjecture what it will bring!"

I was curious about how Marie came to encounter the dolphin/whale energies. We took a break from the channeling and turned to her personal experiences. "In Sedona, did you feel any connection then with dolphins and whales?"

"Not that I was consciously aware of. The dolphin and whale thing didn't come about until six months or a year later.

"While you were in Sedona, you connected with extraterrestrial energy? What was that like?" I asked.

"That was a really beautiful experience. It broke through all my previous belief systems and has completely restructured my perception of the world. I think it was an experience that is still being assimilated and I can only begin to express it through my work. I'm currently writing a book about that experience and others that brought about the work with the Southwest paintings. I guess you'll have to wait awhile to hear about that one."

It was nearly time for me to leave and rush to another appointment, first I wanted to trace the sequence of events. "It appears that first you connected with extraterrestrials, then you went to Sedona and then you connected with the dolphins and whales. Is that right?"

Marie agreed.

"That's the same pattern that happened with me. So it seems that the extraterrestrials are wanting us to communicate with the dolphins. We have something to learn through the dolphins."

I asked Marie what kind of changes had happened in her life since these experiences.

She said, "For me, it's been very rapid growth, very rapid attunement with my ability to connect. Making the connection that I feel with my guidance has become the major force in my life. This whole thing is totally beyond anything I ever thought I'd be doing."

"This whole thing meaning your visions of the Southwest...?"

"That series and the meditational work involved with it. There's a whole body of information on how to use the symbols in each painting for expanding our awareness, developing our inner vision and processes for planetary healing. It's expanding every day! And now the new work with dolphin and whale is welling up inside and wanting to come out into form. It's really wonderful!

6 *Interspecies Communicator*

WITH THE SALE of my property completed, Art leaving for the Virgin Islands, my daughters ensconced in creating their own lives, I was ready to leap again into the unknown, into a new life elsewhere. Once more the dolphins began to call. I was free of obligations for the first time in my life and there was nothing to keep me from now responding to the urging of my inner guidance and surrendering my life totally to the flow. Curious about the Orca Whales, I decided to head north to the San Juan Islands, explore the area as a possible new home and begin the actual writing of the book as I traveled. I was prepared to leave within the week when my upper back and neck became too stiff and sore to drive, probably from leaping off poles and skydiving.

I called Bob. He is an eclectic sort of bodyworker/counselor who teaches breathwork seminars. He had helped me in the months prior to the death of my friend Jane, from cancer. When I called for a session he fit me in the next day. We hadn't seen each other in over a year so he naturally asked me, "What are you up to these days?"

I told him, "I'm' writing a book on dolphins, extraterrestrials and Atlantis."

He leaned toward me with interest and said, "I've had visions of dolphins leading the survivors of Atlantis to their new homes…to Egypt and the Yucatan."

"You dreamed that?" I asked.

"No not dreamed…these were visions…I was fully conscious."

As I jotted what he said in my mental notebook and thanked him for giving me another piece of the puzzle, he told me that his daughter had spent a lot of time around dolphins off the Florida Keys, attracting them to the sailboat she lived on by playing flute music. As we spoke, she was planning a trip to Hawaii to swim with dolphins in the wild.

The pain in my back demanded attention and I was anxious to get on with the session. The first deep thrust of his thumb into the knot in my back behind my heart chakra brought up the grief. I started to cry softly.

"Who are you crying for?" Bob asked gently.

I gulped a deep breath and released the pain, "My mother...she died when I was 11."

"What would you like to ask your mother?"

The words stuck in my throat. It took a minute to spit them out. "Why did you have to leave so early?"

Through the veil I heard her speak softly, "Because you needed to learn about death so that you could choose to live fully. For the better part of an hour, I allowed the sounds of howling pain to unfurl.

The next morning I headed north. I'd received a newsletter or two from Interspecies Communications out of Friday Harbor and wanted to connect with whoever was writing it. A friend had just given me a copy of "Animal Dreaming" by Jim Nollman, a beautiful book about interspecies communication with music. I didn't know at the time that he was also the author of the Interspecies newsletter. Jim has been playing music to the Orcas for several years and annually takes a group of people out on excursions into the wild to communicate with them. It was on one of these outings that Joan Ocean connected with the gray whale.

It took some tracking to find Jim's place in the country. As we drove up the driveway he stepped out on the porch for a break from writing. My friend Carol and I got out her of car, each carrying a copy of "Animal Dreaming" for him to sign. We spent an hour or so talking. Jim told me, "You're the third person this month who has shown up on my doorstep wanting to know what is going on with dolphins." Despite his protestation of "I don't want to be a dolphin guru," that is the role he's been thrust into as a result of his experiences and chosen profession.

In 1978, Jim was asked by several environmental groups to go to Iki Island in Japan and attempt to lure the dolphins away from the fishing nets to prevent them from being slaughtered. He described the scene as "ketchup-colored seas littered with the bodies of dead and dying dolphins." Once his reputation for attracting dolphins through music became known to the fisherman they began to trust his intentions and he was told that if he could warn or frighten the dolphins away from the fishing grounds, the fishermen would relinquish their own extermination program. The musical mission failed for logistical reasons, but the killing of the dolphins diminished substantially the following year. Eleven years later the Japanese are still killing dolphins—right next door to their Marine Park. But today, within Japan itself, there is an empathic movement of people gathering who are beginning to demonstrate their concern. While some humans are short on compassion for dolphins, dolphins seem to have an abundance of compassion for humans and for wounded, dead or distressed members of all other species as well. This characteristic behavior of dolphins is one that often puzzles the people who study them in the wild. Dolphins are known to attack sharks and yet have also been seen supporting wounded sharks in the water. They seem to have an innate ability for sensing when another animal or mammal is in a state of distress and requires support or assistance. By nature they are helpful creatures.

The dolphins' caregiving behavior is an enigma that cannot be explained by the logical mind. The question that arises for Jim Nollman is, "Why does a mammal with such a large brain and high intelligence attack and kill its own species and then save the lives of other species?"

Even Plutarch a century or more before the birth of Christ commented on their caregiving behavior, "To the dolphin alone, beyond all others nature has granted what the best philosophers seek: friendship for no advantage. Though it has no need at all of any man, yet it is a genial friend to all and has helped many."

Like so many characteristics of dolphin behavior and communication Jim's question adds one more element to the dolphin mystique. Maybe the answer is so simple that we are overlooking it. Could it be that the dolphins sense their survival is tied to all living things? Could it be that dolphins sense the oneness of all life and their own immortality?

Jim witnessed a trapped and dying dolphin respond to the tender care and stroking of Russell Frehling on board an Iki fisherman's boat. The dolphin who was shivering and appeared in a state of shock, returned to awareness and stopped shivering. As Frehling stuck his whole hand in the dolphin's mouth and began to stroke his tongue, the dolphin looked directly in his eye, Jim said and, "gave us all pause." Then the dolphin seemed to enter his astral body and surrendered to dying gracefully.

What is it about the nature of their presence that touches our hearts so? Jim Nollman feels "they are like humans in dolphin skins, their skin is so smooth and they have the energy of hummingbirds. It's something about that energy…something about their metabolism…the way they breathe that attracts us to them." Our attraction to these creatures goes beyond their sensuousness, however. In all the myths and legends that have been passed down through eons of time, the dolphins are most remembered as guides. Stories are repeatedly told about dolphins guiding fisherman to safety during storms, guiding fishermen to schools of fish, piloting ships through hazardous straits, guiding the survivors of Atlantis to their new homes, steering ships through fog, circling people in the water until they are rescued and on and on. In recent years the dolphin mystique has captured the imagination of science fiction writers and movie makers but our growing connection to them seems to be much more than fantasy or fiction.

Says Jim in one of his newsletters, "Nowhere are the issues of psychic phenomena more in evidence than at the point of contact between human beings and the dolphins and whales. Stories about a direct human/cetacean mindlink have always existed as a quiet undertone at the various scientific and environmental conferences—the stuff of backroom discussions where personal anecdotes garner more attention than quantified data. Yet, unfortunately, this intuitive subject matter rarely makes it out onto the central podium where it most needs to be heard. First, no one seems to possess either the language or the certitude to know what to say about it. Secondly, psychic experience remains too risky an area for many professionals to even acknowledge as valid material for study."

Jim feels his Interspecies Newsletter serves as "a bridge between current scientific objective and the ancient shamanic-mythic view" although he insists, "There's nothing mystical going on here." He garners a certain level of pride in calling himself a "ghostbuster" who likes to bust people's mystical bubbles. And he also readily admits he doesn't have time to worry about the mystical connection humans feel with cetaceans. "I need to stick to my musical connection." He says, however, "the Spiritual Revolution is the best thing we have going on the planet right now because it's helping people connect with nature." His next book will be entitled "Spiritual Evolution."

"Living as we do in a tamed world, the telepathic connection that some people say they sense in the company of certain animal species (not only dolphins) serves to awaken the future primitive in all of us. This is where we all were when we were less civilized and this is where we shall be when we are more civilized. Everywhere the yearning for communion deepens," says Jim.

It was this yearning for communion that spurred John and Toni Lilly, pioneers in dolphin research, to create The Human/Dolphin Society. As part of this project, they sent Jim Nollman to the Sea of Cortez in Mexico to explore the possibility of establishing the first human/dolphin community. It was not the right place or time, but the interest never waned and even today, Jim finds himself, reluctantly at times, involved as leader in the informal human/dolphin network that has spontaneously sprung up out of the Lillys' and his own work.

He seems to prefer connecting with Orcas and whales in the wild, rather than connecting dolphins and humans in community. The week following my visit he left with friends to kayak near Vancouver Island and play music to the Orcas. Over the years he's taken an array of musicians out to meet and greet Orcas. "How well they play doesn't seem to matter, it's how much fun people are having on the boat that attracts the Orcas" and inspires them to vocalize. Two Tibetan lamas accompanied him on one occasion. Their double-toned chanting intrigued the Orcas.

It was Jim who lured the gray whales out of the Alaskan ice jam, not with the sounds of other whales calling, but with the sound of jazz.

The next morning I drove along the coast looking for a place to camp. I had just reached the crest of a ridge, when I looked out and saw a small pod of Orcas breaching in the distance. They were rolling over and milling around a small cabin cruiser full of "Orca watchers." I watched for a while, then decided to find a place along the beach to check out the water. It was mid-August and it was still icy cold and required a wet suit for swimming. I decided on the spot to look for a new home where the water was warm enough to swim year round. The pull to head south into California grew stronger each day. I was anxious to reconnect with John, the environmentalist, and meet some of the dolphin people he had told me about earlier. It was time, also, to visit my aging father with whom I'd been attempting to heal the past.

7 *Answering the Call*

IN LATE SUMMER, I headed south into the heat of a scorched and cracking California landscape. On my way to the Bay area I stopped to see my Huna teacher and spent the night. She was in the process of having some carpentry work done and had hired a man who was temporarily laid off from work as a woodcutter. Bill and I sat on the back deck the next morning sipping coffee and the topic of conversation drifted somehow to dolphins. He told me he'd been swimming with them in the wild about 20 times, four to six hours each, off Siesta Key just below Tampa Bay, Florida where he once lived. I asked him what he got from swimming with them and he said, "A peace I've never known from my birth, 'til then. There's nothing like it. They gave me my humanity. I didn't want to do drugs, drink or do anything to spoil the high I got from dolphins. I went out in the boat and jumped in. As soon as the boat left they came and supported us in the water and carried us back to the dock." I was ready to leave for Tampa on the next plane but Bill had more to tell me.

"The biggest thing is to let go of your own shit and just trust that they'll take care of you. I used to think, 'I got to have a life preserver.' I'm not a good swimmer, but they took care of me."

He paused for a minute, reluctant to tell me the next anecdote for fear I wouldn't believe him. "I haven't talked to anybody about dolphins in a long time. Not too many people understand. If I hadn't gone swimming with dolphins off Siesta Key, I never would have had the trust to jump ship in the North Atlantic.

"I saw a pod of whales and there was a baby with them and I just had to be in the water with it." He leaped from a 700-foot-long oil tanker into the sea and no one missed him for an hour.

"I knew inside, 'They'll take care of me and they will, until I die.'" When a fellow crewman reported him missing, the ship's captain executed a "Williamson Turn" and calculated approximately where they would find Bill based on the approximate time he'd been missing. When they returned to the estimated location, they spotted Bill in the water with the baby whale a short distance away from where he had jumped.

"Were there any changes that happened in your life from swimming with the dolphins?" I asked.

"They showed me that I'm OK. Never thought much of myself. I was raised in South Bronx and then went through the war killing people. What they gave me was something that nothing else can give you…unconditional love. I never got it from my parents. That was a bad trip. You might say I raised myself. From the dolphins, I got a sense of who the hell I was. And I'm OK."

He added, "I always tried to be somebody…I knew who I was wasn't the right one. The dolphins straightened me out and I've gotten better ever since. Now when I see a picture of dolphins or whales, it mellows me out and I calm down."

We talked for a moment about how connecting with nature healed emotional wounds. "I've always connected with nature, I knew it was the only way to go but I never knew how to plug into it. The dolphins showed me the way."

When I think of loggers, I see the stereotype of a strapping muscle-man with red suspenders, high-topped, thick-soled boots and earthy, red-necked mentalities to match. Wearing the garb of the woodsman only slightly camouflaged Bill's sensitivity. He is a man who deals with the pain in the world by going to work in the woods every day and communing with the trees and the spirits who live there. It pains him deeply to cut down trees, especially old growth trees but he says, "Better to have someone with some caring for the trees cutting them down. Sometimes I save one of the old trees and that makes me feel really happy. That one tree will grow forever and ever."

His eyes softened as he reminisced, "I cut timber because I love the office space, the outdoors. I'm out there where no man has ever set foot. I know every trail and how to survive out there. I've been doing this for 12 years."

Wistfully, he said, "I gotta quit killing trees. I'd love to take people on hikes, be a tour guide. I feel things out there I can't relate (to others). When I feel backed up, I go down to the brush in the morning and something happens. I feel in control. Never see another human being all day. I work alone. When you go back to town you have to deal with people." He said he cuts down massive trees 15 to 20 feet in diameter.

As I listened to Bill talk, I thought that this man would make a great advocate for Greenpeace, the Sierra Club or the Save the Old Growth Forest group. They'd love to have him on their side. He had some kind of mental block about feeling worthy enough or capable enough to do anything other than being a treecutter. "I don't know how to do anything else," he insisted. I sensed he had unlimited potential and wished I had more time to spend talking with him.

His eyes softened again as a memory stirred. "When you cut into a tree and you get so far, you think 'this is the time of George Washington. This is the time of Columbus discovering America. The oldest one I've cut was 900 years old."

Cutting it down must have seemed like murdering his ancestors.

"Half of the timber is rotten. Fifty to 60 percent of old growth is rotten. Being able to save a tree makes me feel so good, but going out and killing them...God that makes me want to go and find another profession."

I asked him, "Why do they cut the old growth then?"

"Because it's in the way. They buck it and leave it. They cut down wild cherry trees 20 inches around and they leave it there and burn it."

He had an idea. "People in jail...bring 'em up to a logging share and have them yard it up and give it to the old people who can't buy fuel. They'll (the prisoners) get the benefit of being out there. So much is wasted."

Loggers are paid per thousands of board feet. "The incentive is to fall the big stuff and wreck the little stuff. Kills me to do that. When I don't do it, I don't make money."

At some level he felt trapped, unable to find his way out of the darkness of his own inner forest. We talked about his options and he agreed to go home that night and write out a list of things he could do instead of tree cutting, since it obviously caused him such great pain.

"I hug trees...I love 'em. I don't want to cut them. There was a Great Horned Owl and an owl's nest in one of the old growth. I went to my boss and asked him if we couldn't save the tree. He said, 'If you don't want to cut the tree Bill, I'll get someone else.'" He couldn't stand the thought of someone else cutting it down so he said "Screw that, I'll cut the tree. It's in my space. I'll cut it. I hugged that tree for half an hour before I could cut it down."

Regretfully, I let Bill go back to his remodeling while I headed east to visit Tina and Steve, my tour guides in the Yucatan. It was the dry season and there were fire watches in effect throughout the mountains.

An intense heat spell had settled over the Sacramento Valley. I thought I'd take my time heading to the Bay area. First I'll visit my father, I thought, then connect with the dolphin people. But the impulse to go to San Jose grew stronger each day. I used the heat wave as an excuse to bypass the valley and head down the coast through the redwoods to the Bay area. I arrived at Meredith's the day after Labor Day and immediately called John. We met the following morning.

John reviewed what had been happening since I met with him in late January, seven months earlier. He'd connected with an unofficial group of philanthropists, concerned citizens and foundation representatives in southern California. They involved him in their project because of his environmental background and to help them create an international foundation that would raise people's consciousness about emerging environmental, global issues in general. "They aren't really tuned into dolphins but they are somewhat metaphysically oriented," said John.

Each time he went down to meet with them, dolphins showed up to greet him in the bay just beyond the window of the office building. The man John was working with said, "I've been here eight years and I've never seen dolphins."

John told him, "Look over your shoulder." A pod of eight or nine dolphins were frolicking in the bay just outside.

During one of his trips a huge pod of about 200-300 dolphins showed up in the bay as John meditated early one morning next to the water. He said, "The only thing I can compare the experience to is the birth of our son. I was just overwhelmed by it. They are definitely trying to tell me something or maybe just validate that what I'm doing is right on. There are so many synchronicities happening."

I told him, "You're going through an initiation into a higher level of consciousness."

"Yeah," he said, "a water initiation."

As we talked, we discovered once more that we were being led to the same books and connecting with the same people. John had spoken twice with Mary Caroline about the Dolphins-In-The-Desert project. She was still attempting to put it together and was now teaching some special form of breathwork.

He knew the people who organized the citizen diplomacy tour to Russia. They were leaving the next day to talk with Igor Charkovsky about underwater birthing with dolphins. I knew some of the rebirthers who were going on the trip. One of them was Athena Neelley, a friend and one of three co-creators of the Healing Connection, along with me. She and I thought when we simultaneously resigned from the steering committee that our paths were leading us in different directions. Now it seemed that we had come full circle and were crossing paths again through our connections to the dolphins and underwater birthing.

John said, "Russia has been coming up a lot for me lately. Some of the people at this foundation have been to Russia as citizen diplomats. And this

morning I'm due to talk with a group about trade agreements or negotia-
tions with Russia. I keep asking my guidance, 'What's it all about'? After
resigning his career position as an environmental manager for a large government agency, John was living off his IRAs and savings. Essentially we
were in the same position having made a 360-degree turn in our usual
approach to managing our lives and finances. I'd been in retreat for nearly
three years, had already spent my IRA money and was now living on
money from the sale of a piece of real estate. I was totally trusting that the
book I was being led to write would support me. We both worried about our
future at times and dealt with the anxiety by distracting ourselves and
becoming even more involved in our connection with dolphins.

CRYSTAL SKULL MYSTERIES

John invited me to attend a meeting conducted by Joshua Shapiro of
J&S Aquarian Networking in Pacifica, California. The gathering drew people who were interested in UFOs and psi phenomenon. John commented
several times about some Crystal Skulls he'd been hearing about and
seemed to have a keen interest in learning more. Joshua was, at this time, in
the process of writing a book with a group of friends entitled "The Mysteries
of the Crystal Skulls Revealed." John thought Crystal Skulls might somehow relate to what I was writing about. My mind went into confusion about
what they were and how they would relate to dolphins and whales. Finally
John told me they were believed to be receptacles for ancient knowledge.

The Crystal Skulls are shaped in the almost exact image and size of
actual human skulls and are believed to have been created several thousand
years ago. Part of the mystery is how they were made. Tests have determined that they were not carved by metal tools and they cannot be dupli-
cated by modern technology. Through the Mayan legends, one of the Crystal
Skulls (the Mitchell-Hedges) is described as being shaped by over five generations of native people rubbing the quartz by hand with sand and hair.

This Crystal Skull is best known as a clear one in the possession of an
82-year-old Canadian woman, Anna Mitchell-Hedges. It is considered to be
the largest worked gemstone in the world. She discovered it in 1924 at the
age of 17 while on an archaeological dig with her father in the rubble of a
Mayan ruin called Lubaanton, located in what is now known as Belize (formerly British Honduras). Belize lies in the southeastern corner of the Yucatan
peninsula, approximately 100 miles from Palenque. Lubaanton is believed to
have been destroyed by a sudden catastrophe, just as Palenque was.

The Crystal Skull always remains at the same temperature regardless
of the outer temperature. When viewed from different angles it produces
holographic images and acts much like a computer, transmitting phenomena in a very precise way.

My interest reached its apex when Joshua mentioned that friends of his who are working on the Crystal Skull book with him, viewed the Mitchell-Hedges skull in person. They were amazed when holographic images became visible, including what appeared to be dolphins and whales. The Skull is believed to be activated by light, color sound and human energy.

Joshua believes the Crystal Skulls are of extraterrestrial origin, as are dolphins and whales. "Cetaceans were brought to this planet to help Mother Earth in its spiritual evolution," says Joshua. Dolphins and whales, being very evolved and compassionate are able to communicate telepathically through human channels.

The Crystal Skulls, which the co-authors of the book believe are like a compact computer, also shares information with people telepathically. Thus, both cetaceans and objects like the Crystal Skulls, are in communication with other levels of consciousness and other galactic beings. Like John, Joshua believes the dolphins—ever since they had contact with Man—are aware of the location of sacred objects and know how they were used by ancients for the positive advancement of this planet.

In turn, Joshua sees the Crystal Skulls as a repository of historical information about the Earth and the races that have shared it with us, including not only cetaceans, but legendary beings and mythological creatures such as Unicorns, Pegasus and mermaids. In the past, when humans were more psychically and telepathically attuned, the skulls may possibly have been used to communicate with dolphins and whales. The appearance of the holographic images of cetaceans in the Crystal Skull, says Joshua "probably indicates a closer relationship between the dolphins and Man in former times, which is happening again. I guess the dolphins and whales become more drawn to us as we increase in our spiritual awareness."

Although the intention of the meeting was to talk about UFO phenomena, we never got off the subject of the Skulls all evening. About eight people were present, some of whom had seen a slide show about the Skulls that Joshua had presented at a Star Trek Conference.

Miss Mitchell-Hedges had once related in a televised interview with William Shatner that a young woman from Australia once saw the Skull and laughed. A few months later she grew ill and died. Before her death she related her experience with the Skull to friends, warning them of its power to kill those who mock it.

Joshua Shapiro saw this Crystal Skull in 1986 for the first time and said, "Something happened...it activated a memory bank." Since then he's been involved in gathering information and material for the Mysteries of the Crystal Skulls Revealed, co-authored with Sandra Bowen and F.R. "Nick" Nocerino.

The Skull seems to affect people much like a sacred site. Some break down and weep. Scores of Mayans upon hearing of the discovery of the

Mitchell-Hedges Skull traveled through hundreds of miles of jungle by foot to see it.

Only a few Skulls have been discovered so far. It is believed at least 12 or 13 exist and will be uncovered in the near future. Shapiro and others think the Skulls were brought to Earth by extraterrestrials, each from a different planet, each created from a different gemstone which gives them distinct healing qualities and psychic abilities. "Each skull," says Joshua, "seems to work with a different part of being. Some are used for information, some for healing."

One of the channels in Joshua's book states that 13 main Crystal Skulls will be found, containing the genetic coding of 12 galactic races living in the inner Earth with the 13th tribe forming a family. This would be similar to the 12 Lost Tribes of Israel connected by the 13th tribe or the teacher. The term Israel represents a plan for the enlightenment of the planet.

The Mayans, through their worship of the sun and moon and their deep connection with the cyclic patterns of nature knew a great deal about the numerical arrangement and coding of the Universe. They are believed to have migrated to South and Central America during the last fall of Atlantis. Carved jade artifacts found in the Temple of Inscriptions at Palenque are exact replicas of those found in Egyptian pyramids. The Skulls may in time reveal to us much about our ancient past. One postulation is that the skulls are a gift from a dying civilization. When the high priests of Atlantis realized the fatal Fall was near, they dispersed the Skulls which are storehouses of the ancient knowledge, to the far corners of the world so that their power could not be abused. When humankind has reached the appropriate level of consciousness and joins together in a spirit of cooperation and trust, the Skulls will make themselves known and will reveal their power to benefit humanity once again. Joshua believes that people who have worked together before and trusted each other, in Atlantis, in Egypt, in the Yucatan, are being drawn together at this time in history to reveal and use the secret powers of the Crystal Skulls.

A legend or story passed down by the Mayans says that when the High Priest was about to die, he would lie down in front of the Crystal Skull with his predecessor beside him. Immediately the knowledge of the dying priest would pass on to the younger man through the power of the Crystal Skull as the old priest passed peacefully away. Anna Mitchell-Hedges was told by the Mayans, who she lived with as a young girl, that the Skull has the power to kill or to heal, depending upon how it is used. The co-authors of the "Mysteries of the Crystal Skulls Revealed" believe the energy of the Skulls were activated by the priestesses of the temple. The Mitchell-Hedges skull, which is normally clear, clouds up when activated.

According to Joshua, "The Skull scans you. It is able to see what is going on with you and to test your chakra system and memory. "It may send you a sound or a color. Your response will determine whether you are ready to receive its secrets. It knows what it can give you."

The challenge for researchers has been to discover a code or method that will access the information at will. Shea, a woman psychic at the meeting, had become interested in the skulls while attending a seminar with Nick Nocerino, who had brief possession of one of the ancient skulls several years earlier. During the question-and-answer period after one of Nick's presentations, the group used autonomic means (sketching of the skull) to receive subliminal information regarding access to stores of information contained in it. Says Shea, "My pen drew a skull, then a wavy line, indicating distance. It pulled it in from a point maybe six or seven feet above the skull." Nocerino tended to feel it wasn't valid.

A couple of years passed. In 1971, Shea read about the recovery of a large crystal sphere from a pyramid structure in the area of the Berry Islands, Bahamas, by Dr. Ray Brown, a naturopathic physician, while he was scuba diving. "I made the 'Eureka' connection," says Shea, "and consulted my husband, an engineer and physicist. Is it feasible?" she asked R.H.

In engineering jargon he spelled out for her the use of a specific apparatus which would enable the emanations to be analyzed, retrieving the information through the same hard axis point at which it was originally programmed.

According to a written account by Shea, people who viewed the sphere at the Phoenix Psychic Seminar in 1975 and in other exhibits since then report "phantom lights, voices, tingling. Compass needles nearby spin counterclockwise and reverse direction only two inches further away. Metals are temporarily magnetized. Symptoms of illnesses may be relieved in one individual but acquired by another subsequently in the sphere's vicinity. Internal images dissolve into myriad fracture lines. Photos have been obtained of a large single eye which occasionally appears. At another angle, three pyramids superimpose in decreasing sizes. Some claim to see a fourth."

Shea goes on to say, "The similarity of these reported phenomena to those credited to the more widely known Crystal Skull(s) indicates a similarity in the techniques used to enter, and thus a requirement for similar means to remove or retrieve information."

R.H.'s commentary adds that, "All crystals are known to be capable of storing energy and aligning themselves into various axes of wave transmission—the most forceful (powerful) being located on what is known as the 'hard-axis.' Various external energy fields, usually magnetic in nature, help to stimulate radiated energy along the hard axis and make measurements of the force and predominate wave length more readily measurable."

8 *Path of the Heart*

I'D BEEN INVOLVED in the holistic health and spiritual movement for nearly five years and had observed that some people became workshop or personal growth junkies the way others become food and drug addicts. Not only is going to workshops and seminars an expensive habit to maintain, it's also self-defeating. Leapfrogging from one workshop to another in search of new highs without integrating and practicing what one learns seems to be another form of denial cloaked in positive terms. After several years of intense growth and bodywork, I felt as though I'd done enough. "How many dyads and techniques and processes can one person incorporate into their lives," I wondered?

Nevertheless, my inner guidance would persist in pressing me to attend particular workshops. Since my earlier visit, my friend Meredith had begun teaching Tantra. I'd been curious about Tantra for some time but my resistant streak immediately kicked in. "No more workshops!" It seemed like I'd been in one workshop after another all summer. Following the two-week intensive training on changing states and breaking through belief systems, I'd gone to a third-level Huna training on the use of sound and light in healing, followed by a weekend retreat. "Enough!" I said. The voice persisted, however, until I got the message that Tantra would help me open my heart chakra and facilitate connecting with other dimensions, especially dolphins. "OK! OK! I'll go!"

Tantra is an ancient Eastern tradition incorporating a form of Yoga that teaches people to use sexual energy to attain higher consciousness through various breath exercises, meditative postures and eye contact with a partner. Utilizing Tantric positions and rituals as a meditation strengthens the spiritual bond and creates a holy relationship between partners. One's "beloved" is treated as a God or Goddess tenderly, respectfully and with dignity.

The word Tantra means to expand and is indicative of an all-encompassing knowledge. Its rituals are the basis of several Eastern philosophies. It was through the practice of Tantric rituals that the chakra system was discovered and humans learned that the Universe is within us. In this state of awareness, Tantra introduces us to what is known as the "subtle world." The language of this subtle world speaks to us through the heart.

The Tantra workshop revealed to me how frequently I judge other people by their appearance. I became aware how I use that as a way of alienating or separating myself from them and their energy fields—even before I give them an opportunity to express who they are from a heart level. I saw, too, that as a result of these judgments about other people, I was also blocking out the possibility of communicating with beings or intelligences from other dimensions of reality.

A few days after the Tantra workshop my Kundalini energy began to rise. For several months I'd been experiencing spasms in my lower body whenever I laid down and practiced deep breathing. Kundalini, or "serpent power" as the Hindus call it, acts as a transformer of the nervous system and sends ripples of energy and sensations coursing through the body up into the crown chakra—which then radiates white auric light. It is frequently stimulated in the course of Yoga practice involving meditation and deep breathing. In addition to all the workshops I'd been attending, I had been doing a great deal of meditating, breathwork, toning and listening to classical and instrumental music through earphones and hanging out a lot in powerful vortex areas like Mt. Shasta and Sedona.

One evening I was lying in bed and began to tone. The most beautiful sound spontaneously arose and I was sure it was my soul singing to me. I sensed very clearly that my High Self was making its presence known to me. It was as if she was watching over me. Every cell in my energy body vibrated to and radiated that tone. Wave after wave of it coursed through me. It was an exquisite, blissful experience. The next morning, however, my mind was filled with negative judgments about people, especially men. Part of me observed what was happening and began to act as a mediator to the voice inside that seemed to hate them. It turned out to be the rebellious inner child. "They're wimps," she told me. "Not strong enough for me...too full of fear. Always wanting to control." Slowly, I began to realize these criticisms were a defense against my own feelings of inferiority. It was really me the critic didn't like. The observer let her rant for nearly a half hour before intervening. Somehow the positive feelings from the Tantra workshop and the toning experience had flushed out the critic who felt a need to balance out all the positive, loving energy.

When I returned to writing three days later I allowed myself to follow the flow of my thoughts and words without trying to organize them or figure out how they were meant to fit into the book. I could only trust that my superconscious mind knew where it was leading me and what conclusion it might arrive at, if I just stayed with the flow.

KUNDALINI RISING

That night when I went to bed, I decided to breathe the breath that had spontaneously taken over during the toning experience. It was very rhythmic and deep, circulating noiselessly between the ki and the heart center. When I listened to the ringing in my inner ear, it became very gentle and soft, soundless. To my amazement, I could feel the chakra centers on the bottom of my feet open up and energy began to flow up through my legs into my pelvis and arms. My heart chakra opened and began to radiate its own sweet, special energy. I breathed into it, pulling the energy up from my feet. I could feel it moving into my abdomen and very slightly into my will chakra. My whole body zinged with electrical current.

I lost the sense of the outline or boundary of my physical body and felt my energy body expanding, being blown out, swelled up by the pressure of the energy flowing through it. This time, it moved up into my shoulders, neck and head easily and I could feel my throat chakra open, then my head felt surrounded by a crown of energy and my third eye began to pulse inside the shape of an inverted pyramid that merged with the crown chakra energy.

"Whoa! This is wonderful," I thought, and totally surrendered to the sensations. Speaking to the Goddess Isis and to the father God, I asked them to lift the veil between us, to make me One with them. I asked that my psychic gifts might be opened, that I might see between the dimensions and be a direct channel for their wisdom and power. My mind went into ecstasy and consciously merged into the Oneness of all that is. There was absolutely no separation between myself and the God and Goddess energy. I had the sense of being in the flow of the One Mind, One Heart, One Breath, the One that pulsates The All, the Universal Life Force. I stayed with the breathing and the sensations for well over an hour or maybe more.

The next day I went looking for a book on Kundalini and found one entitled "The Kundalini Experience" by Dr. Lee Sannella. The author has been studying the Kundalini phenomenon since the early 1970s. He quotes a passage from Carl Jung's work. Jung liked to relate an allegory of a medieval monk who lost his way in the forest while on a fantasy journey. "While trying to retrace his steps, he found his path barred by a fierce dragon." He

believed that the dragon symbolized the Kundalini force, which in psychological terms launches a person on his or her greatest adventure—"the
adventure of self-knowledge." We can only turn back from this journey into
the wilderness at the risk of sacrificing our momentum of self-discovery and
self-understanding, which in turn would mean "a loss of meaning, purpose
and consciousness." Kundalini awakening marks the beginning of our journey into the "unknown forest of hidden dimensions of human existence."
According to Jung, "When you succeed in awakening the Kundalini, so that
it starts to move out of its mere potentiality, you necessarily start a world
which is totally different from our world."

The Kundalini force, says Sannella, uses the human body as its vehicle
for expression. He quotes Gopi Krishna who said:

> "This mechanism, known as Kundalini, is the real cause of all so-
> called spiritual and psychic phenomena, the biological basis of evolu-
> tion and development of personality, the secret origin of all esoteric
> and occult doctrines, the master key to the unsolved mystery of cre-
> ation, the inexhaustible source of philosophy, art and science, and the
> fountainhead of all faiths, past, present and future."

Kundalini energy burns through the blocks in our structural system
and purifies and cleanses the body on an upward journey to the crown
chakra. It is the force of enlightenment and may work simultaneously on
many levels, says Sannella, affecting motor, sensory, interpretive and non
physiological functions. According to Sanskrit scriptures, three of the major
blocks in the body are in the area of the root chakra, the heart chakra and behind
the third eye. The root chakra relates to our survival issues, the heart with connection to others and the third eye, to an expanded vision of the Cosmos.

The Kundalini energy subtly shifted each day. The sensations were
extremely sensual and arousing. One evening I had an impulse to listen to
music through headphones for three to four hours. Each of the tapes I listened to vibrated a different chakra center. A day or so earlier, as I was
browsing through one of Meredith's books on Tantra, I found a written list
of music that related to chakra cleansing.

Each center reverberates to different instruments. The crown chakra
opens to string instrumentals, the brow to classical piano, the throat to
bass, the heart to harp and harpsichord, the solar plexus to live organ and
the root chakra to the drum. I was reminded of what the dolphins had been
saying through various channels, that sound and light will help raise our
vibrational rates.

When I awoke Sunday morning and shifted my attention to the current, I noticed it was no longer just hanging out in my feet and calves.

Wave after wave of subtle sensual energy rippled through my body, tickling and tingling the nerve endings to arousal. My pleasure spots were working overtime. Listening to the music the night before attuned my whole body and brought it into harmony as if it were one large chakra center. Apparently an energy block in my knees had prevented the sensations from arising earlier unless I did deep breathing. Now the ripples of ecstasy were flowing through me spontaneously while I breathed naturally, radiating out the top of my crown. Beautiful images of future life in the "new" Atlantis flowed through my mind.

In essence what I saw was truly life in paradise. Huge green lawns surrounding beautiful white marble buildings and rainbow-colored flower beds everywhere. When I came out of trance, it struck me that there were no cars, no streets, no noise pollution, no air pollution, just peace and harmony and great joy. The vision felt very soothing and reassuring.

For some time, I'd been confused about the role of sexuality on the path of enlightenment. Some spiritual teachings I'd read declare that sexual energy must be diverted into creativity and ideally we must live like virgins and eunuchs. Other teachers believe enlightenment is reached by fully expressing and embracing one's sexual urges. By satiating one's sexual appetite, we move beyond the issues of sex into a state of oneness in which orgasm is spontaneous and no partner is needed. It seemed to me there was no middle road here. One either chose to live a monastic life and cut off sexual feelings or one engaged in orgies to satisfy the inner sexual strivings. I am a Libra. I must live in balance. Tantra offered other options.

The dolphins themselves have much to teach humans about sensuousness and sexuality. People who swim with them both in captivity and in the wild, commonly report that male dolphins are not bashful about showing their erections and in fact, will rub themselves against a human female's legs. Much of their playful interactions amongst their own species and with humans is a demonstration of their fondness for tactile experiences. They love to be stroked, fondled, caressed and touched, not only on their bellies but in their mouths. Stroking or scratching their tongues seems to have a particularly soothing effect on them. One lone male dolphin who hung out in the English Channel was so enamored of female humans that he attempted on more than one occasion to swim away with them on his rostrum out into the open ocean. Male dolphins can be quite sexually aggressive and jealous and are known to be territorial about their claims on female dolphins within a pod, however. They do not mate for life but have multiple partners. In their relationships with the opposite sex, just as in the dynamic thrusts of their bodies leaping from the water into the air, they show us that being free and spontaneous is a blissful experience for them.

9 Earth: Experiment Station

WANTING TO LEARN more about the Crystal Skulls and to reconnect with some of the people I'd met at the UFO network evening I'd gone to a week earlier, I drove up to Pacifica on Sunday evening. We met in the clubhouse of a condominium project that overlooked the ocean. The thin fog reminded me of the veil that obscures our view of other dimensions and realities. Just as we were arriving, the rosy glow of the sun burned away the mist, exposing the calm, peaceful waters of the ocean stretching to infinity before our eyes.

Joshua started by giving us an encapsulated version of how he saw the "big picture" unfolding.

"UFOs have to do with the prophecies," he told us. "They are heralds of the golden age."

He felt they are coming to Earth now to guide us through the next evolutionary stage and are not allowed to interfere with our free will. Some of them are concerned that as we expand our technology into space and mess around with nuclear energy, we have become a threat to other stars and galaxies. "If we blow up the Earth, what effect does it have on the solar system when one planet is missing?" Joshua asked. "Every action that we take causes a repercussion out in space."

Joshua feels that the increasing interest in paranormal phenomena is related to the acceleration of the planetary vibrational rate and that some kind of galactic hierarchy exists that won't allow us to blow up the planet. He senses that this guiding force has managed to release some of the earthquake pressure on the planet by directing energy into specific areas where small quakes then occur. In the process of writing "Mysteries of the Crystal Skulls Revealed," Joshua has researched and drawn to him people and information in much the same way I have. He learned that many Native American tribes believe they originated on other worlds.

As the evening progressed the group wove a tapestry of experiences and information together that interlocked, merged into and validated the information I'd been receiving. We agreed, among other things, that the ancients knew about energy vortexes, grids and ley lines, that the stone blocks in the temples of South America between which you cannot pass even a piece of paper, must have been created with extraterrestrial help, etc. Heinrich, the oldest member of the group who'd been exploring paranormal phenomena for years and felt that his mind was tuned into the intergalactic consciousness, told us that "Earth is an experimentation station. Different civilizations from different star systems passed by and dropped their life forms here. The time of harvest is coming now and they are allowed to come back and see what has happened."

We talked about the very intense experiences of Whitley Streiber, author of "Communion" and others. Shirley, a nurse in the group, questioned the compassion level of entities from outer space that implant instruments in people's bodies and scare them to death. The group consensus seemed to be that certain entities have agreed to experience negativity before they incarnate as part of the lesson they came here to learn—and Whitley was probably one of them. He perceived them through fear initially, rather than through his heart center, and later, in a second book called "Transformation," revised his perceptions.

One man said, "Many of us have coded information in us and it is time to start decoding…the memory bank is popping open…it's linked up to a point of evolution where we made a mistake so painful that we had to lock up the information until we reached a certain level of awareness." The Aquarian Age which is about balance and returning to a state of higher pristine knowledge is now enabling us to reclaim that encoded information.

Joshua feels that the evolutionary plan to raise the vibration rate of the planet is so important that we must have guidance from evolved incorporeal beings or listen to our High Selfs to help link us into it. He also senses that those of us who choose to come here and serve during this time have extra protection surrounding us. "We are going to become galactic citizens and are being prepared to become brothers and sisters with star people from other worlds," Joshua said. Many of us are simply remembering our origins.

When someone asked why these masters or extraterrestrials don't appear to us in physical form, Joshua said he'd been told inwardly, "If we appear to you, it would change your vibration rate. You wouldn't be able to do your work —be patient."

I asked Joy Johnson, the psychic, to channel Sam, the dolphin energy who appeared for her when she needed to relax and play. A vision of a bay would appear in her consciousness and she knew Sam was calling to her. She explained to us before engaging his energy that, "Dolphins are accepted vanguards for extraterrestrials." Joy relaxed into the cushions in the couch and closed her eyes for a few minutes, before Sam's energy invited us to ask him questions.

I wanted to validate my sense that the dolphins were here to teach us about the spiritual evolution of the planet and asked Sam why they were appearing in our consciousness in vortex areas.

He told us, "Dolphins open people to receive, they are remembering...learning to follow that which is within them, surrendering. Sacred sites are places where surrendering is easier."

"What is the dolphin's connection to Atlantis and extraterrestrials?" I quizzed.

Sam replied, "Extraterrestrials had to leave because of fear. The dolphins are perceived as lower life forms—now acting as emissaries. We are non-threatening and when we invite people to come and play and share and open to this love, they are more ready to accept that there is intelligence beyond self, love beyond self. Mistakenly our space brothers and sisters were seen as posing a threat. Those people who come to us now have already found the truth. Communication and sharing and love is meant to be done through play, through joy. Spinning and jumping and playing like children, we touch the child and the child is curious. Left to itself it is unafraid."

I asked whether or not only some of us are being called by the dolphins to recreate Atlantis or Atlantean consciousness and Sam replied. "The Atlantean consciousness of knowing was that we are all One. Toward the end of Atlantis, we (dolphins) became worshipped and had to separate ourselves. We wish not to be worshipped, we wish to share."

"Do dolphins allow themselves to be captured as a way of serving?" I asked.

"We allow ourselves to be captured and killed...to be companions as a way of teaching. Through our sacrifice, compassion is awakened, such as in yourself. Children will not hurt other beings. Only those who are separated from themselves, injure others."

Curious about Timothy Wyllie's vision of a mutated species evolving on the planet, I asked Sam about it. "Mutation...not physically." There was a pause, as if he were contemplating a human/dolphin image. "Possibility, but not necessarily." I thought I detected a slight note of pleasure in the response.

He went on. "We are more like you than different. We are not better, we have only chosen a different view. Not all dolphins are as aware as those that teach. As in human beings there is a hierarchy, an organization of which we too follow the laws. We are not rebels, we see the harmony. This is why we love life. We live, experience and share. We are also in dense bodies. We, too, are students. We have the advantage of ridding ourselves of the distractions you have given yourselves."

Joshua questioned Sam about his personal role as a networker and Sam admonished him. "You need to lighten up, be freer, play more, if you expect to lead people in the future."

I asked Sam if the dolphins would lead us to the Crystal Skulls and noted a scolding tone in his reply. "Not until you come to us with a light attitude! Not seriously, but with lightness." Is that a message for me to lighten up, I wondered.

Taking the cue, I asked Sam about engaging in Tantra as a way of lightening up, being more playful like the dolphins. "If you want to see how dolphins align themselves," he told me, "You would see how they do it is belly-to-belly."

Sam completed the channeling by telling the group, "It's the consciousness of the dolphins that humans need, not the saving of the dolphins. How to be considerate and loving to planet Earth."

Joy came out of her channeling state and said, "Nothing new. He's not saying anything new." She added, "One last thing, I'm not special, I have no special connection to dolphins. They don't leap out of the water when I'm at the ocean. I only connect with them in my visions."

" Hmmm," I thought, "maybe we can't all swim with dolphins, but there's nothing to stop us from playing and romping with them in the ethers, like Joy." Maybe all that was needed was for us Earthlings   to start being lighter, stop worrying about all the extraterrestrial activity, the dark prophecies, the ancient knowledge…just start following the ecstasy of the dolphin within ourselves, dance with them in the ethers inside our minds, tune into the dolphin energy in our souls.

As we were winding up the evening, a martial arts master, motioned to me from across the room and said, "Water, you need to do more water movements. Tai Chi—that would help you get rid of those blocks in your body. You've got an awful lot of Earth."

Funny how he read my mind. "I spend a lot of time around water," I told him. I needed to loosen my body up. I'm grounded to the chair in front of my computer several hours every day. He gave me the answer I needed without my asking. I didn't bother to tell him I was thinking of moving to Hawaii so I could swim in the ocean every day…and connect with dolphins. On the drive back I made a commitment to myself. Enough of this serious stuff. You've got all the information you need. No more meetings, no more intellectualizing. It's time to play, to be free. I vowed to put an ad in the paper to sell my motor home. That would free me to move to Hawaii. I visualized the sale and a beautiful place to live and play with lots of dolphin people and maybe even some real live dolphins. I surrounded it with a ball of light, put it in a basket and handed it up to God. "Take care of it for me, please?"

My High Self answered, "It's all ready and waiting for you." The ecstasy feeling rose in my feet and legs, creeping up into my groin. A warm sensation spread around my heart chakra. The only way I can describe it I told a friend on the phone earlier that morning is "like liquid fire." It crept up my spine into my neck. It opened like a blossom at the top of my crown. A numbness and tingly sensation spilled down my cheeks. My tongue fibrillated, very subtly tuning into the body harmonic.

I wondered, is this the state of perfection that Astra, the whale energy Marie channeled, is talking about? If so, we could all be transformed in the "blink of an eye."

EXPLORING VORTEX ENERGY

I'd been thinking I needed to learn more about vortexes and their energy, when Sigrid, a dolphin woman I met through Meredith, invited me on a dowsing tour of the Monte Bello vortex (areas along the San Andreas fault above Palo Alto). The guide, Gary Plapp, is a friend of hers. Gary is a space research engineer with strong metaphysical leanings. He became interested in studying vortex energy after returning from a tour of the ruins in the Yucatan in the early 1980s. He is in the process of developing the technology to photograph and measure vortex energy and document its existence to skeptics.

On a sunny but crisp Saturday morning we hiked along the curved trail of one of the coastal mountains in Monte Bello Preserve. Gary told us that, "being in a vortex is like being in the eye of a hurricane. When you are in the center, you move beyond time and space." Vortexes serve as link-ups to the center of the Earth and to outer space. "Sedona," says Gary, "is a major communications center. Vortexes radiate measurable radiation that is experienced as pressure and sound by sensitive individuals. He says he is extremely sensitive to the energy and comes away with radiation burns on his forehead after these excursions. It can't be sun because he wears a hat with a bill to shield his head.

He added, "The pyramids generate vortexes so that the priests could go inside and meditate and move beyond time and space. They could also levitate along the ley energy lines."

Some vortexes radiate male or positive charge, while others radiate female or negative charge. Some are balanced. One way you feel a spinning sensation. When you turn the other way, you may sense some resistance. If you sense the energy flowing in both directions, you've discovered a balanced vortex. We explored several vortex sites that afternoon and I half hoped to encounter some being from another dimension and was somewhat disappointed when nothing profound occurred.

Hiking up the hill later to meditate at an etheric temple located at the crown of a small hill above a female vortex, I remembered previous experiences with seeing other dimensions. The first time had been on the ocean when I saw the lightbody spheres. The second had been at Sedona when the dolphins appeared in the ethers. But receiving the Huna initiations, touring the Yucatan, encountering the mystic on Mt. Shasta, meeting so many people who seemed to be on the same wave length had an even more profound effect on my life. I never knew what I was supposed to be **getting** out of an experience while I was in it. The greatest impact always occurred after the fact. The synchronicity of these occurrences was mindblowing enough. What I got from the experiences was an "inner knowing" that other dimensions do indeed exist and are more real than what we perceive as ordinary reality.

After the hike we drove along the ridge road from Monte Bello Preserve to Saratoga, which overlooks the Santa Clara Valley. At that moment it came to me that the valley was once ocean. It had the same energy as Sedona, though not as strong or dramatic. There is a high degree of interest in dolphins among the people who live there. Even the editor of the San Jose Sunday supplement had picked up on the energy and had a reporter follow up, first with an article on extraterrestrials, then one on dolphins. He knows something is going on.

That evening as I was laying in bed tuning into the Kundalini energy, I had a thought that our chakra centers link into 12 different planets. Is it possible, I wondered, that there are 12 major vortexes or cosmic communication centers on the Earth? The number 12 seems to have some extraordinary significance in mystery teachings and the numerology of the planet. I also wondered if a Higher Intelligence somehow monitors what is going on with us through our chakra centers.

As I lay there pondering the cosmic connection, a spasm thrust my whole lower body off the bed. Seems like the Kundalini current activated by the breath clears the meridians or charges them in a way similar to acupuncture, except I felt no charge of electricity run through me. A few minutes later, I began to receive what felt like channeled information or an integration of information I'd been gathering for several days. Here is the information that was conveyed to me:

"The electro (sky) magnetic (earth) currents of Kundalini are drawn into the body and circulated through the breath charging the system and chakra centers with a cleansing heat that purifies it. That radiant heat merges in the heart and emits a vibrational signal which hooks us up or links the body into the electromagnetic field of the Earth and Universe as well as to other people. (As in telepathy.) The grid/ley lines of the Earth and vortex centers serve as storage centers and conduits along which the waves of vibration travel.

Each of us is a charged field of vibration. When our chakras are blocked or our circuits are jammed, we fail to receive or transmit at peak efficiency. This limits the flow of energy and information and our capacity to communicate with each other and other dimensions of reality. What is happening on Earth today is an intense purification of the electro-magnetic field in preparation for the shift to a higher vibration as the Earth spins closer to the central sun and decreases in density."

What came through after that seemed to be a message for Gary, as much as for me:

"Study mandalas to learn more about vortexes. Meditate on them. The center of the vortex of the mandala is an eye of spiraling energy that emits sound currents which are radiated into the atmos-phere and transmitted to receiving centers on other planets. The sound currents enable us to emanate visual images with which we communi-cate to the receptive side of your mind the right brain. It is important for you to remain in a creative state in order to receive clear messages from us. If you become too analytical, you will not decipher the mes-sages properly. Just write down your experiences as they occur. The logic behind them will unfold when those who read the book are ready to know and use the knowledge appropriately. We are with you always through the opening in your heart. Peace be with you. Be in Samadhi to receive."

After the voice finished speaking, I remembered that mandalas are vortexes used by the Tibetans and other Eastern philosophers to reach Sam-adhi and enter into altered states and other dimensions of reality. These images take us back to the point at which a thought generates sound, which generates light patterns, which generates colors, which generate images in the form of art, etc. In other words, we return to the essence by meditating upon the form which was created out of it.

Several months earlier I'd taped a card on the wall at the foot of my bed. It is a mandala of dolphins swimming in the waves around and around in a circle. I looked closely at the image for the first time and found that at the center there is a gold spiral similar to that of a seashell. When I looked at the mandala with soft, unfocused eyes, the whole thing began to spin.

The next evening I went to a sacred sites meeting at Gary's home. I had asked him if he felt any special connection with dolphin and whale energy and he said he hadn't. When I walked into his house, however, I noticed one of Jean Luc Bozzoli's dolphin cards on his bookshelf and Gary himself was wearing a T-shirt with a dolphin on it. Sigrid, one of his closest friends, is totally preoccupied with dolphins. She has a huge stuffed dolphin she sleeps with. She hugs and loves it as she plays with the energy in her dreams and meditations.

Gary is coordinating a group of people who will travel to the Yucatan and other ancient sites in the future and attempt to retrieve ancient knowledge which he believes is trapped between dimensions. The purpose of the meeting was to attune and bond the group—to strengthen their telepathic or energy connection with one another. He stressed the importance of creating a symbiotic relationship in order to glean or retrieve information during visits to the ruins. During the meeting he talked a bit about clairaudience, or the ability to hear the sounds of other dimensions of reality. Gary is able to hear sounds from particular places. For instance, he says he once tuned into the voices of the men who died on the USS Arizona.

Listening to those inner sounds requires intense meditation skill. The mind must focus its complete attention on them. All thoughts stop. Our transmitters shut down and our receivers open up. In other words, we become more receptive to messages and images being transmitted to us from other dimensions. To help access the ancient knowledge that is trapped between dimensions, developing clairaudient skills is beneficial, Gary feels.

10 *Lightening Up*

EVERY TIME I went to a meeting on the ancient records, Marcia Well's name popped into the space. Finally, the night before I thought I was leaving to visit my father in Sacramento, I called her. We talked briefly and made an appointment to meet the next afternoon. I sensed some doubt in her voice and wondered what it was about.

Our timing was impeccable. I arrived at her house the next day just as she was returning from grocery shopping. We talked as we carried the bags in from the car. I knew nothing about her other than she channeled a dolphin named Belinda. She only did this for people who were tuned into dolphin energies.

When we finally sat down she told me that for 17 years she'd been involved in the education field in the area of Instructional Technology, focusing on breakthrough techniques. Currently she was working with people using a process she calls "Clearing." This identifies glitches in people's energy fields that signal erroneous beliefs and attitudes in the subconscious computer. Many clients are referred to her by an employment counselor when the counselor detects a lack of clarity is getting in the way of someone finding a job. In less than two hours, no matter how many years the energy block has persisted, Marcia is able to clear it out so that the person can move forward in his or her life. The block, according to Marcia is sometimes only a symptom, the tip of the iceberg, and what gets cleared is the real issue, nine-tenths of which was not visible. She told me, "Last night when you called, I sensed your energy was flat, like there was this thick block of some sort."

"Oh, great!" I thought. "She's going to tell me I need to do more work." I told her, "Maybe I didn't come here for a dolphin reading. Maybe I came her for clearing."

She said, "I don't know...well that isn't a very intelligent answer..."

"It's perfectly acceptable to me," I joked "I say it all the time. But I feel like I'm as clear as I'm ever going to get. My Kundalini started to rise last week and I know my chakras are wide open. I can feel them."

"Don't you feel vulnerable?" she asked.

"Not really," I told her. "It feels very safe. Like it's time for me to be totally open and undefended."

When I asked her to channel Belinda, she said "Well, I can't make any guarantees. She comes through when it's appropriate or someone else might come through. I'm what you might call a multi-dimensional channel. Lots of different energies come in."

We seated ourselves in straight-back chairs facing each other and she said, "I must tell you I'm an extraterrestrial."

I had long since ceased to be amazed when someone announced their other-planet origins to me. Instead I replied by telling her, "So am I. I'm told I'm from the Pleiades."

Marcia persisted, however, and told me that, "A year ago, I entered as a walk-in soul."

"Oh, terrific," I thought. "Here's another ingredient to add to the mish-mash of pieces I have to this vast puzzle." Joy had told me about a group of walk-in souls in Carmel that functioned under the name Earth Mission. Then someone suggested that the anti-Christ president who is prophesied to take over the government in the last days very well could be a walk-in soul who is of the dark force. Now here I was sitting in front of walk-in extraterrestrial who was about to channel a dolphin. What am I supposed to do with this information? Since my experiences have convinced me that we are being observed and tracked every second and there are absolutely no accidents, no coincidences, I can only conclude more information about walk-ins is about to pop into my life.

The walk-in's entry into Marcia's life created a healing crisis for her body. Not only did her Kundalini energy rise to handle the strain, she discovered she had candida and Guillan-Barre Disease. She looked a bit emaciated to me, not healthy. Hopefully, my asking to have all my psychic gifts opened would not leave me in the same condition.

Marcia interrupted my thinking. "Don't be frightened if I make some loud toning sounds. That's how I break through the energy field."

What came out sounded like muffled dynamite blasts. I could feel the percussion in my chakra centers, but apparently it didn't budge the block in my energy field. Marsha said, "You've got this really thick wall around you that I can't get through."

Suddenly I remembered a few nights earlier talking to St. Germain and Merlin and my High Self, telling them I'd be willing to be a direct channel for their energies but no one else's. Could it be they'd thrown up the wall to protect me? Or had they been shielding me ever since my trip to Mt. Shasta? I'd certainly been given many images of protection at that time and I'd felt very protected since then. I told Marsha, "I think you have to ask permission of St. Germain."

She went inside and called, "St. Germain of the violet flame." A few minutes later she told me, "He's opened a kind of window or slot. Some information will be permitted to come through at this time. My sense is it's kind of like it will be monitored in terms of the amount and the appropriateness and you'll get whatever else you need at the right time. It will be a progressive thing."

Marcia asked me if I was clear on what I wanted to know.

I told her, "I want to know how we can access the ancient knowledge or secrets that are supposedly trapped between dimensions."

Marcia closed her eyes and breathed deeply. She saw Belinda standing on her tail and said, "She's in a very playful mood. There's two ways these transmissions occur, one is telepathically where I relay the information, the other is where the sounds come through this body and there's an interspecies mingling that takes awhile. It may take as much as five minutes for the energy bodies to merge. It's much more difficult. Seems like Belinda wants to speak in her own voice."

After several minutes of deep breathing, Belinda's voice broke through.

The sounds were very close to those of the dolphins I taped and heard in Florida. I was amazed. I couldn't understand a word she was saying. The contortions that Marcia was going through in order to channel the dolphin sounds were causing her to look like she might choke to death. Her neck was stretched and taut and her face contorted and flushed. I could see it required tremendous effort and was a great strain on her body. For some reason, the whole scenario seemed hilariously funny to me. I had to stifle the laughter building up in my solar plexus. I sent Belinda a telepathic message asking her to please take it easy on Marcia and to speak in a language I could understand.

A few seconds later, Marcia said, "That's enough for now, I don't want to tire the woman's body." She came out of the trance state and gave me a telepathic translation of what Belinda said.

"You are being honored out of your commitment to bringing forth the truth of the information. There are those who are not of an understanding and they could misuse it or exploit it. This is not for show and dramatization. This is for the ears of those who are willing to hear not only with their ears but with their heart as well. There is much that we would tell you about yourselves and about us and about our relationship with each other. We are more attuned than you realize. We are coming into a time where the communication will become increasingly easy. It will be a way of attunement that has not previously been done on the planet. The information will become simultaneously available to people in different places on the planet at the same time. Guard against any feelings or thoughts you may have about ownership of the information or needing to be the only one to bring it through. It is imperative that it happen with many people at the same time so that no one being can have it be diffused by their own ego needs.

"We are here to reopen you to your experience of joy and of play. There has been, as one of your bards so aptly phrased it, 'Much ado about nothing' in a sense of the focus being so predominantly on work. Very little has been done to equalize this and balance it with true play. There are those who do social and recreational activities without the experience of play. The work energy and focus and ethic is so predominant that they turn their leisure time into another occupation, another structured form which exhausts them so that they need a vacation from their vacation. This is not a true experience of the energy of play and of joy. The energy of play has no agenda, has no intended outcome…has no goal other than the experience itself. There is very little of this experience on the Earth at this time. We have come to help to bring these energies into balance for the healing of the beings on the planet, and for the planet itself. The Earth is working very hard to cleanse itself of all of the damage which has been inflicted by mankind. We have come to assist with the purification process and we will be making ourselves available to those who would join with us in this experience, not out of something they ought to do or have to do as a duty, but something that comes from the love of their hearts and something that they do purely out of joy. Those who are willing to bring the energies of joy and play into their own experience and their own lives will find it most easy to connect with us. It is time now for me to leave as I am tiring the body which I am using. Thank you for being present here."

I said, "Thank you, Belinda."

For the second time in a week, I received a message from a dolphin telling me the key to accessing the ancient knowledge was in lightening up. "Doesn't pay to be dead serious about this stuff," I joked.

"Right," Marcia said. "You could end up seriously dead. After all the word enlightenment does contain the word lighten."

As I was preparing to leave Marcia asked if I'd seen the movie "The Big Blue." I told her I had. "I loved the dolphin scenes but didn't care for the ending," I said.

She said, "Chuck, my partner, and I went last week and at the end of the movie when we got up to leave I could feel Belinda trying to come into my body. My body started convulsing. When we got to the car I asked Chuck to find a darkened parking lot somewhere so I could let her speak. She had a message for us. I could feel her rostrum forming around the front of my face and the melon over the top of my head. It was almost like I was inside her body."

"You were becoming one with the energy," I said.

"Yes, fortunately Chuck understood what was happening. He said, 'You're shape-shifting.'"

"Oh, he must read Carlos Castaneda."

"Yeah, and he's done a lot of work with Native Americans…so he knows about this stuff."

"Anybody else might have been blown out of the water."

I wondered what had brought the two of them together. Marcia read my mind.

"Chuck swam with Joe and Rosie, the dolphins from John Lilly's Janus project that were released back into the wild in 1987. He said it was the most loving, unconditional experience of his whole life. Marcia asked where the two of them could go and swim with other dolphins so I told her about the Florida Keys.

The message Belinda gave to Marcia was that sometime in the future she would be given a piece of equipment that she would belt to her waist which would directly translate the dolphin communications into language we can understand. She urged me to stay in touch. "I have a feeling there is a lot more you'll want to know.

11 Death, Dying and Dolphins

PART OF THE planetary cleansing process that is now underway during the transition between the Age of Pisces and Aquarius is the healing of relationships. Addictions, dysfunctions, negative attitudes and beliefs are being flushed up and aired out on Prime Time TV, radio talk shows, in magazines and newspapers all around the country as well as in therapists offices and support groups. Some people, I've been told, are so anxious to rid themselves of addictive/dysfunctional patterns that they are fabricating an alcoholic parent or digging ancestral skeletons out of the closet who were alcoholic so that they can qualify to attend Adult Children of Alcoholics or Al-Anon meetings and do the Twelve Step Program. Treating people for addictions and addictive patterns has become big business in the past few years. The symptoms of our emotional and spiritual bankruptcy are rising to the surface to be cleansed. This clearing of old patterns, negative as it may seem, is a natural part of the rhythm of change. It indicates, to me at least, that we are preparing ourselves on schedule for the Age of Enlightenment that has been prophesied by the elders and through the legends of many cultures worldwide.

I had been in the process of healing my relationship with my father for many years without success. We hadn't lived together since I was ten years old. I saw him only once as I was growing up after my mother died but he reappeared in my life after my first child was born and wanted to reconnect. A few years later my sister committed suicide. Her death reopened all the old wounds of childhood. I blamed my father's irresponsibility for her inability to cope in the world and it wasn't until a year or so after my divorce that we really got down to the business of getting to know one another again. In the process, he revealed a side of himself that no one else in the family seemed to know. By then he'd been an outcast for nearly 40 years. My father, I learned, was a closet mystic, loved to play with numerology and knew a lot about Haley's Comet and its effects. After several healing visits, I came to realize that he was an extremely sensitive man who hid that part of himself behind a smokescreen of rage and vengeance. Once I came to accept him as he was, to look beyond the anger and wrathful behavior, to the pain beneath it which he could not express, we became friends.

I had sensed during the months since my last visit, that the time was drawing near for him to leave the planet. I dreaded yet another loss in my life and put off visiting him in Sacramento until the heat spell had broken. By the time I arrived, he was moving into the dying process and there was no time left to heal the past.

Just as he had created struggle and trauma in his life for himself, he turned his dying into a drama as well. When I arrived, he'd been sick for several days and couldn't keep food in his stomach. Small cartons of untouched gelatin, applesauce and milk sat on top of his oxygen tanks. He'd been battling with emphysema for years. It was all he could do to get up and go to the bathroom. In a rasping voice he said, "I've been holding out 'til you got here. If you'll just stay three or four days I think I can get through this without going to the hospital." Yet in the next breath he told me, "I'm ready to die. There's nothing left for me to live for."

I asked him what had kept him alive so long. He said, "My relationship with you." A few weeks earlier I'd written to tell him I was thinking of moving to Hawaii. Without my visits to look forward to, and losing his ability to take care of himself or go out into the sunshine, play poker or drink an occasional highball, there was little for him to do but await death. It was time for him to let go not just of life, but of the long years of suffering and pain he'd endured without a caring family. "Have you thought about whether or not you want to go on life support in the hospital if it's needed?" I asked him.

"Yes," he said, "I want to."

"How can he be 'ready to die' and want life support at the same time," I wondered. "Only part of him is ready."

"Are you afraid of death?" I questioned.

"No," he assured me.

"What are you afraid of?" I prodded.

"The nothingness...the emptiness."

It surprised me to hear him say it. I thought he believed in God. He stopped me from going further. "You're getting too deep. I don't want to get deep."

I sat with him for a while, observing his struggle for every breath, wanting to be present for me, wanting to talk and unable to do either. Between gasps he vacillated about going to the hospital and not going to the hospital. He said, "When I get through this maybe we can go for a picnic in the park." Each time I'd been to visit him in the past few years, we'd gone to the park, drank a beer or two, ate a picnic lunch and watched the children play. A sun worshipper, he loved being outdoors. I assured him I wasn't going anywhere and promised to return early the next morning to run errands.

I slept in a little late the next morning and by the time I got to his room, ambulance attendants were preparing to take him to the hospital. My father, barely able to breathe, began flailing the air with his wallet and ordering me in a rasping voice to pay his rent before I followed him.

When I finally connected with his long-time doctor later in the morning, he told me my father had been given too high a dose of a new medicine designed to regulate his breathing, but after a few days of clearing out his system, he should be fine.

I asked the doctor to step out into the hall and got right to the point. "Have you spoken to my father about going on life support?"

"Every time I've asked him, he says yes," the doctor replied.

"Last night he told me he was ready to die," I told him.

"As long as he is capable of making a decision about whether he wants to be on life support, we honor his decision."

"How long can you keep him on it?" I wondered.

"As long as he decides," the doctor replied.

"How long WILL you keep him on life support?"

"We can keep him on indefinitely, as long as his body holds out."

"But that's not dealing with the real issue. He's terrified of dying into nothingness."

"We have to honor his decision."

"But his decision is based on his fear of dying."

The doctor had no answer.

"Do you ever work with hospice people?" I asked.

"No, they're only interested when someone has six months or less to live. You can get a durable power of attorney that covers his health care for when your father is no longer able to make his own decisions."

How can he make clear decisions when he's doped up, I wondered? I wasn't sure I wanted power over his life. Some part of me didn't want to be responsible for making the final decision, didn't want to play God. Who am I to determine what is right or wrong for him? How could I know his soul's ultimate destiny? I'd been warned before not to interfere with someone's freedom of choice.

Besides, now that my father was actually in the hospital and I'd just watched the nurse slip an IV needle into his right hand, how could I ask him to sign a power of attorney over his life? No, there had to be another way to help him work through his contradiction about wanting to die and being unwilling to do it without life support. My mind moved into a state of confusion and inaction trying to deal with the whole idea. As I was leaving the hospital, I stopped in the waiting room to call a hospice center. Surely they would know what to do. No answer on the first number. A recording on the second. Time enough tomorrow, I thought.

The next morning I slept late. The first traces of exhaustion were creeping over me. I asked for help from above and found myself pulling the "Course in Miracles" book from its resting place. I hadn't opened it in months. I said, "I hope you don't give me this shit about 'there is no such thing as illness or disease and death is an illusion,'" which is what it had told me the night Jane died. Then I'd flown into a rage and threw the book against the wall. This time it fell open to "In the giving you receive." I thought, "I'm not sure exactly how it applies, but I'll say it and do it anyway."

I arrived at the hospital around noon to discover my father had been shifted to intensive care the previous evening. When I finally found him surrounded by attendants and hooked into a respirator, he torched me with one look and then asked the nurse for a pad to write on. When he was done scrawling he handed the clipboard to me. It read, "Well, you lazy bitch it's all over now. The doctor was already here."

My body felt like it had just been grazed by a flash fire. The grizzly bear had returned. Instead of reacting by walking out, my old way of coping with his rage, I sat down in the chair in the corner, got out my tape recorder and played some soft harp music and wrote a few letters. About an hour later, when the swarm of worker bees in attendance were finished sapping him of a variety of nectars—from blood to urine to mucous, I got up, unwrapped the rose I'd brought him and asked the nurse for a vase. When she returned with it, I handed him the rose to smell along with a card that had a mandala on front with butterflies emerging from their cocoons symbolizing transformation. Squelching back a barrage of feelings that wanted to gurgle up and out my throat, I took his hand in mine and said, "You think you feel helpless, how do you think I feel?" A glazed look of understanding passed across his eyes and he gripped my hand hard. With his mouth taped rigidly in place to hold the respirator tube, it was impossible for him to speak and his scrawlings under the influence of morphine soon became illegible.

That first day, I couldn't think. I could only feel my world of spiritual fantasy collapsing around me. The giant pink ball of protective light I'd felt surrounded with turned into collapsed bubble gum, trapping me inside a sticky mess with a dying father who had no mercy for himself. "Why is it," I asked St. Germain and Merlin, "you can protect me so well out in the ethereal realm and you can't protect me down here?"

All I could think to do was hold one of his hands in mine and place my other hand on his heart, hoping to relieve some of his suffering while trying not to take it into my own body. I struggled to hold back the feelings for nearly an hour and then thought, "This isn't doing me any good." I felt myself slipping back into time, into childhood when there was no one around to talk to about the melodrama being played out before my eyes. I'd worked so hard to break through the frozen, barren wasteland of those years. If I stuffed my feelings now, if I didn't reach out and ask for help, then all my own years of pain and suffering were for nothing. Gently, I slipped my hand from his and excused myself to go to lunch.

After choking down some chicken and potatoes and plugging the parking meter with quarters, I walked back into the hospital and found myself heading for the phone booth to call the hospice center one more time. The minute I heard the saccharine-voiced volunteer on the other end, my mind and body went into resistance. The last thing I wanted was to have to deal with some sugary, patronizing do-gooder in fear of her own death. Three referrals later, I was given the number of a social worker in the hospital to talk to. The minute I heard the reassuring, steadfast quality in Liz's voice, I lost it all. "My father's in the process of dying and I need someone to talk to."

She met me at the fourth floor elevator and we walked the short distance to her office. I liked her immediately. Her soft eyes and rounded frame felt safe, comforting. No sharp edges here, no phony facades.

It didn't take long to get to the anger that was building inside me. I wanted my father to die gracefully, to get on with his dying so that I could get on with my life. We'd both suffered long enough. It was time for me to live fully. I was ready to let go, why couldn't he? I wanted to be present for him and yet, I didn't want to be held up too long.

Liz found the soft spot. "You think you ought to be this compassionate person…"

"It's not an ought, it's a value. If I'm not this compassionate person, who the hell am I?"

"You are really hard on yourself. You have such a narrow, limited view of who you can be. Does your compassion have to be limitless in order for you to feel good about yourself?"

I looked down at the floor, not knowing how to answer. It was a question I needed time to ponder. I felt no need to defend my position so she changed tacks. I'd given her a brief family history about my father's violent alcoholic behavior, my mother's death, the series of deaths in my early 20s that preceded my sister's suicide. "I wanted to be there for my sister, but I couldn't. It was a draw between which one of us would kill ourselves first.

We were like two survivors of a shipwreck. Only one of us could survive. I chose to save myself."

"There's still a lot of unfinished business there isn't there...a lot of pain."

"Yes," I choked. And then it hit me. I was here to help process my father's unfinished business along with my own. I'd taken on his grief and guilt, acting as a transformer for him because he couldn't seem to do it for himself. Yes, he could express the rage and anger without any problem, but he couldn't even begin to touch his pain. It was too overwhelming. "Why," I wondered, "do I keep taking on all this guilt and pain for other people?" I felt better, releasing it, passing it on to Liz. She wasn't tied into the drama. She could handle it better, view it from outside as an observer, help me extricate myself from the sticky mass of bubble gum.

I could feel relief wash over me. My heart lightened a little. We joked about how no matter what I did it would never be enough to please my father. "It's not him I'm trying to please anymore," I thought. "It's myself." I truly want to be a compassionate human being. My father is giving me a gift, the perfect opportunity to practice being the heart of compassion.

That night my restless mind and body refused to sleep. It was easy for me to intellectualize being compassionate, quite another to be compassion itself. I could feel exhaustion creeping into my bones again. "Somehow, I have to transform his dying into a celebration," I thought. It occurred to me that my father and I were the torchbearers for generations of ancestors who had passed on leaving behind legacies of their unexpressed sadness, guilt and pain for those who followed. It was as if my father and I, our souls, came into this life to carry the burden of pain and suffering for the rest of the family. At least that is the role we both assumed. Our lesson together was to somehow come to completion with the past...to heal the familial wounds.

My father acted out the woundedness, had been blamed for my mother's death and my sister's suicide, been labeled weak and irresponsible and unfit to be alive. He'd been ostracized and ignored as an outcast since I was a child as a result of his raging alcoholism. Each time I'd witnessed his persecution, I'd felt his pain like a knife in my heart. Here was a man I couldn't feel anything toward as a father, neither love nor hate, yet for whom as a human being, an underdog, I felt overwhelming compassion.

My need, for whatever reason, to bring it all to an end, to heal the old wounds, felt overpowering. Lying in bed, I called for guidance and found myself shifting into the world of the already dead, calling forth his grandparents, his parents, an aunt named Wealthy who died when she was six on the Oregon Trail, my mother, my sister, the aunt and uncle who raised me, their son and an assortment others who strayed into my vision. I asked each of them to release my father and me from the burden of suffering, to forgive us so that he could die gracefully and I could live in peace.

When all of those who had crossed over were gathered together, I came back to Earth and spoke separately to each of his living relatives, asking their forgiveness and inviting them to join the celebration. I saw us gather in a circle around him in heaven while he danced the Irish jig. I can't remember a day in our life together when I'd seen him truly happy, but I remembered seeing pictures of him as a gay blade in high school and heard stories about his love of dancing.

I felt tons lighter when I got up the next morning though still in a state of mild exhaustion from all the invisible healing I'd been doing in the ethereal realm. It was the same feeling of body exhaustion I'd felt while Jane was dying. It seemed to permeate every cell. It struck me then that the candida in my system had flared up, gotten out of balance. No wonder I felt so emotional and distraught. I'd drank some wine and eaten a few desserts the previous week. "Why is it I seem to fall off my diet just before an onslaught of external distress?" I set myself up to be emotionally out-of-balance and unable to cope."

For as long as I could remember, I'd held a terrible picture inside me— the image of my father dying alone with no one around him who really cared. I wanted to be there for him. Having survived being his daughter, I felt strong enough to handle being present for him at his death.

Feeling as light as the bouquet of balloons I carried into my father's room the next day, hoping he would allow his fear to float up and away inside them, I was totally unprepared for the brutal picture that confronted me. His arms and legs were tied down and fresh red blood seeped through the sheets near his crotch. My first assumption was that he'd become violent and a nurse had lost her patience with him. When the doctor arrived a few minutes later, I asked why he'd been tied down. "Standard procedure," he informed me. My father had pulled the catheter out of his penis and the air tube out of his mouth.

I insisted that the doctor ask him one more time if he wanted to stay on the life support system. I couldn't stand the torture he was subjecting himself to. When the doctor asked my father he nodded yes. The realization began to creep into my consciousness, that he could be kept alive this way for weeks, maybe even months. As long as he could shake his head yes, he was in control. "You have the final decision," the doctor told him."

The exhaustion I felt in my body earlier, suddenly overwhelmed me. I knew I couldn't hold up much longer. Choking on tears, I told my father, "If you decide to stay on life support, I won't be able to stay here with you. It's too hard on my body."

It had taken me nearly two years to recover from the stress of Jane's death. I couldn't pay that price again. I couldn't tolerate living any longer in a black hole, depriving myself of being close to people so that I could process through layers of grief and sadness. Silently I wept for both of us. He clenched my hand with great strength and refused to let go. I stood there locked into his grasp for over an hour, watching him tug at and pull away the sheet and then the towel which covered the still- bleeding penis. His blood had lost its clotting ability. When I pleaded with him to, "Be nice to yourself," he looked at me like I'd gone insane.

Some time later he attempted to tell me something with the movement of his tongue against his lower jaw. I couldn't understand him, but I guessed he was ready to call it quits. The physical pain, the restraint, the loss of control, my threat of leaving was too much for him. I asked him, "Do you want them to turn the machines off?"

He nodded yes. The doctor had just returned and was examining charts at the nurses' station. I walked out and waited patiently for him to finish writing. Searching for a way to excuse my distress in 15 words or less, I told him, "I seem to pick up a lot of his energy and I can't seem to let it just pass through me." I told him my father had pulled off his sheet and was struggling to say something. "He shook his head yes when I asked him if he wanted the machines turned off. Please ask him one more time."

Obligingly, he walked into the room and asked my father several times, "Do you want the machines turned off?" My father nodded yes each time, though he seemed to hesitate once or twice and acted unsure of what he was being asked. The doctor persisted in asking the question and my father slowly, but persistently nodded yes. The doctor wavered and said, "Maybe we need to call in the Ethics Committee to decide."

The nurse on duty that day called the doctor into the hall for a conference. When they returned, the doctor said, "Mr. Miller, you've only been on the respirator for three days. That's not very long. If you decide to go off now, it could be fatal. Better to wait a few days than make a fatal mistake."

Liz, the social worker stood in the doorway with tears in her eyes. One more time I asked for emotional support, "Can't you send someone to talk to him?"

"No," she insisted, "it's a matter of process."

"I meant to help him process his fear of dying."

"You can't hurry process. It just takes time."

Somehow we'd entered into a battle of wills. My father's will versus mine versus the medical system versus the process. "Where is the compassion in all of this?" I wondered.

The doctor felt it was his duty was to save a life, regardless of whether that life had anything to live for, to look forward to. The system dictated that in order to save the life, the body was open to an endless onslaught of mutilation and plundering regardless of the emotional trauma and physical suffering involved for the patient and family.

Despite the fact that he was technically being given top-notch medical care, I began to feel that emotionally and spiritually he was being raped to support a system without a heart that had been designed by humans to save human life in a mechanistic way. It seemed the system had gained control because the humans in charge didn't want to make the final decision. How is it that every human life came to be mechanistically treated like every other human life? Is there no room for discernment, no room for customizing to an individual's needs? This was hardly a holistic approach to death and dying. My father needed compassion, an understanding heart, to free him of his fear so that he could voluntarily release himself from his emotional suffering and pain. Instead he got physical pain and suffering piled on top. Before the doctor left the room, he said, "Maybe you should stay away. Your father needs people here who can support him so that he can recover."

"I come in here in a supportive state and when I see what's going on I lose it," I told him.

Liz was still standing in the doorway and motioned me to follow her. I wrestled my hand loose from my father's grip and the minute I stepped outside the room felt a gush of pain surging up and out.

"It's a hard decision," Liz said.

"I'm tired of making hard decisions," I told her. "I've had to make too many in my life."

She guided me into a tiny little room just off the waiting room. For the first 15 minutes I allowed myself to just pour out the frustration and grief over having to deal with so much death and loss. Liz perceived my need to be there for my father as part of the roleplaying that goes on in dysfunctional families. I felt it was more than that, but I didn't feel the need to enter into a confrontation with her. What I wanted and needed was to be heard and listened to and received.

"I want to be there for him, but now he's even taking that away. He's so controlling, so full of fear." Suddenly I began to see the irony in all of it. Accusing my father of being controlling, I'd failed to see my own pattern. I started to laugh. "You know, there's a whole lot of healing going on here. Of course, I don't have any need to control."

Liz laughed with me and seeing her lighten up helped me to lighten up even more. I told her how much I appreciated her just being there. "I'm not easy to work with. Usually, I call people on their shit."

"Well," she laughed, "I'm glad I didn't know that."

I got up to leave and gave her a hug. "A little humor helps a lot," she said.

"It's saved my life more than once," I assured her.

I hugged the nurse that was on duty that day and noticed that all but one of the helium-filled balloons I'd left at the nurses' station the day before had sunk to the floor. "Well, maybe he plugged his fear into them after all," I thought. Liz had asked if she could give them to a nine-year-old boy with a brain tumor and I had stewed about it all evening. After awhile I thought, "Well, maybe he'll transform the fear somehow." When I saw them hanging on the nurses' station, she said, "For some reason I changed my mind about giving them to him."

"Good," I said, "it looks like they were full of my father's fear."

"Maybe a day away from all of it will give me a chance to regain my balance," I thought. "There must be something I'm not seeing. Some perfection I'm overlooking. I need time to regain my strength." The strength returned to me in surrender. After decades of struggling, resisting, fighting, disassociating from feelings to survive, my body had worn itself out. Physically and emotionally exhausted I'd discovered the gift of surrendering, letting go and letting God. As I walked out of the hospital to go to lunch, I visually placed my father's crumpled body in a basket and turned it over to Him. "You take care of my father. I can't deal with it anymore."

Later, on the way back to his room, I pulled up a chair in front of the pay phone in the waiting room and started calling. I talked to my father's two brothers, my brother, my father's sister, my children and my brother's daughter. I gave them the gory details and said, "If you can't write to him for his sake, do it for mine. I need you to. It would mean so much to him if he heard from you." To my great surprise and tearful relief, they all agreed. They cared. Even my brother who had been so bitter for so many years agreed to write. They didn't care as much as I did, but they cared. My father's sister said, "I've been thinking about Johnny a lot lately."

It didn't matter that most of them hadn't seen or spoken or written to my father in years. It only mattered that the hostility, the hatefulness, the judgments had somehow melted over time. It mattered that they were willing to support me in supporting my father through his process of dying. I felt for the first time ever that I'd been fully acknowledged and accepted by the family I was born into. They understood my need to be compassionate. Back in my father's room, I hesitated to tell him I'd called his family. When I told him his younger brother had thought about coming to see him for a long time but didn't know what to say to him, he turned his head away, as if to tell me "It's too late now."

I stayed just long enough to say goodbye and to tell him I wouldn't be coming back the next day. "I need to rest and so do you."

Fortunately, Joan, a dolphin friend from third-level Huna, had just moved to Sacramento. She wasn't quite settled in her new home but she invited me to park the motor home at her place. We'd become friends and sisters over the summer. Joan trains counselors to work with battered women and abused children. Having dealt with similar issues in her own life, she was able to stand by as an observer and hold a lantern for me as I floundered in a dark sea of confusion and turmoil. Like a dolphin, she circled me while I was in the midst of my distress, wrestling with my decision to stay or leave.

Since I couldn't work with my father directly in his present state, nor could anyone else approach his pain, I had to find another way. Joan and I did some energy work using Huna techniques, helping me to regain my balance and attune my chakra centers. I felt somewhat cleansed, yet still unprepared to cope.

Working on the etheric level seemed to be the key. That night I called Marcia in San Jose, the woman who did the "Clearing" work. I asked her, "Can you work long distance on people?"

"Yes…"

"My father is in the process of dying and I'm wondering if you can help us through some blocks."

She tuned into his energy field and mine. "I don't perceive them as blocks. What is going on has to do with your relationship with one another." We chatted for several minutes and finally got down to the core issue. "Which level of your energy is holding onto him, the emotional, the spiritual, the conceptual, or the physical?"

"I guess the mental."

"What does your mind need in order to release him?"

Unable to think, what I got was an image of me holding his head in my lap, stroking his head, soothing him. "I guess I need to touch him, to hold him, to give him what he was never able to give me."

"Will that be enough to allow you to let him go?"

Pausing for a moment, I said, "Yes."

The only three times I can remember being touched by my father when I was a child were when he spanked me because my sister broke an ashtray, when he tugged gently on my hair and I started to cry, causing my mother to call the police and have him thrown in jail, and the night he molested me when I was nine. Then I realized what I'd been looking for from men my entire adult life was to be physically touched, held and caressed in a loving way. I didn't know how to have that happen without being sexual and yet being sexual never nourished me in the way that I needed. One more double bind to release, to heal.

I had never wanted anything more out of life than to love and be loved and yet there had been only one person, my father's brother, the uncle who raised me after my mother's death, who had known me, accepted my pain and my need to withdraw and act-out and loved me inspite of it. As a teenager, he stuck by me after two unsuccessful attempts at running away and after I feebly tried to poison myself in reaction to the emotional abuse of my aunt.

It was he I had tried so hard to emulate and failed. His highest ambition was to, "Live beside the road and be a friend of man." I searched for him in other men, holding them up to the light of his being. None came close to matching his compassion and caring. Being a friend of man, of nature, had fallen out of fashion, it seemed. When I was 21, he died of emphysema. A farmer, for years during haying season he'd taken the dirtiest, hottest job at the top of the haymow. He'd stack bales himself so that someone else didn't have to endure the thick dust and intense heat in the mow.

The year following his death, my sister, who had been raised by another uncle in California, slit her wrists toward the end of her freshman year in college. The message was clear: "I can't cope alone out in the world." Due to a law that stated she must receive psychological help following a suicide attempt, she ended up in the state mental hospital and thereafter became the scourge of the family. I wanted to do for her what my uncle had done for me, stand by, be present in her time of distress. A few weeks after she came to live with my husband and I, my uncle's youngest son, my kid brother, was killed in a drunk driving accident. Not long later, my mother-in-law, the only woman in my life who loved and treated me as a daughter, died of a stroke. I grew numb from the pain of these losses. The aunt who raised me advised, "Take care of yourself, forget your sister." She was reacting out of fear and I bought into it.

It seemed like only a matter of time then, a draw between which of us would kill ourselves first. Having a child who depended on me, saved me. I couldn't abandon her, couldn't leave her such an awful legacy of pain and suffering and death. Long frozen years later, I began to see how my emotional detachment from others kept me isolated, alone and invisible from those close to me. Still overwhelmed by the guilt of my sister's suicide, I began to see how I was punishing myself and everyone around me, how in failing to live up to the model of behavior my uncle had established, I failed myself. I wanted to be like him. Determined to break free, I began to explore the unexploded mine field of my past without a map to guide me.

At 18, I'd wanted to go to college and become a writer and psychologist who inspired people to achieve their highest potential. Instead I got married, exchanged my worldly ambition for a more personal one. I believed then something I read in a magazine. "The greatest treasure a woman can create is the love she builds in a man's heart."

Some 20 years later, my soul cried out to be free. I had a dream. In it, I stood in a swimming pool bent over at the waist with my head underwater. While one force pushed me down deeper into the water, another pushed me up toward freedom. Within arm's reach two men stood talking; my husband with his back to me and the psychiatrist we were seeing for marriage counseling. Neither perceived my dilemma. Paralyzed, I could not reach out. Years later, after I'd left my marriage, the double-bind meaning of the dream came to me:

"If I give up struggling I will die/I must give up struggling to be free."

Giving up struggling meant leaving a marriage that limited me, kept me in self-imposed captivity. Giving up the marriage, meant giving up the only stable family relationship I'd ever had. I couldn't do it...at least not willingly, consciously. So part of me sabotaged the relationship. I began to drop bombshells on my own life. While writing a book about the past— thinking about it and talking about it—I began to relive all the unexpressed emotions and created abandonment and powerlessness in the present. Thought, I learned later, is creative.

Leaving my children behind, I felt once more that I'd failed to live up to the values modeled by my uncle. I failed my own highest purpose in life. Now, here I was again, facing failure. Facing walking away from my father's pain to escape my own.

That night as I lay awake allowing the grief to pour out of me, as I lay touching my own pain, feeling the tenseness in my legs and pelvis area, I asked to speak to it. "What are you about?" I asked.

"Your resistance," the pain answered me.

"But I surrendered," I insisted.

"Only in your mind," said the pain.

"OK, I surrender into the resistance, into the tenseness and pain in my legs and hips." I felt like every emotion in me was draining out. I could do nothing but curl up like a child in its mother's womb and wrap my arms around myself for comfort. I couldn't get rid of the image of my father's bleeding penis. It kept returning to my mind as if it was trying to tell me something I didn't want to hear. I wept until I was too tired to weep. My father was afraid of the emptiness after death. My fear was of the emptiness that followed someone dying, someone leaving. It seemed I could never fill the holes they created in my energy field and in my life. Death had, more often than not, been more inviting to me than life. There were more people on the other side who knew and cared for me than there were on Earth. At least it seemed that way at times. Trying to fill the holes in my life exhausted me. I was ready to give up. "One of you scavengers out there want this body, you can have it. Walk in anytime. I'm done."

My High Self made her presence known just then and I told her, "You come down and take over here. I can't live in this world anymore. It's too hard. I don't want to be here."

Between periods of fitful sleep, I envisioned myself laying between my father and Art, holding their hands, feeding my father with the energy I got from Art. Being present for him, the way Art had tried so hard to be present for me. Then I saw my mother, my father, my sister, my brother and myself. We were all children together, comforting one another, not knowing quite what to do. Acting dazed.

Later the dolphins came. I asked them to look after my father. I was too tired. I saw myself lying on the belly of a dolphin, floating upside down in the water. Hundreds of other dolphins circled around, caressed me with their flippers as they passed by. Gently,the one whose belly I'd been lying on, rolled ever so slightly to the side and I found myself floating on a transparent mattress,being slowly towed by a pod of dolphins. We were in the middle of a vast sea. There was no land in sight, just endless open, gently rolling water, soothing me, nurturing my soul.

In the morning I awoke feeling as if my body had been raped. The exhaustion had sunk deeper into me. I remembered that Joan had gone to see "The Last Temptation of Christ" the night before. Two weeks earlier I'd walked out of the movie just as Jesus was being marched up the hill with the crown of thorns on his head. "I don't need to see the crucifixion", I told myself. "I don't need to see any more suffering and pain." And then it hit me. "My God," I thought,"my father is crucifying himself. That hospital bed is his cross."

Suddenly, I began to comprehend what his soul was up to. This final suffering was his absolution, our absolution from guilt. Those needles in his arms, the ties on his arms and legs, the respirator in his mouth, the catheter in his penis, they symbolized the spikes pounded into the flesh of Jesus.

I then saw that each time in the past when someone close to me was dying, I had walked away from their suffering, turned my back on them, just as I'd walked out on the movie, just as I was now threatening to walk out on my father. Yes, I had stayed longer than most people would, but I had not stayed to the end, which was what I needed to do for myself to live up to the values I believed in as a compassionate human being. Each time I'd walked away the suffering followed me, grew more acute. As loss after loss mounted, heaped on top of one another, I suffered over not only the current loss, but the unfelt, unexpressed previous losses. Like mummified corpses, the old grief waited to be healed before it could be buried. I couldn't escape.

Joan had loaned me a copy of Stephen Levine's "Healing Into Life and Death" and I had turned to it often in the previous week in search of relief. He talked a lot about touching the pain softly, allowing it into awareness, softening the edges, "just this much," learning to love the suffering rather than resisting and separating from it.

I'd been embracing my woundedness, dancing with my dragons symbolically for some time. Now I needed to go to the heart of the holding, the tightly clenched fists in my body, the pain in my low back and legs, the knot behind my heart. The pathway to healing the body lay in walking through the suffering a millimeter at a time. Embracing the pain, loving it, welcoming it, entering into it with awareness.

I'd embraced the grizzly bear who symbolized my father on Mt.

Shasta; danced with it in the moonlight; celebrated my liberation. I'd been led to the dragon crystal and worn it for a year until I leaped from the pole blindfolded into the unknown and caught the trapeze. Each time I felt healed, enlivened, freed by the experience, as though I'd graduated to a different level of awareness. Yet here, I'd found another layer. Despite years of intense bodywork, changing my lifestyle, changing my eating habits, changing my thought patterns, sound therapy, nearly every kind of therapy imaginable, I had still not fully released the pain. It was there waiting patiently in my body until I could meld into it, love it, allow it to be part of the whole of who I am.

The healing crisis that came about after my swim with the dolphins in the Keys had moved me closer to the suffering, to the unexpressed grief. I got stuck in it and couldn't find my way out. In the two-week intensive training I learned to shift states, to move in and out of the grief and sadness at will, but I had not returned to touch the pain until my father decided he was ready to die.

I thought my soul had this great lesson to learn about death because nearly everyone I'd ever been close to in my life had died, but the lesson is not about death. It is about freeing oneself of pain and suffering, going beyond it; being blissful in spite of it.

It was so easy and yet so difficult, I thought. If I am destined to be a healer, teacher and communicator, then I need to stay with my father while he purifies himself on his cross, no matter how long it takes. I need to take myself outside the suffering, to observe it, to observe him, not just as my father, but as a human being. How can I ever hope to rise above the Earthly plane if I can't live the Christ consciousness, if I can't enter into my own pain and suffering to heal my own woundedness. It was 10:30 before I drug myself out of bed.

When I went inside to take a shower, Joan asked me if I wanted to talk. Feeling drained and yet needing to share, I said "Yes." I told her about my realizations of my father impaling himself on his hospital bed, using it like a cross to alleviate his guilt. I told her that my lower body felt like a rag that had been twisted hard to get the last drop of moisture out. She told me then what I'd missed by walking out of "The Last Temptation of Jesus."

When she said, "God took Mary Magdalene when she was happy, so that she wouldn't have to come back again," I began to realize I hadn't been ready for that message. No one in my life had ever died happy. Death and suffering were synonymous. Maybe what I was resisting was not suffering, but happiness.

Our talking drifted to punishment and forgiveness. I told Joan, "I never ever wanted to punish my father, even once. I forgave him for molesting me because even then I knew what he needed was love. He only did it once."

"You're so hard on yourself. You may have forgiven him intellectually, but your body is still holding the trauma. What he did is awful, even if he did only do it once. Have some compassion for yourself. Stop discounting what happened. That pain and tightness in your back and legs, that's the area of the holding."

I'd never related the pain in my back in that way before. "It makes sense," I told her. Maybe I could just allow it to unfold slowly, untwist itself. I'd explored every avenue of healing in an effort to rid myself of my low back pain. Maybe this was where the answer lay. I need to love the experience of my father totally, love the pain and suffering he passed onto me to be free of it.

The Kundalini energy gave me the feeling of bliss, of being wide open and safe at every level. It opened the door to other realms, to a closer relationship with my Higher Self. But since my arrival in Sacramento, I'd felt myself closing down again, retreating into the darkness, falling once more into the void. Yet I knew that I could walk through the pain and suffering in a state of higher consciousness. I knew that I could move in or out of it at will. "Whatever it takes, I'm willing."

I stayed away from the hospital on Friday and rested and wrote. Writing helps me integrate, digest and assimilate experience though the wisdom behind experience often doesn't make itself known for months or years. By Saturday morning, I felt I'd surrendered enough to return to my father and allow him to be where he was in his own process.

Carol, a new nurse was bathing him when I arrived. I thought, "If I really want to touch him, touch his heart, I could bathe him. He needs my touching him as much as I need him touching me." Part of me wasn't quite ready. Instead, after she left I leaned over the railing of my father's bed and said, "You know you remind me of Jesus Christ on the cross. If I'd known you were going to crucify yourself for our sins, I'd have sinned a lot more and had more fun." He was exhausted from a week of struggling and resisting. I saw only a flicker of reaction in his eyes.

A tear filled the well in the corner of his eye beside his nose. I bent down and said, "You've held onto that suffering an awful long time. It's time to share it with the rest of us. We need to learn from it, too. After all, you didn't screw up the whole world on your own. You had a lot of help."

He strained to tell me something with all but his tongue taped down. I couldn't decipher the wobble. Carol came back with a pad and he scrawled something vaguely resembling letters. After several minutes we decoded the message. "Save me."

"We're doing our damndest," I assured him.

A few minutes later, she came in to feed him intravenously. He hadn't had anything but glucose for a week. "Sometimes we're so busy saving people's lives, we forget to feed them." We joked about people being saved only to die of starvation.

I held his hand for nearly two hours, looked in his eyes and breathed in rhythm with him. I forgot all about needing to be touched. I forgot all about the visualization Marcia had given me to do to accept his energy without holding it in my body. None of it mattered. I'd returned to a state of grace, a state of harmony within myself. I'd walked through the suffering and come out the other side. Whether he lived or died now, was no longer an issue. I knew that I would stay for as long as needed. For myself as much as for my father.

When I sat down in the chair later as Carol drew a blood gas sample from my father, I could feel the Kundalini energy rising once more up my legs, through my pelvis. I felt my heart chakra opening. The energy felt blocked all week. I worried that it might not return because I wasn't ready, wasn't healed enough. Noticing the sensations rippling up my body, I felt comforted.

Maybe this week was just part of the cleansing, part of the transformation of my nervous system. Funny, how in the midst of a raging healing crisis I always cry out to be taken out of this life, relieved of the misery, and yet, once it has passed, I feel so much more alive, so much stronger and enriched for having moved through it. Each step in the process of healing gives me the courage and confidence to take the next step toward even greater freedom.

As a reward for surviving, I promised myself a gift; a winter of swimming with the dolphins in the wild, somewhere in the world.

"Life is full of hard decisions," I said to myself. "Let's see, should I go to Hawaii, Baja, Bahamas, Australia, Siesta Key or maybe the Virgin Islands. Why limit myself? Maybe all of them." It seemed like the dolphins were calling from every direction.

"Well, what about the ancient records?" an inner voice quizzed.

"Oh, I'll write another book, later, when I've lightened up."

That night they took my father off the life support system and supplied him with oxygen through a tube to his nose. The next day when he was having trouble breathing, he refused to be hooked back up. "Its too hard," he told the nurse.

Carol removed his arm restraints just after I arrived and said, "Guess you won't need these anymore." My father rubbed his wrists, then crossed his arms up behind his head. He seemed relaxed...laidback...no longer struggling. He tried to tell me something about his chest and stomach. I couldn't understand. Motioning me closer, he said, "Bring money. Going home."

I laughed. "You've been in intensive care all week. They're not going to let you go home. You don't need money."

I stayed with him an hour or so. Carol assured me "He's doing better than he thinks he is, although the X-rays show his lungs are filling up." I promised to return the next day. "What time do you want me to come back?" I asked my father.

"Afternoon," he rasped. He apparently meant that same afternoon. I blanked out, missed the meaning of, "Going Home." At 9:30 that night, he died peacefully. I wasn't there for him physically, but emotionally I was never more present.

A few days later as I was sorting through my father's belongings I came across a piece of paper on which he'd written "God sends down fools and Winos to confound wise men."

I discovered, too, that he had programmed himself to die at the age of 78. He predicted that he would live 6 cycles of 13 years. On a sheet of paper dated Thanksgiving Day 1978, which was blocked off in squares, he noted what were to him significant dates and events in history. One of the boxes read "J. Miller will die a millionaire in 1988." He never made his million, but he prophesied his death fairly accurately, dying two months beyond his 78th birthday.

My father has been my greatest teacher. From him I learned compassion, surrender, forgiveness and acceptance—major lessons on the path to enlightenment—and in the Twelve Step Program. Life's greatest challenges, I've found, are cloaked in negative experiences, hiding out in the darkness, waiting for us to recognize and embrace them. Through the process of my father's dying, I learned to transform suffering into celebration. He enabled me to let go of the past, climb a step higher on the mountain and provided me an opportunity to be a dolphin and support him in his distress. And in the end, he showed me how to die gracefully. Some lessons take a lot of practice.

12 *Dolphin Dreaming*

AS ONE DOOR closes, another door opens. Joan gave me a copy of a local transformational newspaper to browse through. A display ad featuring palm trees and ocean waves caught my eye. Someone was looking for investors to help create a retreat center/community in Hawaii. The morning after my father died, I had breakfast with the visionary for the project. After touring the islands a few months earlier, she had chosen Moloka'i as the place of her dreams. I'd never even heard of the island before but after she described it as "undeveloped and quiet," I was anxious to explore it as a future home. She invited me to come to Moloka'i and spend the following week getting acquainted. It was just the transition I needed. I booked the earliest flight out on Monday morning and then headed to Nevada City to meet Maraiel Ruth, a Rebirther who had advertised her Dolphin Dreaming workshop in the same transformational paper. I was naturally curious and ready to explore again.

Maraiel is a transplanted New Yorker, a B.R.E.T.H. practitioner and counselor who moved to Nevada City two years earlier. B.R.E.T.H. (Breath Releasing Energy for Transformation and Healing) is a process developed by an Australian nurse and healer, Kamala Hope Campbell. Kamala, a Rebirther, began to notice that more and more people were, with startling frequency, connecting to dolphins and whales during the meditations in her training sessions. When she went inside to discover why, cetacean guides told her that it was time for humans to connect more with dolphins and whales. Soon after Kamala developed Dolphin Dreaming. Initially Dolphin

Dreaming took place within the safety of the B.R.E.T.H. trainings. However, when Maraiel arrived in California, she was guided to create a slightly different version of Dolphin Dreaming.

Working with the connected breath, group and personal intention, sacred music combining cetacean song and human voices, and using the mandala form as a vortex, Maraiel creates a safe and sacred space for people to experience their inner connection with dolphins and whales. Participants report receiving telepathic communications and/or healing, experiencing a deep sense of peace and joy, going on magical undersea journeys, and having a variety of other experiences in the dreamtime.

Guided to leave her marriage and New York and to move west, Maraiel found herself living in a rustic cabin with no electricity or water for a short time after her arrival. "Did you suffer from culture shock?" I asked.

"Oh, yes. Especially in such stark contrast to my life in New York. It was the first time in my life I'd ever lived in a rural area. But I needed the time to be with nature and to do my own inner work," Maraiel replied, flavoring the words with a twist of Big Apple accent.

She eventually bought a beautiful home in the country and created a room out of her garage for doing the Dolphin Dreaming workshops. The room is decorated in pale turquoise and entering the space is like suddenly finding yourself in the bottom of a giant swimming pool. The dolphins and whales call out from the posters on the wall, inviting you to come and play.

Maraiel offered me a B.R.E.T.H. session. The first step was to write down my intention. Feeling ready for another quantum leap, I wrote down on a yellow legal pad, "I'd like to directly and consciously channel dolphins and other master teachers."

"OK," Maraiel said, "Now write down that you're willing to meet and heal and enter into whatever keeps you from channeling direct knowledge or wisdom."

I wrote it down just the way she said it.

"Now," she instructed, "write down what's keeping you from channeling."

I was amazed at the objections. The list appeared endless.

I'd become famous and lose my privacy. I wouldn't have time for myself or my children. I'd have to be disciplined and organized. I'd have to deal with paperwork. I'd have to work! I'd be on a treadmill. I'll have to put up with rejection! I'll have to be nice to people! I wouldn't be able to be myself. I'd have to be responsible. I wouldn't have time for fun. I'd have to lighten up! What? "Isn't that what you want?" I asked myself. "Who is that talking now?" I wondered.

Maraiel needed to step out of the room for a minute and interrupted to tell me, "When you're done with the objections, write down why you want to channel."

Not quite finished with the objections, I continued to write. I'll have to have fun. I might be happy. I might even enjoy life. I could become wildly successful. I might live up to my expectations. I might have too much freedom. Someone might genuinely love me for who I am. "Wait a minute here," I said to myself. "Am I really that resistant?"

Then I asked, "OK, let's see why I want to channel direct?" To save time, effort, energy. (Well, that's a Libra for you.) To take off all limitations. To expand consciousness. To connect more strongly with guidance. To assist others in claiming their power. To have fun. (Well, that's more like it.) To lighten up. To fulfill destiny. To facilitate the healing and evolution of the planet. I can't believe I said healing. For two years, I'd complained every time someone said to me the planet needed healing. "The planet can take care of itself, it's we who need to heal ourselves so that we don't abuse the planet," I insisted.

The list was winding down. To be more fully alive and in touch with other dimensions. To bridge realities. To heal, teach and communicate. I'd finally gotten to the core.

Maraiel returned and I soon found myself lying peacefully on the floor while she coaxed me to enter into a continuous breathing pattern. As the whales sang to me in deep baritone from the tape recorder, I heard a message coming through for Maraiel. No, I told myself, this isn't real, it's just my mind playing tricks again. I'm just imagining the whales want to speak through me.

"Remember to surrender," my High Self interrupted.

"OK. OK., I give up."

I told Mariael the whales wanted to speak and asked her to turn the music off. The first part of the message was for her.

THE WHALES SPEAK

The whales told her in essence to "stop trying and surrender into your work. Focus. You're too scattered. Trust. Know that your needs are taken care of." Maraiel had spoken earlier of needing to sell her home because her payments were too high. Her income didn't meet her current expenses.

The whales continued, "This woman (meaning me) is resistant to doing workshops. She needs support. She needs to do it."

They suggested that we work together.

"You'd do powerful work together. It's time for a Dolphin Network to surface and make itself known. Open up to the flow. It's already there. Let go and surrender into it. Time to come out of isolation and come together. It's time to play."

The rest of the message was for me. The whales told me, "You sing the song of the Earth and the darkness. Whales represent the darkness of the ocean and the Earth. You've resisted the darkness in the past but now that you've entered into the suffering and pain, it's time to surface and be a dolphin. Be more in the light." The voice told me, "You're a bridge between the dolphins and the whales, the darkness and the light. We need to speak of the whales also, to merge the two, to marry the darkness and the light."

They told me, "Teach people to enter into their suffering— be one with it so it can be healed—so they can be more dolphinlike. Peace and harmony comes from marrying the forces of darkness and light—not resisting it— but allowing and moving through it, surrendering into it. They are the yin and yang."

The yin/yang symbol came into my consciousness and refused to leave. I kept seeing two pinpoints of light. Suddenly, I understood that the white yin swirl was the dolphins, the black the whales. Earth and sky. Darkness and light. When they spin, they spin into nothingness. The entire symbol began to swirl like a pinwheel in the wind. "Merge them in the middle— marry them," the whale voice insisted. The symbol persisted in speaking to me. "Yin/yang takes us through to other dimensions."

"Other dimensions!" my mind clicked in. Ears are a vortex. Through them we hear the inner sounds that take us to other dimensions. They're shaped like the yin/yang symbols inside. I found myself integrating the information I'd just received. I suppressed the feminine/yin aspect of myself when I was young so I wouldn't have to hear the sounds of suffering. My chronic ear infections as a child and young adult had caused a hole in my eardrum and a partial loss of hearing that enabled me to tune out. Twelve years ago I had my eardrum repaired. That's when my lower back problems began, when the tight fist, tightened even more and refused to release until the dolphin zapped me with sonar. "I need to swim with the dolphins again," some part of me insisted. "I need to let go of my mother."

The session came to a gentle ending. I rolled reluctantly off the mat and sat up, more anxious than ever to connect with dolphins and whales in the wild, and knowing at the same time, that I already had. I hugged Maraiel and thanked her for sharing the B.R.E.T.H. process.

DANCER DOLPHIN SPEAKS

Maraiel was anxious for me to stay until her housemate, Paula Peters, channeled the dolphin energy that had recently started coming through her. I parked Freedom, the motor home, at the top of her steep driveway and spent the night.

We discovered while getting acquainted that we'd both visited Friday Harbor the same week. Maraiel had gone up with a friend of hers from New York. The two of them take people on dolphin swim journeys to Florida.

Both of us had gone swimming with the dolphins earlier that spring in the Keys. At a summer workshop I met a man who had talked about two women friends of his who'd gone swimming with the dolphins. "It changed them," he said, "They looked so peaceful, so wholesome. You have that look, too," he told me. It turned out that Maraiel and Kim were the two friends he'd been talking about. I'd just met Maraiel and never heard of her before arriving in Sacramento where I saw her ad in a small transformational newspaper. Everywhere I went I connected telepathically with members of the pod. We seem to be part of a vast international family linked together by dolphin/whale consciousness.

Maraiel's housemate, Paula Peters, began channeling dolphin and extraterrestrial energies after returning from a scuba diving trip to the Cayman Islands. At the time she worked in the film industry in Los Angeles. She'd been told by a spiritual teacher that while she was in the islands she would go through an initiation. Paula didn't understand what she was being told but she remembered an image passing through her mind, an unfamiliar shape she couldn't identify.

Diving on the barrier reef in the Caymans she sensed the strong presence of dolphin energy, though she never encountered them physically. Unexpectedly, her trip became what she called, "the most spiritual experience of my life." She received the impression that ancient knowledge was stored in the layers of coral around the islands that had been building itself in cycles over millions of years and that dolphins would one day play a role in revealing it. On the day of her departure, she looked down as the plane circled over the island and saw that it was the exact shape of the image that came into her inner vision when she'd been told she would go through an initiation.

"It wasn't until I left the Islands that I realized that this island was the place of my initiation that took place on the astral levels and within Dreamtime," said Paula "I was never the same after that. My initiation centered a great deal in opening those doors to the ancient knowledge stored within the corals and also to the vibration of dolphin energies throughout and around the islands."

Paula quit her job and moved north to Nevada City, a small vortex community at the edge of the of the Sierras, swirling with New Age consciousness. "I began channeling extraterrestrial energies after being contacted very profoundly during a guided hypnosis session when I regained my memory of a very powerful and overwhelming personal contact with ETs when I was a small child.

From them she said, "I experienced more love, more energy and more expansiveness of mind than I had in my entire life!" It was beautiful! Gradually they introduced their plans for me, first through telepathic messages over the typewriter and then, to my surprise, by coming through verbally. They've taken me on an incredible, accelerated journey through life. I feel blessed."

Some time later she began channeling dolphin energy for friends. Maraiel was anxious for me to experience the dolphin presence so Paula agreed to channel early the next morning. Four of us sat in a semicircle around her in Maraiel's aqua room, like a small pod of young dolphins attending school at the bottom of a Caribbean cove. She closed her eyes and arched her body like a dolphin about to spring from the water. Her fingers came together forming an arch in front of her breasts and her toes connected with the floor like a ballet dancer about to pirouette, while seated in a chair.

Paula referred to the first voice that came through as the Association of Worlds, a blending of consciousnesses. The voice spoke to us at length about unconditional love, reminding us that we need to ACT and BE unconditional love, rather than just talking about it and paying it lip service. Saying "I love you" to someone is not enough. "When you give unconditional love, when you act upon the idea of unconditional love, do not expect anything in return. That is not the idea of unconditional love. When you give a gift, do not expect a gift in return. Do not expect special favors in return. That is not the idea of true giving. Also, that is not the idea of true unconditional love. When you express true unconditional love, there is no idea of what you are going to get in return. True unconditional love has to do with the idea of true giving," we were told.

The voice of the Association continued. "Now we understand that one of the purposes of this meeting is to communicate with the dolphin energies and the cetacean energies and you always know that the dolphins are always anxious to communicate. So if you will allow us one moment to change in consciousness...allow the cetacean energies to come through and we shall at the end of their discussions...return."

With her eyes still closed, Paula took a series of gasping-like breaths and suddenly a dolphin voice burst through.

"Oh....dolphin energy comes as Dancer Dolphin. Dancer dolphin here. Dancer desires to communicate. Dancer desires to speak with you on level we always speak with you...on play...on love...on becoming more one with us...all together...you and I join on level of understanding of love and play. Join in play, understand our energies, learn our energies. Learn to heal. You can heal when you join with us. Our healing energies join with yours. We blend as one...become powerful...become as one upon this planet. We come as love...we come as joy...you understand dolphin? We know sometime dolphin hard to understand but we'll come clear as we align more closely together...this one and us...we come in more clearly. But not care so much you not understand...for dolphin here to share energy and love. We love come through just to share energies. You have question for

Dancer? Dancer enjoy playtime."

"Dancer," I asked, "Where can we come and play with you?"

"Dancer always enjoy playtime with all of you in dreamtime. You understand that dolphin know dreamtime, just as you know physical time. Always dolphins try to touch all of you anyway we can, when you dream, when you mediate…we are there knocking with our flippers trying to swim, to play with you, to say come dream with us. We dream a dream of togetherness and play and love. We're always there. You can come play with us physically, but not necessary for we always everywhere. We know that closeness is in telepathic. There is no far away. There is no distance in telepathic communication. You understand?"

Bill, the only man in the group, said "Dancer, I've been seeing dolphins swim all around me…"

"Oh, dolphin glad. Dolphin know swimming with you. Dolphin know you invite dolphin energy in…always there. Many of us were excited when more of you open up to our energies. You have question?"

"How can I use that energy to benefit me?"

"When you see dolphin in your dream, see them play…play like dolphin. You can join them in imagination and dreamtime. When you see dolphin flip and twirl and turn, you can do same in dreamtime…you know that?"

"Yes."

"If you can do that, you can feel it. Let dolphin take you on trip, let dolphin take you on journey. Do what dolphin do Play follow leader…you get idea. You play along with dolphin. Dolphin greet with games. We take you…we show you many things about yourself. We take you on trips. We take you deep in sea…show you many treasures. We will be there…you let us lead and we show you. Understand?

When you travel with dolphin this way and you do more and more with dolphin, you can see it happening in your physical time. You bring back with you our energies. You begin to play more in physical time. Understand? Work begin to seem more like playtime. You understand?"

"Yes."

"More questions!"

"Dancer," I piped up, "Can you tell me anything that I haven't included in my book that I need to include about the dolphins?"

"There is many, many things for you in store as you investigate dolphin idea. Dolphin idea very expansive. Dolphin idea not understood at all yet. So much to dolphin energy. So much to dolphin mind. You will know many, many things in book, but there is so much more…much more than one book can hold. Much more than two books, three books, four books. We see much information coming through for many…for there is so much for us to tell…about past…what we know. There is so much yet to be revealed. But we can tell you that dolphin originally come from star system…star system long ago…eons…eons time ago…on planet far away, now known as star. We come from a place of great love and creation and like to come here to join with humankind to develop on this planet a system of life. But long ago ideas went wrong. We see long time ago that there was choice for all of us to go one way or other. We choose way of sea. You choose way of land and to build buildings and to create science.

"We choose to go into sea to live simple life of heart.

"We know…we know this. We not lose our ability to see…not only what has occurred in past but to see future. You forget so much. We remember much of what you humans have forgot. Because we live life of simplicity, we have not forgotten so much. But when you humans created life of so much complexity you have so much still in mind, in your life. You have what you call 'worries' in your life. You cannot fill your minds with past. You cannot remember what things occur. So what happens? You fill your life up with continual cycles and patterns doing the same thing over and over and over again. That is why it takes so long for you to awaken. We've been trying to reach you for eons of time to awaken you. And now it's time for you and us to join and we are joyfull1! Because we are so joyful our energy has increased so very much. Because we see what we have longed for now has begun to take effect and has increased in acceleration. We jump for joy. Our acceleration has occurred also and we desire to join with you to create that planet of light that we desire to create long ago here. Do you understand?"

"Yes. Thank you."

"You have more question for Dancer? You know we love to talk and plaaay!"

"Can you speak more of the time when we choose to live on the land and you choose to live in the sea?" Maraiel asked.

"Long agoooo we are a form of interchangeable ability. Dolphin not too solid as you see dolphin now, although was some kind of what you say, replication of idea on other planet, was less solid. More of what we can equate with light being; light being what you could see in what you would know of as dreamtime state. You can see in dreamtime that form of long ago in dreamtime state. Not too much similar as physical form but enough similar to see that there was some sameness there. When we exist long time upon your planet, there was many similarities in our souls…in the way we move…in the way we breath. There was similarities in the way we learned…in the way we exchanged our ideas…the way we exchanged energies…the way we created. Much similarity.

"We were altogether jointly creating joy and abundant adventure here. But long ago there was a choice. And that is what many of you know as choice of ego track. Ego track or ego lane or ego path. When most choose that idea, we see there was mistake and we say that this is not our way to go. Many choose that way because they feel it was more powerful but was mistake. It was what you would know of as a lie. That ego grew in power...ego grew in strength...in actual identity and offered to our souls, our spirit, ourselves a way of power...was more powerful...was a lie...was not truth. Some of us saw this...some of us did not. Those that did not, choose way of healing. Those of us that did see and choose not to pursue that path, remain dolphin in sea. Understand?

"So long ago there was a choice. We went separate ways, but we remain...we remain to keep balance on earth. Our way of giving love and remaining in love centered ideas and humankind with their ideas of growing in science and more violence. You understand? Moore questioons!"

"Can you tells us about the connection between dolphins and Atlantis?" I asked.

"Oh...many dolphins in Atlantis! Atlantis alwaaays filled with dolphin energeee! There was consistent interchangeable times from human with dolphins, from dolphins with humans. Even though were then physical human forms and physical dolphin forms, we were able to exchange spirit at will."

Before Dancer left for the day, I asked, "I'm in that place of deciding whether I should sell the motor home and move to Hawaii or should I stay here and travel in the motor home and finish the book first?"

"We say we cannot tell you that answer, but we ask you, 'Do you wish to do this? Do you want to?"

"Oh, I'd like to move to Hawaii!"

"Is it in your heart that you wish to move there?"

"Yes."

"Very strong feeling?"

"Stronger and stronger, yes."

"Very, very, very strong?"

"Well, now that I think about it, yes."

"Well then, we say you go there. Follow your heart. Your heart knows best."

"Will there be dolphins there for me to swim with?"

"Yes, dolphin always there. Favorite place of dolphin...Pacific sea. One favorite place of many dolphins."

"Can I just jump in the water and swim with them?"

"Oh...high possibilitee...yes. Dolphin love to swim with human. When you approach dolphin...approach with happiness, joy and playtime. Dolphin love that energy. Not be afraid of dolphin but approach with love and joy and play. Dolphin love that. Dolphin come to you. You go out in boat. Dolphin come to you. Dolphin be there!"

"Thank you."

"We share. We share. We always share and this time we share this time with what you call Orca energy. This time Orca energee come through one time." Paula took a few breaths and paused.

A deeper voice boomed "Orca...Orca energeeeeeeeeeeeeeeeeee!. Orca knooooooooooow. Orca knoooooooow whyyyyyyyy. Orca heeeere....give our loooove...our idea of love to those who can use our energeee. Orca say go forth use our energy for accomplishing those ideas of overcoming what you call fear, fear in ideas surrounding goals, ideas surrounding accomplishments, ideas surrounding your chosen path. Orca here...give energy of what you know as fearless love. Understand when go forth in life using fearless love obstacles crumble...obstacles disintegrate. Fearless love. Understand the idea of fearless love has in it the idea of warrrriooor energeee. Warrior energeee...not negative warrior...positive warrior energee. Warrior of strength. Warrior of purpose go forth. Use our energeees to create ideas of powerful love. Strength in love. Love not weak. Love never has been weak. Love is powerful. Love is strong. Use to create ideas of strength. Orca heeeeeere give you energeeeeee!

A few breaths later we heard from the Association of Worlds. "Well we trust that you got all of your questions answered and in future communications that we shall be able to be of service to more and more of you in time. Now before we go, are there any more questions?"

"I have a question," Bill said. "Well, not really a question but I've always had this fantasy of meeting a UFO or meeting a member of another physical dimension. Will there ever be in my lifetime a time when I'll be able to meet physically with an extraterrestrial being?"

"Yes, we understand and yes there is a great possibility for many of you upon your planet within the next 20 to 30 of your years as you become more of that society which is conducive to receiving our energies. Yes, there will be actual physical contact. But as it is at this time because there is so much...still so much fear connected with the idea of meeting extraterrestrials face-to-face, that is why we can't meet you face-to-face right now. There is still not enough of you that are really able to accept our energies at this time without that fear aspect. You understand?

"So we leave you with this...that once again we thank you for allowing us to interact with us this way and for communicating with us and for accepting us into your vibratory field. For understand when this has occurred, when this has taken place that we are blending consciousness. We are sharing consciousness so that a little bit of us remains with you and a little bit of you remains with us and this is how we learn from each other. This is how we begin to blend together. So we thank you. Until the next time."

A few puffs later Paula emerged as herself in the room and shook off the last of the energeee! We talked briefly about the experience and thanked Paula for being willing to allow the energy to come through. As we sat chatting I began to integrate what the dolphins and the other energies had said and how it related to my experiences the previous week with my father. He'd certainly given me many opportunities to be a fearless warrioress, demanding that I go beyond the mere expression of the words "I love you" to the actual demonstration of loving him no matter how he badly he behaved or treated me, and other people.

13 *Following the Bliss*

LANDING ON MOLOKA'I in the bowl near the center of the island I knew I'd found my new home. The air was only slightly on the muggy side. A gentle tradewind from the east swept the heaviness out to sea. Splotches of cumulus clouds dotted the sky, shading the landscape just enough to screen the sun's tropical intensity. The air smelled clean and sweet, as if it had been freshly laundered. No smog banks here. In the distance, a single column of smoke from the burning residue of a pineapple field, billowed, then blew out to sea but that would be the end of it. The pineapple growers were moving to the Philippines to take advantage of cheaper labor. While I might miss the pineapple, I would never miss the smoke or the pesticide and fertilizer pollution it takes to grow them. I was happy to hear they were leaving.

Coming to Moloka'i was like entering a time warp. That was exactly what I'd been wanting to do…to push back time, not because I wanted to relive any experiences I had with people but to live in the simplicity of an unpolluted, untainted, uncrowded environment. My body craved it. I'd survived the distress of family crises by seeking order and balance, escaping into my aloneness. The complexities and complications of life in a high- technology culture are more than I can handle. And now here I was…back in time. No chain stores, no movie theater, no traffic, nothing to do but enjoy nature, to be with it, to tune into its cycles and rhythms and patterns. Here, I could listen to the song of the wind blowing through the treetops, the gentle lapping of the waves against the shoreline.

Moloka'i is known as the invisible island. Almost untouched by commercialism, it is said to be protected from development by spiritual forces. Being on the island caused me to ponder my own invisibility. I'd learned from a Huna sister there is power in being invisible, in choosing to wear invisibility as a cloak or remove it at will, in discerning when it serves a purpose or not. "Perhaps this is where I will make peace with and come to accept my own invisibility," I thought.

The golf resort where I would stay for the week was anything but invisible. It reminded me of my previous ivory tower existence while pursuing the American Dream, which on very rare occasions, I missed. A lush oasis of green, the resort sparkled like an exquisite emerald beside diamond sand beaches and a lapis blue sea. The manicured golf greens and palm-fringed fairways offered a sharp contrast to the wild unkempt hillsides surrounding it.

During my first night on the island I was awakened by the silence. The soundless stillness was an alien phenomenon to my psyche. Unlike Mexico, there were no dogs barking, no sirens screaming, no chickens crowing out of sync with the dawn, no people squawking, no traffic noise, nothing. Absolute, deathlike quiet. Being in my room with the windows wide open, was like being in a giant, stimulus-free floatation tank without the water. My body soaked up the silence thirstily, as if it had been starving for it for a very long time. I got up and stood near the window, listening. All I could hear was the faint sound of waves sloshing along the beach. Looking up, the stars seemed to be winking from the night sky.

I laid awake listening to the stillness for a very long time, breathing softly and focusing on the sounds in my inner ear. It was the perfect setting for tuning into and receiving messages from other dimensions. Just before dawn, a vast chorus of birds began trilling and singing in the trees just outside my window, tuning up to celebrate the dawn of another day.

I spent the week getting acquainted with the island and a handful of people who were interested in helping to create a community and retreat center. The first two residents I met happened to have been involved some five years earlier in a project to release Joe and Rosie, the Lilly dolphins, into an ancient fish pond along the island's East Side. John and Toni Lilly had come to Moloka'i to check out the possibility but the project never materialized. It seemed a bit strange to me that I kept meeting people who were somehow involved with Joe and Rosie.

One of them had been inspired to move to Moloka'i to pursue her interest in the Huna traditions. She loaned me a book entitled "Huna: A Beginner's Guide" by Enid Hoffman. Browsing through it, I found frequent references to Max Freedom Long. Max was a mystery writer who came to the islands in 1917 and spent years studying the secrets of the Kahunas.

Eventually he devoted his life to deciphering the hidden messages of the Mysteries in the Bible which he found could be decoded using root words from the Hawaiian dictionary, first published by the missionaries in the mid 1800s. I began to wonder why, whenever I was pursuing dolphins, the subject of Huna, the Mysteries and information on reclaiming ancient records and artifacts popped up instead.

The Kahunas, among other things, were expert psychotherapists. The modern-day psychological model of Transactional Analysis resembles the model used by ancient Kahunas to understand the human personality. The basic premise is that we have three selves: the high, middle and low, which are identified as aumakua, uhane and unihipili. Each self uses a different level or voltage of life force energy or mana, which is transmitted along the aka cords. The aka is the connecting thread between all organisms and mana is the energy that binds and unites us into a sense of oneness with all other forms of life and dimensions of reality. It is the low self, Max Long, found, that likes to be invisible. Skillful at hiding, it retreats from expressing itself and its beliefs and emotions and must be coaxed slowly and delicately to reveal its innermost, thoughts and feelings.

To understand and rediscover unihipili, we need only observe the unrestrained, uninhibited behavior of infants and children. Through experiments it has been established that children have a built-in response to distress in another human being and will turn to adults and appeal for their help to act. Unihipili is sensitive to other people's suffering, it feels another's pain as its own. Dolphins and children, it seems, have much in common. The low self is in charge of all autonomic behavior, skills, rituals and learned habits.

The high self, or aumakua, is immortal—forever alive in the world of spirit. In our mortal bodies, a relationship is established to the high self with the help of energy from the low self or subconscious. The middle self ego, or uhane, has no direct link with the high self. In other words, to truly "know thyself" at our highest level we must first come to know ourselves at our lowest level. One is not above the other as in a hierarchy, however, but equal as in a partnership. It is through uhane that the low and high selves are integrated and then expressed in the world. The Hawaiian Kahunas used their knowledge of the inner selves and their ability to direct energy to establish their power of healing and sorcery in a loving way. The essence of their philosophy, according to Long, was "to harm no thing," to live in harmony with all things.

By the end of the week I knew I wanted to move to Moloka'i. It would be the perfect place to hide and complete the book. I made arrangements to return in early December and then called Joan Ocean to see if she knew any people on Maui I could talk with about dolphins. I had nine days left to cruise around to other islands and hopefully find some dolphins to swim with. Joan told me about Starheart and Jim Loomis, the "dolphin man."

I flew to Maui the following day, arranged to meet Starheart and then decided to take a sailing excursion the following day in hopes of encountering some wild dolphins along the way. We departed in three trimarans at the break of dawn for a half-day of snorkeling and lunch on the beach. I knew when I climbed on board the trimaran I wouldn't be swimming with dolphins. Too many people.

About an hour out, we spotted a pod undulating in the waves near the entrance to a harbor. I had my video camera along hoping to get some good close-up shots but shooting dolphins from a circling sailboat, I soon discovered, is like trying to take pictures of someone on the ground from one of those spinning airplane rides at the carnival. Chaos! It was worse than being at the starting line of a sailboat race while two dozen boats circled around each other in a frenzy, tacking to and fro waiting for the signal gun to bang. It was total mayhem!

People were shouting at me from all directions. "Here they are over here! No over there! At the bow! Near the stern!" The dolphins were everywhere but inside my viewing screen. Just as I thought I discovered the knack of filming them by staying in one spot near the bow, they disappeared like phantoms beneath the boat. For a split second I thought my mind was playing tricks. They were there and then they weren't. "Hey, this isn't Sedona!" I thought. Somehow they knew what I was up to and didn't want any part of it. Suddenly I had great respect for the film crews that shoot dolphins in the wild. They must have a dozen cameras trained on them from every angle to get a few seconds of good footage.

So much for dolphins! Schotts, a blond, bronze-skinned crew member with a wit that matched his Nordic good looks, told me not to get discouraged. "The dolphins often come into the bay and swim with the snorkelers." He went below and hauled out a couple of frayed snapshots of dolphins that he'd taken with an underwater camera.

We snorkeled in the marine preserve until lunchtime. It was a beautiful little hidden cove along an otherwise rugged shoreline, but its peacefulness was marred by the sound of heavy equipment gouging out the hillside and workers hammering and sawing on a hotel under construction. I couldn't believe a resort was being built on a site so close to a marine preserve.

After lunch, a few of us returned to the bay while the rest toured the island. No dolphins appeared. I needed some time to get comfortable in the water, anyway. Before leaving I talked with the groundskeeper who said they usually show up every morning around ten. I vacillated about returning the next morning on the trimaran and camping on the beach for a night or two. Permits were required and I didn't have any camping gear. Too much trouble.

STARHEART'S STORY

Tuesday morning, I drove out to meet Starheart so that she could lead me to Jim Loomis. Starheart began swimming with dolphins when she was a three-year old living on the coast of Florida. Instead of being told by her mother, "go play outside," she heard, "go play with the dolphins."

"I used to slip out of my clothes and run into the ocean when I saw them," she says. Her mother, an Australian, told her stories about how dolphins often saved people when drowning...how she liked dolphins more than some people.

Jim lives in a jungle hideaway a mile or so down a dirt trail that is close to impassable. It was a challenge driving the little Nova over the humps without getting high-centered. I thought I was on safari in the African Bush and expected any moment, to encounter a giraffe peeking at me from around a palm tree. Since he has no phone there was no way to announce our arrival, I wondered whether he minded the intrusion, but Starheart assured me it was fine.

We parked the car at the top of a hill and hiked down through the trees a short distance to Jim's open air meditation room. It's a platform sheltered from the sun and rain by discarded windsails that have been sewn together. Jim was reclining in a huge overstuffed chair reading "The Magical Child." He was friendly but reticent and informed us, "I'm tired of talking about dolphins." He'd been interviewed three times in a month by an assortment of writers pursuing the dolphin mystique. Nevertheless, in the time we spent talking, swimming and getting acquainted, dolphins were the main focus of our conversation. His advice at the end of the morning was "Forget all this mental stuff and go get in the water with them. That's where it's really at." I agreed with him but I also wanted to hear other people's stories. Before I left he took me down to the pool and showed me how to swim and undulate in the water like a dolphin as a way of establishing rapport with them in the wild.

Starheart had her own fascinating story she seemed anxious to tell, but we met on a day when she was moving to a new home. I offered to help, hoping she'd have time later that evening to sit and talk. As it turned out, we got distracted when I asked her to teach me undulation breathing, a technique she discovered in her own body while watching dolphins glide through the water.

I expected to catch her the next morning at her old house on my way to the airport and was disappointed when I found I'd missed her. Giving up the idea of hearing her story, I headed toward town and stopped at a restaurant in Paia to get a bite to eat and jot down a few notes. I walked in the door of the restaurant and, to my surprise, found Starheart and Jim eating breakfast in the far corner.

A bodyworker by profession, Starheart (Darrienne Heller), is co-creator of Hellerwork, a form of psycho-physical integration work that she developed along with her former husband, Joseph Heller. She became so involved in her profession as an adult she says, "I completely forgot about dolphins until I was 40 years old. That all changed at a workshop in Vermont with Peter Russell, author of "Global Brain." He led us through a meditation and afterward gave us colored pens and told us, "Don't think about it, just draw what's in your mind."

"What I drew was a dolphin jumping up and out of a wave, arching over and looking down, and a baby in utero with umbilical cord looking into the dolphin's eyes. It was a beautiful yin/yang symbol. I looked at the pictures and didn't know what it meant. However, around that time I began to hear about underwater birthing and Estelle Myers. I wrote to her to find out what it was all about...saw the film "Water Babies" and decided it was about time I came to Hawaii. A friend had a business card with dolphins on it and all of a sudden, dolphins started coming back into my life.

"Everywhere I went people were talking about dolphins. I came to Hawaii to give a workshop and Jim Loomis, "The Dolphin Man," was one of the first people I met. We became great friends."

Jim lives the life of Robinson Crusoe on a few acres of jungle property he bought in the early 1970s. The nearest grocery store is his backyard. Most of his food comes from the nut trees, berry bushes and small garden he's planted and nurtured over the years.

One corner of the property drops off into a jungle pool, fed by a tiny stream cascading over a rocky ledge. He took Starheart there to swim. "There was something special about swimming in the waterfall without my clothes on," said Starheart. "I felt like an aspect of jungle fairy emerged after being on Maui." It was Jim who led Starheart to swim again with the dolphins in the wild.

She added, "I decided to bring people over to introduce them to the natural Hawaii and 15 people signed up—just like that! I took people to places tourists never go. Finally, I was coming to Maui more than I was in California, so I moved over permanently."

Later, Joseph called to ask her if she wanted to teach a Hellerwork seminar in New Zealand. She jumped at the chance as an opportunity to visit Australia as well. "Australia is the land of Oz to me," said Starheart. "The dolphins led me to a bay where I met Peter Schenstone caretaker of the "Legend of the Golden Dolphin". It's an incredible spot on the most eastern shores of Australia. People live elbow to fin with dolphins. They live in the waves and you see them everyday.

"One of the most beautiful things I've ever seen are dolphins surfing in waves at sunset...waves shot through with the light of the sun. Dolphin shadows appear and disappear mysteriously."

Starheart says after her return from Australia she had, "My most magical experience." "Before," when she swam with the dolphins, "it always looked like a telepathic experience. Having a very scientific mind, I could discount saying it was a coincidence. All the rest of the times I swam with dolphins were like introductions for me. This time I swam out with Jim Loomis and Tim Wyllie. The dolphins were playing chase tag with us. I could see their fins above the water. It was getting late.

"I decided to swim to shore, diving under and undulating like a dolphin, I saw silvery shadows start to swim toward me. It turned out to be the pod. I swam closer and they didn't swim away. I just stopped, opened my arms and sent a message out of my heart and asked them, 'Please invite me into your world.' The moment I sent it, they swam toward me. My skeptical mind opened. As I snorkeled around them, two of them broke out of the pod and began undulating together. They were making love underneath me!

"When they swam back to the pod, a small one swam out. It seemed like a teenager. It turned around and zapped me with a dolphin look, then swam away. I followed her and swam into long legs that happened to be Jim's. The whole pod had spread out around me, but when the other people came up they went back into a solid grouping and moved as one...then just disappeared."

"What happened in your life after that experience," I asked.

She said, "Four months later, 'The Dancing Dolphins Present The Undulation Celebration,' was born. Dancing Dolphins became a co-creative endeavor—a theater piece.

"In the theater piece, what I experienced with being with the dolphins kept coming forward. It had an arena in which to discover what I had learned from the dolphins that day..ask to be included in their world, rather than intruding. Dancing Dolphins is only presented when someone asks us to perform it. The main theme is the dance between the individual and the group and what that means. We've seen what happens with the mindless mass in which the individual is suppressed. Most of us have had the experience of pulling away from the group in fear of not being received. What I learned was the dance between the individual and the group and how it serves both."

Starheart struggled for a moment and said, "It's hard to put into words. To me the dolphins teach through visual telepathy. Perhaps it has something to do with their ability to 'see' with sonar."

Before her trip to Australia, Estelle Myers invited Starheart to the Homo Delphinous Conference in New Zealand. "I couldn't go," she said but, "I put myself there and in my imagination I found myself with a group of people discussing what they were going to be doing that night. I saw in my imagination that people were being taught visual telepathy. The dolphins' message at the meeting was that there is such a thing as visual telepathy. After I sat in on that meeting, I realized I'd always had visual telepathy but until then I hadn't recognized it was something I could use in life."

Just as I was about to ask her about dolphins and underwater birthing, she volunteered, "I never understood why people wanted dolphins involved in birthing. It's logistically difficult to do. Why would people go to that extreme? Then I realized that if dolphins use visual telepathy and can 'know' how the baby feels they can ignite the visual telepathy of a child in utero; so there's an outside friend making contact; so the child is born into relationship and has a friend when they first come into life on the planet.

"As a child myself, my strongest wish was that people could see what I was thinking. I didn't have words to share thoughts. My whole life has been expressing feelings and thoughts through dance, art, poetry, music and finally I have discovered there are some people with whom I can share visual telepathy. Then I discovered that most of these people are people who have had dolphin contact. People like Jim Nollman, Peter Schenstone, Jim Loomis...and others.

"It's not necessary to swim with dolphins, but those who have in someway connected with them seem to have that capability. A dolphin is the one being on the planet with whom you can connect without having to actually be with them."

Going back to her encounter with the dolphin pod she said, "Someone recently asked me as I was telling my story, 'Did that really happen? What was it like for you?' In that moment, I had absolutely no fear of being in that group. I felt totally connected, accepted and embraced by the pod. There was nothing between us. It was like being together in mind...not thinking but becoming one with the group.

"In contrast, if I were to walk into a group of people I did not know, I would feel outside playing 'Who do you know that I know?' Trying to discover ways that we connect. With the dolphins I completely skipped over that. It was so real...so in the moment I didn't recognize any separation.

"Something is definitely going on with dolphins. It has something to do with being embraced in that energy field. There's mutual trust through the telepathic connection and energetic embrace. If we never receive anything else from dolphins, that would be the greatest gift to humankind at this time. There is so much mistrust on this planet. By embracing each other through mutual trust, we can become a planetary pod."

SWIMMING WITH WILD DOLPHINS

Leaving Maui behind, I was flying to Oahu to visit Joan Ocean and Jean Luc feeling disappointed that I hadn't connected with dolphins in the water. At that moment, the pilot of the small commuter plane nosed toward the airstrip on Lanai, the island I had visited two days earlier—and where dolphins were known to hang out in the bay. It was a routine stopover which I didn't know about. As we were coming in for a landing, I impulsively asked the captain, "Do you suppose I could get off and spend the night and catch a plane to Oahu tomorrow? I had no camping gear, no food, nothing to sleep on or cover myself with, no camping permit and no transportation. It was Uxmal all over again!

We walked into the passenger area and before I could change my mind, the captain informed the clerk behind the counter that I was getting off. She crossed my name off the manifest. A few minutes later my bags were tossed off the aircraft and I was left standing in the prop wash with my finger up my nose wondering what to do next.

One of the incoming passengers, an older native woman, offered me a ride to town and drove me to the gas station so I could rent a car. When I told her I'd come to swim with the dolphins she said that Joana McIntyre, author of "Mind in the Waters," a book on dolphins and whales, had earlier been the harbormaster. One evening at dusk the native woman had gone to the wharf to fish with her husband. She and Joan were sitting chatting when Joan suddenly spotted the dolphins darting through the water near the mouth of the harbor. Joan jumped in and swam out to be with them. "I wish I had enough trust in them and in myself to jump in and swim with them in the dark," I thought.

The island was one big pineapple plantation. The tourist trade would not hit the island for another six months or a year. The only food I could find that appealed to me was some chips, fruit juice and nuts. I stopped at a small dry goods store and bought a beach towel for a blanket, drove to the pineapple plantation office to get a camping permit, then drove to the marine preserve to spend the night, hoping the dolphins would show up in the bay before 11 the next morning so I could catch the early flight out.

As I was settling down for the evening, one of the construction workers from the hotel project nearby attempted to strike up a conversation by offering me a beer. I declined. He asked again several minutes later. I declined a second time. He persisted. "Well, can I at least bring you dinner?"

Dinner....Ah yes...the Universe provides and who am I to judge how. "Sure, why not," I said.

His name was Art. I'd been asking for a man to appear in my life to take the place of my friend Art, but this one was a little young for me. At least it was a sign I was in the flow again. "Maybe my timing is right this time. Maybe the dolphins will appear," I thought hopefully. Art brought enough dinner to satisfy an Amazon and a huge thermos of orange juice. He left to attend a first aid class and said, "I'll be back later to pick up my jug." A little later, I pulled the lambswool seat cover off the driver's seat of the car and made myself a bed on the beach. The night sky was crystal clear, a good time to study the stars. Except for the loud hum of the generator plant attached to the construction site above the preserve, all was peaceful. By the time Art returned for his thermos around midnight, I was soundly asleep. He'd been stumbling around in the dark for an hour trying to locate me. When he found me lying on the beach, he said, "You don't want to sleep here. You'll get stung by centipedes." He described their bites, convincing me to move to the back seat of the car. I couldn't get comfortable for the rest of the night and before dawn up got to put on my swimsuit on, just in case the dolphins showed up for breakfast early, and to take some pictures of the sunrise.

Art had assured me, "They always come in around 11. "I see them almost every morning swimming out in the bay from where I'm working." But the campsite attendant said he usually saw them around 7 in the morning if they came in at all. There was nothing to do but wait and watch. An hour passed...then two...then three. "Oh, well. Another time," I thought. I was packing the car to leave and catch my plane and still had my swimsuit on when I turned to look once more.

A dark shape darted through the water several hundred yards out—then two—then three. A small pod of spinners was coming in to feed. Two young men on the beach saw them at the same time. I forgot my fears about swimming far out into deep water. The three of us waddled in with our flippers on and swam out to greet them. It didn't take long for me to realize that pursuing them didn't work. One of the young men had a camera and he was chasing them for a close up. I gave up and lolled in the water hoping they would come to me. It took me a few minutes to remember to move my attention to my heart chakra. Starheart's story was still fresh in my mind so I sent them a message: "Won't you please invite me into your world?"

By now, they were leaping and spinning in rapid succession. It was enough just to lay back and watch them frolicking. I gave up and was swimming into shore when they caught up with me and circled round and round about 15 feet away. They were, it seemed, as curious about me, as I was about them. I laid on top of the water and just looked at them through my mask. There were 14 or 15 of them, beautiful and sleek and fast. We swam together for 10 or 15 minutes before I felt the need to catch my plane. I thanked them profusely for the experience.

As I walked back up on the beach, flippers in hand, an older Japanese man who'd been sitting in a lawn chair watching said, "If you hadn't chased them, they would have come right up to the shore? They swim in almost every morning." No doubt, he had a knack for attracting them, just by being patient.

"Thanks," I said, "I'll remember next time."

It's all a matter of timing, I realized, as we circled over Lanai and flew toward Oahu. There is a rhythm and pattern to their movement just as there is with everything in nature. Connecting with wild dolphins requires tuning into their habits, moving into their flow, coming to honor and respect them.

Maybe Jim Nollman was right. Swimming with them was no great spiritual experience. Nevertheless, I felt more powerful putting my fear of the water aside to swim out and be with them. My fear of swimming in the ocean, in deep water had diminished. One thing was certain: they taught me another lesson in letting go, surrendering, giving up struggling to make things happen. Everything we ask for comes to us in time. Before I reached Oahu, thoughts of swimming with the whales danced across my mind. Starheart had said they were "too big" for her and she was a dolphin in the water. "Why is it," I wondered, "that I'm always looking for some fresh, juicy adventure? Maybe all of life is just one big Mystery School?" It seemed like I was never happy unless I was undergoing some new initiation, some new challenge to pit myself against.

On Oahu, I drove out to visit Joan and found Jean Luc was engrossed in completing a series of paintings, each more exquisite than the last. I asked him if there was a message in them. He assured me there was but that he wouldn't be able to put it into words very well without Joan's help and that would have to wait until the whole series of eight or nine was complete. It was a treat just to be able to see the work in progress for a few minutes and watch how he painstakingly and artfully compiled such tiny strokes into masterful pieces. The dolphins had certainly led him to find and express his life's purpose.

Joan, I discovered, was in the process of writing her own book and enjoying swimming with the turtles every day in the bay. I was envious of the two of them living on the beach and doing their work together. It made me even more determined than ever to move to Moloka'i.

Honolulu, I was disappointed to find in the three years since my last visit, had become nearly as smog-engulfed as many of the larger cities on the mainland. I choked on the fumes and my allergies began to flare just in the few days I was there. The noise pollution was equally obnoxious. In order to go to sleep at night I played music through earphones to drown out the traffic noise. Moloka'i looked better all the time.

RESISTING THE BLISS

After returning from Hawaii I spent two weeks catching up on writing, parking the motor home at the home of some good friends in Santa Rosa. When the rains started in earnest I knew it was time for me to leave. I had committed to return to Hawaii by the first of December but now it appeared I would not be able to sell the motor home until spring unless I was willing to let go of my downpayment. The practical part in me resisted.

"Go south for the winter, finish the book, sell the motor home, then move to Hawaii," it told me. My heart wasn't in it.

A niece who felt close to my father lived near San Diego. "Maybe I'll take his ashes down and do a ritual with her to honor his crossing over," I thought. She was the only one in the family who felt strongly connected to him. They'd been corresponding by mail for years but she hadn't seen him since she was a young girl. I detected some sadness and regret in her voice when I told her of his death. A goodbye ritual might ease her pain.

The day I reluctantly headed south, the sky opened up and flooded the Earth with rain for hours on end. I thought I was back in the Northwest. I made it as far as my niece's home before I gave up. I couldn't handle the smog, the crowds, the traffic or the idea of waiting until spring to move. The day before Thanksgiving, I headed north in the motor home to put it up for sale, pack my belongings and fly to Moloka'i within the week. The minute I made the decision, it felt like a ton of repressed energy lifted off my shoulders.

14 Waterbabies and Dolphins

IT WAS THROUGH Athena Neelley, a co-creator of the original Healing Connection, that I first heard about the Rebirthers' Tour to Russia. A group of 18 rebirthers, sponsored by the Center for Soviet-American Dialogue, went to Russia to learn about underwater birthing with dolphins from Dr. Igor Charkovsky, a founding father of the movement. John Lilly, the dolphin researcher and Sondra Ray, a rebirthing pioneer, were members of the group.

Athena is a nurse. She left the profession nearly a decade ago to become involved with the alternative health community as a rebirther and spiritual teacher. Five years earlier, we talked about the need for a networking organization in Portland and a few weeks later gave birth, along with Dick Mort and Steven Woolpert, to the Healing Connection. Athena and Dick and I resigned from the Steering Committee at the same time the previous summer thinking that our lives and our energies were moving in different directions. A few months later the dolphins led us back together to talk about Igor Charkovsky's work with underwater birthing. I interviewed her in the motor home surrounded by piles of boxes, ready for shipment to Moloka'i. Athena's vision, along with that of other people like Rima Star, author of "The Healing Power of Birth" is to create an underwater birthing center in the United States.

"Charkovsky has been working with dolphins for probably 25 years," said Athena. "He goes to the Black Sea and uses them and their sonar to reduce and largely eliminate the fear in his pregnant women and couples.

When they give birth they can do it in a relaxed, easier way than when they're doing a dry birth. What he has done lately is help women come into alignment with dolphins without even being at the Black Sea," Athena told me.

"He takes couples on guided imagery journeys and helps establish a mental and emotional rapport so they can tune into the consciousness of dolphins and ask them for help in the area of their pregnancies and their births. A couple will come to Charkovsky during a pregnancy and they want to have the delivery at the Black Sea but it's winter so he will bring that energy to them and they'll tune into it. By the time they get to the Black Sea in the summer, when it's time for the birth, they're ready. That's greatly helped his birthings.

"The biggest benefit to babies born underwater is the elimination of fear. The mothers are deeply relaxed so the birth happens easily. I don't know if I can go so far as to say without pain," says Athena, "but I think that's one of the objects of it. Childbirth is supposed to be easy. It's not supposed to be filled with pain. That's our old teachings, to bear children in pain. That comes out of the Garden of Eden. It's old karma that can be erased and change the whole birthing process. Birth is in the state of transformation now, all over the planet."

One of the objects of Charkovsky's work, Athena feels, is to transform birth on the planet and people in general and their ability to be comfortable with water. The merging of these dimensions and species on land and water will facilitate our feeling connected with all animals and sea life.

"In Russian lore there is the story of people working in Atlantis trying to develop mutations, experimenting with humans to get them back to the sea so that they could live in the sea like the dolphins," said Athena. "The experiments weren't accomplished in time to save the Atlanteans although some did go back to being dolphins. Eons and eons ago they were half human, half fish—like mermaids. There were also half humans and half dolphins and these are shown in the tapestries that we saw in Leningrad in the museum called Hermitage."

Charkovsky showed the group a video. "He was working the babies' bodies like you would exercise if you were a master Yogi, twisting your body all around and twisting your legs up around your head," said Athena. "That's what he's doing with these babies. He's wringing their joints and muscles and spines out. Their spines are quite twisted when he's working with them. A lot of times when he's working with them, the babies are nursing on their mothers and he's working on the hips or different parts of their bodies where they're being nurtured and bonded. It's unbelievable.

"When we watched the video, all of our mouths just dropped open. A lot of us went into spontaneous rebirth because it just looked like he was hurting these babies. It was just something we had never seen before—

babies bodies twisted so. Yet the babies were not resisting and when he was finished with them they were so relaxed and happy and smiling. A lot of this is done in cool or cold rather than hot water. He believes that cold water pushes out the death urge and the limitations that we put ourselves into coming into this atmosphere. Where warm water will produce the merging, the bonding, the connecting with one another, cold water pushes out the death and the limitations. He uses a lot of cold water with babies.

"All Russians use a lot of cold water for their health. They'll break the ice in the rivers and they'll go in through the hole in the ice and take a swim maybe once a day or a couple of times a week, like hydrotherapy. It's very stimulating. In fact, a couple of people we met in Leningrad invited us to go swim in the rivers before going to sleep at night. I went, 'Oh, God, no, I hate cold water.' And yet, when I do a cold water rebirth it's always good. It pushes out stuff that other rebirths will not. It brings it to the surface. It is so terrifying to me to be in cold water. It reminds me of death and that's what it brings up is death."

Going back to Charkovsky, Athena said, "He is experimenting with birth and infants and children. He's also wanting to invite adults into the water because water has so much value. When you're in water you don't have pressure on the body. Cells actually have the ability to revitalize. When you're just walking around everyday, there is a lot of pressure on us—atmospheric pressure. It's aging us. If we could spend more time in water, it would make us more youthful."

Athena continued, "Rima's interpretation of what Charkovsky is doing now is to in some way create humans being able to live in space. In other lifetimes, it was humans being able to live in water. Now it's like humans are learning to live in space.

"What the dolphins have to teach us is grace and sensitivity. They are all right brain and heart. They care for each other and they show deep sensitivity and caring for humans. Many stories have been written on how they have rescued humans. They really care about humans, especially children and babies. They are closer to babies than babies are to their mothers. When babies are born with dolphins in the water and children play where there are dolphins in the water, they connect at a deeper heart level than they connect with their own parents."

"How does that happen? Do you have any idea?" I asked.

"Sonar," Athena said. She had a difficult time explaining exactly how it works, but senses that it is the energy the dolphin emanates from their "biofield" that helps to create a feeling of safety and security in the water for the newborns. This enables them to bond at a deeper level. "In the Black Sea, Igor says that the dolphins are not coming up close and nudging the pregnant woman or anything like that. They have a distance that they stay. But their sonar and their 'biofield' is within the mother's range and her process, her labor and delivery. So they are putting it out, creating this energy field for protection and the elimination of fear."

Babies born underwater have very few problems with infections. The reason for this, Igor says, is because of the biofield. Athena said she believes this is true in waterbirths where midwives, doctors and birth sensitives are free of fear, as well. "The mother and the husband also help create a positive biofield when they have processed through their fears," said Athena.

She explained "biofield" as an energy presence that is extremely healthy and free from fear on all levels. "It's not so important to have all this sterilization that the medical profession thinks is necessary. One example would be how the immune system functions. Germs are always present in each one of us but when our immune system is dysfunctioning we tend to be prone to illnesses and disease. We can build the immune system by alternating the use of hot and cold water, or hydrotherapy, which stimulates the organs. Our way of thinking, our thought process, our consciousness and what we eat, what we breathe and what we believe, affect the biofield. If we are tuned into our hearts and live there most of the time, then we create this very positive field of energy. If that's what's present at birth, then you don't have to have sterilization. When a baby's and mother's immune systems are strong and their biofields are full of positive energy, they aren't as apt to be susceptible to harmful bacteria."

Athena mentioned that she was going to go swimming with the dolphins in the Florida Keys the following week and that she had a lot of fear around it. She believes she was zapped and killed by sonar in an Atlantean lifetime by a human who learned to use its power destructively. "I've been drawn to dolphins for a long time through Rima Star and the rebirthing movement. Many rebirthers have been tuned into dolphins for quite a number of years and have been working with them in New Zealand with Estelle Myers for about five or six years but I've been afraid to swim with them." I asked her to write and tell me about her experience when she returned from her trip.

I told her about my experience of becoming ill and feeling like I was going to die after the dolphin zapped me with sonar during my swim with them and released some trauma I was holding in my low back.

"They know where that is in your body," said Athena. "They can sense that and they send out rays to that part of the body for healing. One woman had breast cancer and didn't even know it." A dolphin nudged her breast during a swim and a week later a lump appeared where the dolphin had touched her.

"Where is your connection to dolphins taking you?" I asked.

"To a real unknown," she said. "For the last month I've been real terrified. I've been doing a lot of work on myself. Some of the things that are known to me is that next week I go to be with the dolphins and learn. The dolphins have a lot to teach me and the other people that are in this birth school about gentle birthing and about sensitivity, about being real and being in the essence with everything, specifically in our work. They are like the feminine. The sea is like the feminine. The land is more the mental, which I would call left brain. The sea and the dolphins are more like right brain. So, for me, it's like diving into my right brain, diving into my intuition, my heart, my essence to connect with them." Athena exhaled a long breath.

"This is the first time on the planet that a school like this will have been developed and pulled together in one specific structure. It's a place where people will be able to come and learn while they work with the dolphins. After they've completed the school participants will be able to go out and establish centers all over the planet. It's about transformation of birth on the planet for the parents and their babies who will be born without limitations. Parents will erase all of their karma so that they will be unlimited and then the babies that they birth will also be in their completion. They'll have ascension births.

She imagines that "The facility will be like a university in some ways. It will offer a lot of birthing techniques and methods, house the birth school and have areas that will be for adults who just want to come and learn and be healed of their past karma and couples who want to prepare themselves for conception."

The curriculum at the present time includes subjects like anatomy and physiology, midwifery skills, complications and preventions, nutrition, cultural/historical aspects of birth, non-interventive birth, waterbirth, past lives and birth, establishing a matrix for birth, being successful and powerful in the business of birth, infant massage, clearing parents and infants on birth, intuitive and psychic development for birth and bonding and dolphin midwifery.

The physical structure will be close to the beach so that people can connect with the dolphins. She is certain the dolphins will be drawn to such a birthing center. It is an opportunity to merge the dolphin species with the human species. The results, she feels, are likely to be profound.

Out of the Russian trip came a Declaration of Mutual Support for Freedom in Birth signed by Australian, English, American and Soviet midwives. This was announced on Soviet television.

The proclamation claimed the right of a mother and father to create their child's birth in whatever way they choose. It stated also that, "In free birth, full of love, openness, and high consciousness, we see the hope of the new world rising—the world free of violence, wars, aggression and hate. We see in it the way toward the birth of the new ecological consciousness, the expanding of human spiritual potential and the human race rebirth."

The proclamation made an appeal to people around the world. "We want to have an opportunity, confirm the right, and call all midwives of the world to deliver together newborns of different countries among relatives and friends, to prepare fathers and mothers to the free and conscious birth of their own children, to use freely, exchange and multiply their unique experience of non-violent birth. In the right of the free birth, we have a hope of survival of the humanity, of saving the life of our planet."

Shortly after her return, Athena wrote to tell me about swimming with the dolphins. "The first time in the water with them (two mature males and females) I was terrified. All my past conditioning and fear of large animals came up for me. Their dorsal fins make them look like sharks so I naturally thought they were going to eat me alive when they came swimming up to me.

"They gently touched my body a few times but after I put out the thought that I was terrified and needed my space, they just swam next to me and under me, looking at me reassuringly with one eye or the other. I was disappointed in myself for being so afraid when I could see they were very friendly and many of my friends were having a wonderful time playing with them. I wasn't going to let this experience stop me from communicating with the dolphins, so I processed my terror and the next day went in the water with four of them.

"This time it was entirely different. I felt more relaxed and willing to touch and be touched by them and they knew it. The more open and receptive I was, the more they played with me, rubbing their soft bodies up against mine, swimming under me and lifting me out of the water, putting their snouts right up on my cheek and giving me kisses, jumping over the top of me and giving me their dorsal fins to hang onto while they took me for numerous exciting rides through the water. This was an incredible experience. They were making sounds and talking to me the whole time. I was very impressed with their intelligence and sensitivity and felt very connected with them. I understand how their presence can be so supportive to the human species.

"I also had the experience of observing a pregnant woman swimming with the dolphins. Because of the dolphins' sensitivity and biofield, they knew immediately the presence of new life in the pregnant woman and gave her their undivided attention by being belly-to-belly with her the whole time—connecting with the baby's energy. They are gentle and caring with new babies and infants and have so much to teach us about birthing our babies and being parents."

15 Home of the Heart

RETURNING TO MOLOKA'I, I arrived just in time for a Kona storm to sweep in from the west. Huge rollers crashed along the shoreline. Surfers skimmed inside the curls of the waves. Early in the evening I took a walk. Billowing dark clouds thundered across the night sky and lightning bolts split open the blackness. I took all the commotion as a sign of welcome cosmically orchestrated—not just for me—but also for the whales who were coming in from the north.

I was anxious to get out on and in the water and connect with them. But it was winter and the weather and water were stormy and the dolphins and whales elusive. They are rarely seen close to shore around Moloka'i. The shoreline isn't conducive to their needs. It didn't take me long to realize I hadn't been called to Moloka'i to swim with them. What kept showing up instead were people and books that had stories to tell about dolphins, plane-tary changes and accessing ancient knowledge and artifacts.

Moloka'i, I learned, was the training ground and retreat center for Kahunas in ancient times. Their curses are still believed to have an effect on anyone whose main motivation is one of greed. The island has a reputation for flushing up relationship and financial issues. Newcomers are tested by island life. I had come to be part of a "spiritual" family and eventually help   create a retreat center. The resort lifestyle did not agree with me, however. It was too much like the existence I'd moved away from when I left my marriage and family. I anticipated living close to nature, not protecting and isolating myself from it. The manicured and sprayed grounds of the golf resort were beautiful, but they offered at best a false sense of security. The reality is there are bugs and insects and flora and fauna that co-exist on the planet with us. They may not be aesthetically pleasing to our senses. Nevertheless, I wanted to get to know them and learn to live in harmony with them, not destroy them. Within a matter of weeks after my arrival I began to feel disheartened, disconnected, out of the flow.

St. Germain, however, continued to make his presence known by sending messengers with books for me to read that were intriguingly appropriate. From "Tales of the Night Rainbow," I learned about Moloka'i and the Hawaiian culture. Forgiving and forgetting were an important part of the early teachings. If you told someone you forgave them and continued to bring the subject up, it was like adding a rock to a bowl of light. Young Hawaiians were taught a parable that said

"Each child born has at birth, a Bowl of perfect Light. If he tends his Light it will grow in strength and he can do all things—swim with the shark, fly with the birds, know and understand all things. If, however, he becomes envious or jealous he drops a stone into his Bowl of Light and some of the Light goes out. Light and the stone cannot hold the same space. If he continues to put stones in the Bowl of Light, the Light will go out and he will become a stone. A stone does not grow, nor does it move. If at anytime he tires of being a stone, all he needs to do is turn the bowl upside down and the stones will fall away and the Light will grow once more."

Each 'ohana (or family line) was distinguished by a color and a spirit guide or guardian angel called an aumakua. This guardian spirit may or may not take the shape of an animal but its presence was known and felt by the family members as if it were an ancestor. The aumakua was held in high regard and became part of the family identity. Its characteristics were emulated. For instance, the mo'o, a giant lizard, was seen as a protector and the clan it guarded also guarded others, as though they were brothers. The aumakua was believed to be a messenger between the worlds of flesh and spirit. It assisted people in the death process by making them welcome to the afterworld. The 'ohana (family) helped members feel at peace when it was their time to go so that the family itself could be at peace as well. If someone stubbornly refused to die, everything possible was done to help them live. Natives loved their aumakuas as if they were part of them, like the food they ate and the water they drank.

Carl Jung in "Man and His Symbols," says that, "Primitives assume man has a 'bush soul' as well as his own, that the 'bush soul' is incarnate in a wild animal or tree, with which the human has some kind of 'psychic iden-tity.' The animal is considered to be some sort of brother to the man—injury to the bush soul is interpreted as injury to the man."

In a book entitled "Kahuna Power" by Timothy Green Beckley, he states, "The aumakua, or spirits assigned to help the living, take the bodies of certain animals and inhabit them. The beasts most often selected by the aumakua are the shark, the owl and the lizard. The Hawaiians have known for centuries what modern man is just beginning to learn. "Animals have an awareness of impending disaster," says Beckley and they warn people of natural disasters.

The aumakuas were described as being laka, or very tame and help-ful. If one lived in a shark, the shark would be tame. It would like to be petted on the head and would open its mouth for a sacrifice. "The shark has cared for and guided many a seaman. Not all sharks are killers, in fact very few," says Pali Lee, co-author of "Tales of the Night Rainbow." Reading these passages, a bell went off in my head. If I substituted "dolphin" for "shark," it described precisely what was happening with the people I'd been interviewing, as well as with myself.

Is it possible, I began to wonder, that the dolphin is the aumakua of ancient Atlanteans and Lemurians? Are they the guardian spirits of the 12 lost tribes who have reincarnated and are being called together to reunite and build communities in various parts of the world? As a family we can be more readily guided and protected during times of change. There are other tribes or families gathering as well, such as The Bear Clan in Washington and The Owls in Texas.

To the early Hawaiians, all of life was a school. Children learned to read the weather and the stars and had contests to see who could make clouds bigger or smaller. They learned to move objects, send them away and bring them back again. These powers were taken for granted and were part of the early training of children that would eventually lead them to become expert Kahunas. There were many kinds of Kahunas, from bone setters to prophets, to faith healers to canoe makers. Even though a student had been studying for many years, he was not given the title of Kahuna until an elder was about to pass away and designated him as a successor. The dying Kahuna would call the student to his side and breathe into his mouth to pass on some bit of wisdom that he had not been taught in school. Then he was called "the keeper of the secret." This seemed very similar to what I had learned about the Mayan use of the Crystal Skull.

The Hawaiians, like the Native Americans, believed that land could not be owned by an individual. The land, the sky and the sea were for all people. When the foreigners arrived and wanted to buy land, the Hawaiians laughed and thought it was nonsense but went along with the joke, trading pieces of paper that were titles to land for a jug of wine or a piece of cloth.

Chief Seattle, in response to President Franklin Pierce's request to buy land from the Indians had replied:

"How can you buy or sell the sky—the warmth of the land? The idea is strange to us. Yet we do not own the freshness of the air and the sparkle of the water. How can you buy Them from us? We will decide in our time. Every part of this Earth is sacred to our people. Every shining pine needle, every sandy shore, every mist in the dark woods, every clearing and humming insect is holy in the memory and experience of my people."

Throughout human history the concept of man as steward of the land has prevailed in the hunter-gatherer mythologies. It wasn't until we became cultivators of the land and stopped roaming to find food, that the idea of "ownership" was born. Now that the price of land in some areas of the world is out of reach of the average man it may be that we will have to return to the old way and begin to hold land in trust once more for the use of everyone, rather than a privileged few.

On Christmas Day, one of the people who had been involved in the effort to bring Joe and Rosie to Moloka'i appeared for dinner with an armload of books for me to read. He was clearly a messenger of St. Germain. The books related to hidden vaults, the secret destiny of America, the reuniting of the lost tribes of Israel and Joseph Campbell's "Power of Myth."

Campbell spoke about the symbols that come to us when we are in the midst of transformation, "the serpent bound to the earth, the eagle in spiritual flight—isn't that conflict something we all experience? And then, when the two amalgamate, we get a wonderful dragon, a serpent with wings." He adds that "All over the Earth people recognize these images." They are latently imbedded in our subconscious and come to the fore when we begin to awaken at the cellular level.

He also wrote of the "animal envoys of the Unseen Power," who in primeval times served as teachers and guides to mankind. Now, we keep our animal guides, the bears, lions and elephants in zoos and our dolphins and whales in marine parks. Still he says, "Memories of the animal envoys must sleep somehow within us; for they wake a little and stir when we venture into the wilderness." And I might add, when we spend the night in ancient ruins and vortex areas.

He called mythology the "song of the imagination inspired by the energy of the body." "Myths," he said "are clues to our deepest spiritual potential, able to lead us to delight, illumination and rapture..." They lead us as well "to the realization of the mystery that underlies all forms."

As Dr. William Tufts Brigham, first director of the Bishop Museum in Honolulu and Max Freedom Long discovered in their search for the secrets of the Kahunas, there are a great many similarities between the ancient Hawaiian teachings and the Mysteries that are hidden in allegory and symbolism in the Bible.

In "Ano Ano" by Kristin Zambucka, another of the books brought to me, nature is used as a metaphor to teach people a sense of values and morality and connection with all things. The tree of life, the vine and the seed were symbols widely used by the Kahunas to teach people about the cycles and rhythms of their lives and the recurring pattern of death, transformation and rebirth. In "Ano Ano," a band of seekers go out in the wilderness in search of truth. Encountering three elders who are kneeling down to smell the earth, they ask "And what of life? Why are we here at all?"

The old ones answer that life is a series of lessons to be learned. And then the seekers begin to ask the questions that I have so often asked in the past, "But why all the suffering that haunts us throughout our years? We didn't ask to be born. Why must we pay such a price for this consciousness?"

The story goes on, "And when the paralyzing ache of despair engulfs you, and you reel shaken from the blows that life deals you, and you scream out, demanding to know what you've done to deserve it. And when you know that you can't take any more but it strikes you again, harder this time, from another side, and you are just hanging on by a thread until you feel yourself curl inward and die a little—Know that there is a reason for it all." The passage evoked memories of all the times I'd cried out begging to be released from life only to discover after the healing crises had passed that I'd been strengthened and tempered somehow by the experience of suffering.

The elders spoke again to the seekers, "Suffering unlocks the door to many answers and fire purifies. If you look back and examine some pain of the past, you will see that it taught you so much that no other teacher could. Only when wounded do we stand still and listen. Only when you can cry no more will you begin to grow."

Only in the silence do we find our way home—only in the silence can we hear a higher source of wisdom and love speaking to us through symbols and images, in the very softest of voices.

Both "The Power of Myth" and "Ano Ano" spoke to me—to my heart—in a deep way. They comforted and strengthened me. They renewed my confidence in having chosen to follow the spiritual path—no matter how challenging and painful the lessons were that kept popping up along the way. I chose a treacherous, uncharted course to the top of the mountain and there is no way to turn around and go back. I might as well find a way to enjoy the adventure and let go of my resistance. One of these days I am sure to run out of tears.

Letting go of relationships, I learned, is no different than scaling a cliff. We have to let go of the security of the rock beneath us in order to reach the peak. There's no point in crying over it. Losses are gains in disguise. Looking back or looking down only scares us more and keeps us from moving forward and upward. Following the spiritual path is not only a test of one's faith, but a test of our beliefs and our strengths as well. Kahlil Gibran once wrote, "Many are those who talk like the roar of the sea, but their lives are shallow and stagnant like the rotting marshes. Many are those who lift their heads above the mountaintops, but their spirits remain dormant in the obscurity of the caverns."

All of life is about ebbing and flowing. Yes, there are times when we get trapped in the decaying bogs and must slither like snakes across the ground. We lose our vision of what life is all about. "God," says Gibran, "has given you a spirit with wings on which to soar into the spacious firmament of Love and Freedom. Is it not   pitiful then that you cut your wings with your own hands and suffer your soul to crawl like an insect upon the earth?"

The beauty of myth and metaphor, I discovered, is that it shows us we have the power to heal those broken wings and rise like phoenixes out of the rotting marsh. Reading all these books, I began to see that the dolphins and St. Germain were leading me on a quest for the Holy Grail, much like the Knights of the Roundtable seeking the Cup in the time of King Arthur. The symbology has changed but the end result is the same. As an Initiate, we are led to give up our earthly loves and materialistic lifestyles in search of spiritual truth and a higher experience of ourselves. We are led to lead more authentic lives, to live in balance and honor all living things.

Joseph Campbell quoted an early writer who says that, "The Grail was brought down from heaven by the neutral angels." During the war in heaven between Satan and God, between good and evil, some angels sided with God, others with Satan. "The Grail was brought down through the middle by the neutral angels. It represents the spiritual path that is between pairs of opposites, between fear and desire, between good and evil."

The theme of the Grail is breaking free from the expectations of others and from society—finding the courage within to do what you want with your own life. To begin living authentically according to your own values and beliefs, rather than the beliefs and values of others and those of the society you live in. The Grail represents that which is attained by people who have chosen to live their own lives, fulfilling in the process, their highest spiritual potential.

Seeing ourselves in every living thing—in the rhythm of the ocean water, in the thundering sky, in the wounded bird, we come to embrace our shadow side and the darkness loses its power over us. Our fears vanish like phantoms into the mist. Honoring all of who we are, we cannot help but honor all that is within others. Refusing to abuse and neglect ourselves, we stop abusing others and the environment around us. The earth, the air, the water, our bodies, begin to heal and purify themselves. No effort is needed. Accepting the cycle of death as well as rebirth, the passion as well as the peace, we come into balance between fear and desire, good and evil.

If, however, we ignore the call to the spiritual life and our connection to the natural world and we continue to focus our attention on the world outside, projecting our inner turmoil, our discontent, our disrespect for ourselves onto others, then the Universe has no choice but to bring that back to us for everything in life is a circle. If we focus on dire prophecies of war, famine, disease, economic destruction and chaos, then that is what we will create in the outer world. Our thoughts are the seeds we sow. We harvest that which we plant. "The fruit is already in the seed," Kristin Zambrucka reminds us in "Ano, Ano."

Suffering is the vehicle through which we come to know ourselves and the life around us; the alchemist's coal capable of transforming itself into gold. Embracing it in mythological form, enables us to free ourselves from the marshy bogs of our pain and fear and to call forth out of ourselves the highest expression of our being. Myth and metaphor are the great liberators of the Soul that connect us with the invisible flow of life. When we are in the flow we become funnels through which the abundance that is the Universe channels itself. Outside of that flow, we are like vacuums filling our emptiness with the debris of life: eating, drinking, sleeping, recreating, smoking, doping and collecting material wealth. These are all ruses we use to fool ourselves and appease our hunger for a spiritual connection to the world around us. Without this inner contact to the invisible realms we fall asleep to the impact we have on the environment. Polluting ourselves, we pollute and harm the world.

The most devastating pollution of all is that of the mind, for it is there that we design and plant the seeds that take root in the world and grow. The question we must ask ourselves is, "Do I want to harvest the fruit that will come out of the seeds of my thoughts?"

16 *Human/Dolphin Community*

ONE DAY I printed the manuscript of this book for the first time and assembled it. I was amazed at how it flowed from one experience to another and indeed how my life had flowed with it. It felt finished, so I wrote what I thought was the final chapter. A few nights later, just as I was falling asleep I asked St. Germain to send someone to read it. I was due to leave for the Pacific Bridge Event the next day to attend a gathering of dolphin-spirited people on the Big Island and didn't expect anyone would appear before then.

Early the next morning, however, a housemate asked me, unexpectedly, to drive to Maunaloa to pick up a woman friend. The friend's partner, Jonathan, came along for the ride. The two of them had spent nearly four years living outdoors in wilderness areas on the islands.

As we were driving down the hill toward the resort, I looked out across the expanse of ocean and saw what I thought was the spray from whales spouting about a quarter of a mile from shore. Something was leaping in the water around them. It was too far away to tell if they were dolphins or large fish.

Somehow during the ride the conversation drifted to the book and the next thing I knew Jonathan was parked on the couch in my room reading it. Later in the morning he told me he connected strongly with St. Germain on Mt. Shasta and that he'd been carrying an "I AM" book, the channeled discourses of St. Germain, by Godfrey King, with him for several weeks on a wilderness hike into Wailau, a rugged, remote valley on Moloka'i's north side. The day before he had gone inside to meditate and asked St. Germain if he should renew the "I AM" book from the library one more time. He was told, "Open yourself to new material." The new material turned out to be this book.

These small confirmations of St. Germain's constant presence in my life are difficult to ignore. It seems that whenever I ask for help related to the book, it manifests almost instantly. Jonathan turned out to be the perfect person to read the manuscript for the first time because he is sensitive and familiar with most of the material.

As I climbed in the car to depart for the airport that afternoon, a housemate asked, "Did you see the dolphins and whales offshore this morning? There was a huge pod of them." Naturally, they showed up just as I was leaving and couldn't come out to play.

Joan Ocean had given me a flier on the Pacific Bridge Event in October but I procrastinated before sending in a deposit. "I don't want to sit indoors for a week. No more seminars," I insisted as the inner voice prodded me to go. I also didn't want anything to distract me from finishing the book. I thought the material I would gather at the Event would be for a future book. Of course, St. Germain and the dolphins knew better.

It was a gathering of old and new dolphin friends interested in interspecies communication and human and dolphins in community. Some of the participants had joined Jim Nollman on his Orca excursions for several years. Gigi Coyle, a board member at the Ojai Foundation and Director of the ORCA project (which brought about the release of Joe and Rosie in 1987) acted as facilitator. The format of the gathering was to share through the Council who we were and what we were about in a process that Gigi Coyle had developed with educator Jack Zimmerman at Ojai Foundation. Jim Nollman shared his experiences on the McKenzie River attempting to attract Beluga whales and talked about his role in luring the gray whales out of the ice jam with jazz music. Joan Ocean spent an evening roasting Jim and emceeing Jean Luc's multi-media art show. But it was clearly the dolphins who called the meeting to order. The one thing we all had in common was "dolphinmania." Micky, a quick-witted, mixed-media artist, described our addiction as "Delphic Bliss Deficiency Syndrome." We just couldn't seem to get enough of those creatures. And, of course, St. Germain was lurking in the ethers. Mention of his name triggered memories of connections people had with him in their travels on the spiritual path. But it was the dolphins we wanted to connect with now. Many of us had a hidden agenda for the week. We came to the gathering hoping to swim with dolphins in the wild somewhere along the stormy Hilo coast.

CAPTIVE DOLPHINS' PLIGHT

Twenty-four human-dolphins appeared. Some flew in from Europe. One of my roommates was a young woman named Helen who had been a dolphin trainer for five years. She resigned her job when she could no longer cope with her role in contributing to the suicide and distress of the dolphins she had come to love. It took Helen several months to move through her feelings of grief and loss after leaving the dolphins. She was in so much pain, she told people, "Don't even mention the word dolphin around me."

After several months, she broke the vow of silence that all dolphin trainers are required to sign before they are hired and began speaking out on their behalf. She uses her experiences as a trainer to lecture and give slide presentations proposing the establishment of a rehabilitation program that will enable dolphins who are no longer used as performers to be released back into the wild. Helen felt inspired by the successful release of Joe and Rosie back into the wild. The two dolphins were placed in a wire cage in the marshes off the coast of Georgia and were retrained to catch and eat live fish for 30 days before their release. Branded on their dorsal fins, they've been sighted numerous times traveling in separate pods by local crab fisherman and wildlife officials in the past two years. Rosie has been seen with a baby by her side in the company of other female dolphins.

Helen came to the Pacific Bridge Event to take a break from her heavy job and lecture schedule and to renew herself. "I feel so alone in this work," she told me. She has lots of environmental groups who support her, but is missing the day-to-day emotional support needed to keep herself going. Occasional threats are made on her life. She faces opposition by the dolphinariums and by the people who trap and sell wild dolphins to marine parks. Their livelihoods, which involve millions of dollars annually, are threatened by her activities, though she attempts to keep a low profile and does not tell the whole story of the abuse and neglect of marine mammals who have lost their usefulness as performers.

When I said to her, "Dolphins serve a purpose by being in marine parks and giving humans an opportunity to connect with them in a way they might never have otherwise," she adamantly disagreed.

"People do not learn anything from going to marine parks," Helen insisted. This issue became part of a running dialogue between those of us at the Event who shared opposite views. There were so many mixed feelings about it, so much pain over depriving dolphins of their freedom and over human neglect and abuse of the environment and the animal kingdom. I arrived hoping to take a break from the intensity of writing. I was ready to play. But this was a group that carried their pain close to the surface. Before breakfast one morning, Helen shared her experiences and the plight of the dolphins at length.

I asked her, "What brought you to the decision to resign your job?"

"I started to work in 1980 with sea lions and dolphins in captivity as a trainer. At that time I really thought it was possible to keep dolphins in captivity without having any influence on the natural balance. After the first season I knew that dolphins were not really happy. They were too much depending on humans. The responsibility always lays with humans for their health and the quality of life of the dolphins. Because humans had that responsibility I had the feeling that I had to continue working. These particular animals needed somebody who was willing to take the time to understand their behavior and to understand their need of food and attention. So I stayed another year.

"The second season I tried to give the dolphins in a working relationship the freedom to react to me. Every interaction we had, if you can call it interaction, they had the freedom to refuse or do something else. By doing that, I gave myself the opportunity to see how the group structure was working, who was the leader of the group, who was able to stimulate one or another of the dolphins. In that year I figured that dolphins don't have a hierarchy anymore. It is closely dependent on humans. You have to stimulate a connection between the dolphins where their natural hierarchy was replaced by human hierarchy.

"Because there were different trainers at different times at the dolphinariums, I thought it would be better to have a basic structure of hierarchy between the dolphins. Humans get fired or get sick, or get married and have children and leave the dolphins behind.

"At that time I started traveling to other dolphinariums and I started looking for a dolphin which would have died of old age inside a dolphinarium. The longer I looked for such a case, the more I came upon dolphins that had committed suicide or died of medical poison. As we all know, cetaceans have a totally different body structure and totally different metabolism. Also they need to be conscious to breathe. They react to medicine differently than we humans. You can give the dolphin only a tiny bit because it works three times as good in them. Sometimes the dolphin reacts totally different than another land animal would to the same medicine. For sea mammals, there is a lot of experimenting. A lot of sea mammals actually have medicine coming out their skin and the skin actually rots away. It turns white and falls off. Tails and dorsal fins fall off.

"If you see it you realize how stupid we are! That's one reason why animals die. Another reason are diseases which are directly linked to stress. Fifty percent of the illnesses which are the causes of death for dolphins in captivity are illnesses which occur after a long period of stress. I know of quite a few cases where dolphins that have been caught and transported and released into a new environment swim against a wall and damage their skull or damage their beak until they die.

"I know of a few cases where animals have filled their lungs with water so they can drown. I know that is happening more and more in dolphinariums. One dolphin which I had the opportunity to take care of for three years unfortunately didn't get enough attention because every trainer has about 15 animals to take care of. Imagine caring for 15 children which you have to give enough attention in eight hour days. It's too much. You have to perform the show, clean the buildings as well. This animal couldn't cope with the lack of attention and started spitting out the fish we gave her and then swallowing it again. This stimulates the acid production in the stomach. If you do that for a long time, ulcers will occur on the stomach wall which will be the final cause of death. Monique died of stomach ulcers. It took her a half year to commit suicide. Once you have gone through that process and you have many moments like this, you can see a dolphin killing itself slowly.

"You're in such a contrary position. Because you're a trainer you have to take care. On the other hand, who are you to decide over the life of another being. But you already have decided by being a trainer in the first place. Do you have the right to choose or does the animal? Then the question comes up: 'Why does the animal choose this way of committing suicide?' It could have just filled up its lungs. It could have just bounced its head against the rim and died of brain damage like most dolphins do. Why does this animal, like many animals, choose acid production?

"I know a dolphin in New Zealand who did it and one in Germany and there are more and more cases. Going through the whole process with such an animal makes you wonder where your responsibility is. What will we humans allow ourselves to do? Which freedoms will we give the animals we work with. Which freedoms do we allow ourselves?

"This is one of the cases where I say now, 'We humans do not have the right to decide over another life if the only motivation is for our own good.' Our own good in this case goes much further than feeding ourselves. It's not to keep ourselves alive. We feed ourselves with dolphins to satisfy our curiosity. We hope we can get better. A relationship with a dolphin in captivity doesn't give you a chance to develop the relationship so that you can give something back to the world. You might be able to give something back in that momentary relationship, but you might not develop to the level that you can be part of the future of the dolphin. If you're building up a relationship with a dolphin in captivity, you're developing a fairly unique situation where natural laws don't count.

"The one who is in captivity is a mirror for the one who is dominant in the situation, in this case the human. You just make reflections of yourself in that relationship and therefore, the importance to the dolphin is with you.

You make the dolphin lower than yourself. You have to do it because you are the one who decides when there is food. You are the one who decides if there is sunlight. You are the one who decides the quality of the water. You are the one who decides every single thing. Because the animal knows you are the decider of everything, the dolphin reacts toward you. As dolphins, they always react to their surroundings. Humans want to make their surroundings react to them…"

I interrupted, "But a child will react to its surroundings."

"Yeah," said Helen, "but the way we pick up dominance if we are any good, we want to make the group listen to what we have to say. If we are any good, we have to make the group follow us."

"Some people do, but not all…" I interjected

"In some cases, it's OK, but in some cases it isn't," said Helen. "If we look to the world in general as it is now, especially if I look to Europe, first we create our houses, then we create a part where there could be some kids. First we build a dam, then we see how many animals will be damaged by the dam and can be taken care of in the zoo. We don't say, 'OK, this is part of nature. What happens if we put in a dam and what happens to the animals? Are there two or three kinds we can take care of in the zoo? From the other side of the world, it's not as beautiful as it is here.' That's the way we humans make our points…."

"We take action, then we take responsibility," I said.

"Exactly, and it's the same with dolphinariums," said Helen. "We now have dolphins in captivity. Some people say, 'Yeah, I'm not quite sure if they should be, but it has been happening for so long, it must be OK.' I think it would be much safer for our surroundings, if we gave ourselves the opportunity every day to ask if what we are doing is the right thing. Every day is a new opportunity. Every day you walk a step further than you were the day before. Now, we have dolphinariums and we see what happens in those institutions. We might give ourselves the opportunity to ask now if it all is worth it."

"In other words, look at the effect of what we're doing. Look at both the cause and the effect," I said.

"We have to look at one side as a conservationist," said Helen. "We are not able to breed dolphins in captivity well enough to be working with humans. Dolphins born in captivity lose their fear of humans and therefore, cannot be trained ever. A dolphin born in captivity cannot be used to perform in shows."

"They're not used at all to perform in shows?" I asked.

"No," said Helen. "Until now, there is no dolphin that performs with discipline in a show. Therefore, you cannot rely on them."

"What happens to them?" I wondered.

"Depends on which kind of dolphinarium they're in," said Helen. "Now they're used for breeding. Dolphins who are not used in the show, die from depression. Dolphins that are not disciplined and are too aggressive in their behavior are set aside from the show group. That means they are brought into a hospital pool or a quarantine pool which in most of the dolphinariums is a very small pool from two by three meters . No sunlight, only artificial light and the light will only be switched on if humans come in to feed them and will be turned off because of energy costs when they go out."

"How long do they keep them like that?" I quizzed.

"Most of the time until they die," said Helen."In Holland, for example, no animal born in captivity has ever reached maturity."

"How old is maturity?" I asked.

"Nine years," said Helen.

"What's the average life span of a dolphin that's caught in the wild?" I asked.

"It's difficult to say because you have several problems. Many die in the first selection," said Helen.

"What's the average number that die before they ever reach the marine park?" I asked.

"We can't say for sure, " said Helen. "Nobody has to register the amount of catch or the accidents which happen from the catch to where they are temporarily landed. It's just a holding area in the region where they've been caught. I know one case in which 70 dolphins were caught and nine went on transport. Two of them were released. In another case in New Zealand, there were 76 dolphins caught. Three have survived to perform in shows longer than one year."

"So the rest of the 76 died," I said.

"The 73 died on the boat going to the dolphinarium or died in the first few months of being in captivity, " said Helen. "You have to understand a dolphin that is captured has to learn to eat dead fish in between concrete walls. It loses its ability to communicate by vocalizing. They are totally depending on telepathy and body language. If you are in such a stressed situation you don't communicate by telepathy because you have to be relaxed. Therefore you are very sensitive to what is happening in your surrounding. There is no species more aggressive than humans.

"The first time a dolphin won't open up toward that kind of communication. After being caught they are very stressed, so they lose their way to communicate. They lose their normal rituals to eat and they come into a world where there is no sounds other than from the pumps that take care of the water system which is a terrible sound to hear day-by-day. It's boring compared to the sounds of the waves and thousands of fishes. Most of the time there is no sunlight and no wind. They have to learn to live in chlorinated water. A lot of the animals in the beginning won't be able to tolerate it and their skin burns. Quite a few animals die also because they burn to death.

"These are all problems that are difficult to solve. What do you do about the communication? What do you do about the concrete walls? If you make bigger walls, it will still be concrete walls. It costs a fortune. For an Orca, for example, you need 480 kilometers because that's the amount he will travel a day. While in a dolphinarium he goes into 15 meters."

"Is there a restriction on the number of dolphins that can be kept in a particular area?" I asked.

"No, not in Europe," said Helen. "America does have restrictions. For each 1,000 cubic meters there can be five dolphins, for each additional dolphin there needs to be 275 cubic meters. I'm not quite sure but it's in this region. There are only a few dolphinariums that are bigger. Of course, we are talking now about bottlenose dolphins but an orca counts as much as several bottlenose, so you have to make it bigger. The orca also poses the problem of the length of his body. It's not so difficult to make a deep pool for a tursiop because a pool where it can be horizontal or faster needs to be only three meters deep. If you do the same thing for an Orca, you have to go seven meters deep at least. And then you come to the problem that it is very expensive to make a pool like that. What you go into the ground, you have to go up and out of the ground, otherwise the ground water will break up the pool. The construction of a deeper pool is much more expensive than for tursiops. Pilot whales or killer whales are very popular in dolphinariums because they have a fear image around them. If you make a nice water ballet, you will attract more of an audience. Everybody wants to have them, but they don't all have the money to finance such a large pool. It costs about $1.5 to $2 million just to make the pool and then you didn't buy an Orca which costs at least $200,000 for one. But then you still have to pay for transport and insurance, your license. You have to pay a qualified trainer. An Orca is not just some dumb animal, it's highly intelligent. So there's a lot of expense."

"Other than not having dolphins in captivity at all, what do you recommend?" I asked Helen.

"I would recommend you go to an underwater content and you will find out about the world of vibrations. You will realize what it is to live in another environment, in another medium. It gives you an opportunity to think out of the dolphin mind, to realize what it is to miss sound or miss the ability to produce sound. We have to give ourselves the freedom to think out of another one's disposition. We have to become that plant and feel the sunlight. We have to become the dolphin and feel the speed and we have to become the dolphin to feel the sun. We have to become the dolphin to enjoy the energy of playing or the energy of being touched. We have to not be ashamed to crawl into the dolphin skin and have more responsibility toward them. If we enable ourselves to do that then we can meet the dolphins in the wild. There are many places in the world where you can meet them in the wild where the knowledge you gain of such an interaction will be much bigger and much more worth it. Then you only have to see them once in your life to gain enough from it. You don't have to go every year to a dolphinarium and see how they are looking."

"Is there any way that we can continue to have dolphinariums and satisfy the dolphins, to meet their needs? What about just having them along the coast in natural lagoons? Would that work?" I wondered.

"It would, of course, be better—a lot like Florida where they have these halfway places," said Helen. "But I do think what needs changing is that it shouldn't only be for our own sake. By rehabilitating dolphins, we will bring dolphins to the coast who have this relationship with humans. If those dolphins choose to stay along the coastline, it is no problem to go and meet them. Like this ex-marine park dolphin in Florida who lives in the backyard of this lady, that's why this dolphin is happy. He made this choice! In the first place we should give the dolphins a choice. By bringing them out to sea, we give them a choice. If they want to stay on the shore and want to depend on us for food. If the dolphin chooses to stay, then we have to feed the dolphin until he chooses otherwise. That's our responsibility. That's the responsibility we took at the moment we took them on land. If the dolphin is choosing for itself, you can feel more confident in the love you get from it. Because you won't get the love if you're claiming it from them, you get the love because it wants to give it to you. From that mark, we can be much more happy. A happy person can do many good things."

"Is there a trend in Europe to swim with dolphins?" I asked.

"Not as much as there is here in America," said Helen. "Being in France, there were a few people who wanted to swim with the dolphins. There were more people who just cruised on the coast. They traveled for 200 kilometers just to see a dolphin. They didn't feel the need to go in and swim. They just stood on the coastline and watched and they were as happy as we were swimming with the dolphins. I realized there that these dolphins had a treatment for everybody. As many people as there were, the dolphin responded in its own way, because it could. If it was tired from it, it chose the open ocean and rested for an hour and had new energy. That was nice! If you have seen such a dolphin, it does more for you than going to the dolphinarium and seeing them jumping through a hoop and attacking one of the trainers because the dolphin became as aggressive as humans."

"So like you said, they reflect a trainer's behavior?"

"Yeah, yeah, very much," said Helen. "In order to bring them back to the sea you have to get that behavior out of them. We have to stimulate initiative because we take their initiative away. Humans who work under a stress condition can become very aggressive and they are very good about understanding another animal's aggressive behavior. So if a dolphin wants to get a point across and show 'this is too much' they only have to jump up and snap at the trainer and he will understand, 'Oh, he is pissed off. I will leave him alone him, otherwise he is going to bite me.' And then this dolphin gets his point across because that's the only way we understand.

"If I go and see a dolphin in nature…if I swam with them in the wild I would see I was in the living room of the dolphin. I'm very pleased that they come up to me and explore this creature with this black flippers and say, 'Who is this?' I realize that I'm in the living room of another creature. It's not my living room and they rule in the place where I'm swimming. If they exhibit a behavior I don't understand, I will take a laidback position to see if I can understand them. If I don't understand I don't say, 'Oh I'm still not afraid, I'm still gonna do it.' I say 'OK, maybe next time' and I go out and I sit on the shore. If they come back to me I know I'm invited. If they don't come back, then it was the right time to leave them. You can do that in a relationship in captivity. That animal grows up to snap at somebody if he wants to have his food or if he wants to have his freedom. Then you have the problem, that if he does it often he loses his discipline. He can see he can play with different behaviors. If he frightens the trainer well enough, he will leave him quiet but if he comes to the point that by testing him it becomes impossible to work in the show, he will be sent to solitary."

"So it's very much like a human prison?" I asked.

"It is," said Helen. "If you don't behave you go in solitary. If you don't listen you don't get any extra food and extra food is the food you need to stay healthy. Normally, the food amount given is not enough to live from, but too much to die from."

"So you're just borderline starving…" I said.

"That's a nice word…borderline starving," said Helen. "We don't feed them enough to become fat or to feed their fetus when they're pregnant. We don't know when a dolphin is pregnant, and if it is pregnant it doesn't get any more food and it has to work hard to get more food for that baby. I've seen many early abortions with dolphins in captivity. You have to work damn hard to get food."

"Are there any other problems that come up?" I asked.

"I think it's just one big problem," said Helen.

"Tell me about your experience of swimming with them in the wild." I said.

"It was an incredible experience," said Helen. "There was a pod of about 45 dolphins. I gave myself the opportunity to only enter the water if I was invited so I stayed on the shoreline for about three weeks and they would come everyday a little bit closer. We would play rhythmic stones and dance on the side of the road and wave at each other and they would show their bellies. They would just perform. I felt very rich to have a free performance of dolphins four times a day without having to work for it...just standing dancing on the rocks. There were these dolphins just jumping out of the water and looking at me. At first it was just one dolphin and then it became a whole group.

"After three weeks, Frank, my companion and I decided this is the moment. We woke up about five o'clock, put on our diving suits and snorkels and went into the water. While I was laying on the surface looking for these dolphins, putting my head up so I could look then putting my head under the surface...I couldn't see any dolphins until I bent my head totally down under my arms and then there were two grown-up female dolphins laying only two centimeters away from my nose. Once I looked down I looked into these two beautiful female, very feminine dolphins and my two eyes came in contact with each of them and I felt so blessed by them. I've looked into many dolphins' eyes, but I've never felt so full. By the time they took off I realized I haven't breathed even one time. If they hadn't taken off I probably would have been drowned because of lack of oxygen. So I was very happy they took off. I was so impressed by them. The most important part of the whole thing was that as a former professional dolphin trainer I finally had the opportunity to learn to swim with the wild dolphin and learn to relate to the waves. I learned to come into the water and become the water and then not be afraid of the power of the water. I was learning how to swim. Actually I was very grateful. After five years of being a professional diver I finally learned how to swim.

"Swimming with the wild dolphin, you're learning something. Everybody is learning something from the wild dolphin and that's the big difference between the interaction with a captive dolphin and a dolphin in the wild."

"You have a more complete experience of nature?" I questioned.

"Some people learn to dive, some people learn what it is to be in the water, some people learn to cope with their own emotions, some people get healed by dolphins and some people get comfortable by being with dolphins," said Helen. "As many different people as there are, there are that many approaches."

Helen feels that people who capture and sell dolphins and dolphinariums should by law be held responsible for their release back into the wild when they are no longer used to perform. However, she is realistic enough to see that this could be a very expensive proposition for dolphin captors and owners and understands their resistance to rehabilitating them. Meantime, she and the environmental groups she works with are attempting to work with dolphinariums in Europe to relieve the problems of depressed and suicidal dolphins.

MINING THE OCEAN BOTTOM

Meantime, on another front, there is grave concern over the destruction of the dolphins' natural habitat. The state of Hawaii and the federal government have revealed plans to lease enormous tracts of seabed between 50 to 200 miles offshore to international mining corporations. They would dredge up the top layer of "crust" of the ocean floor in seamounts around Hawaii to extract cobalt and other metals.

According to environmentalists, the mining operations would stir up large plumes of sediment on the ocean floor and on the surface. An estimated 83 tons of excess waste materials would be dumped overboard per ship each day. Toxic metals such as lead, arsenic, selenium and cadmium would be released into the food chain and end up in fish. The areas where mining would take place are the feeding and spawning grounds for many fish species—as well as marine mammals and other endangered species of sealife.

Nuclear power is not the greatest threat to the planet. It is our ignorance about the effect of our behavior on the environment on which we and other life-forms depend for survival. This ignorance threatens the extinction of the human race. The freeing of captive dolphins symbolizes the freeing of ourselves from unconscious behavior.

UNFREEZING ANIMALS AND HUMANS

Early one morning, Linda Tellington-Jones, known around the world as the Animal Ambassador, called us to the horse pasture near the retreat center to show us how she works with resistant animals. As I stood in the muddy grass, watching her work and listening to her talk about the horse in front of us, I realized the horse was a mirror for my own behavior. Linda told us "Horses respond out of instinct. We know about fight or flight, but the part we miss is freeze."

The moment she mentioned the word "freeze" she had my full attention. I'd just had a discussion a few weeks earlier with a counselor about the freeze syndrome. He insisted that freezing was part of fight or flight. I insisted that it was different and that therapists in general didn't know how to deal with it which keeps many people from receiving the help they need to reach out or to heal. Now here I was, standing ankle deep in horse manure, listening to Linda validate my belief.

"When we begin to acknowledge that resistance—that refusal to do what we want and to block—we begin to see it more and more in two-legged animals. It's fascinating to me to acknowledge that resistance as an alternative to fight or flight. One of the things that I do is work with horses that other people can't get along with and showing other people how to get along with them. Horses like to work and to cooperate...."

"Linda," I thought, "where have you been all my life?" Over a period of several years I had searched futilely for a therapist and found none who understood me. One psychiatrist dismissed me in frustration after encountering my freezing action by telling me, "You've got to find a nourishing lifestyle." The last one I'd gone to for help had said, "You have all these defenses that go nowhere..." I gave up on traditional therapy and therapists and turned to alternative methods.

Linda talked about using telepathy to send messages to the animals, massaging their bodies gently, non-intrusively, in small circles using three fingers of the hand to release the fear stored in cellular memory.

She held out her whip and said, "We call it a wand. It works like magic when you reach out and touch parts of an animal where they are afraid to be touched. Without being so threatened, they get used to being handled all over the body. Linda moved to the horse's head. "Whenever there is resistance work the mouth. Pull your own lip and your attitude will change," she quipped. "I've used it on snakes, tigers and rhinos." She also uses sound and rhythm along with breath in her work with animals. To relieve shock or colic, she'll pull their ears, sliding the hand from the base of an ear to the tip where a shock point is located. The only time massaging the mouth didn't work she told us was with a group of prisoners in the Colorado Penitentiary who were in for murder and rape. "They discovered they couldn't massage their lips with the lightest pressure."

Linda has used her gentle massaging and touching techniques around the world with humans as well as animals. Even the most resistant humans respond. Working with abused and mentally handicapped children and people from other cultures, she sees animals as true ambassadors, the bridge that bring people together with each other and themselves.

WATER INITIATION

Almost every morning before the start of Council, someone would report seeing dolphins along the shore. It was stormy the first three days we were there and the water was too rough to swim. Finally, on Thursday afternoon, we took a break and went to the beach. The sun decided to shine for a change and the surf had calmed down a bit. Sure enough, about mid-afternoon, some spinner dolphins showed up in the bay. Soon after they appeared, a trickle of nude humans trekked down to the shore, plunged into the waves and swam far out to the edge of the cove to where they thought the dolphins were. Of course by then the dolphins were somewhere on the other side of the bay. Thirty or so nude humans bobbed in the water the rest of the afternoon, hoping to get close to them.

I waited and watched and waited and watched while Linda massaged circles on my back to relieve some of the chronic pain that had returned from sitting and writing too much and getting slapped around by ocean waves while boogie boarding. It was clear the dolphins were not going to connect with the humans as long as they were being pursued. When I saw Gigi enter the water with two young boys, I suddenly felt compelled to go out and swim with them. Soon, there were about five older women swimming around these young fledgling dolphins. I felt empathy for the mothers of the boys, one of whom was in the water with us. Her face revealed fear for her son's safety. The other mother sat on shore anxiously watching as Gigi coaxed the boys to swim away from the rocks, got them to relax in the water and stretched their swimming capabilities to the max. Meanwhile, the rest of us "mothers" swam around them acting as a support system while the boys went through their water initiation. We formed our own little pod and forgot all about the other dolphins. When Gigi and the boys spilled through the surf and landed on the sandy beach, everyone breathed a sigh of relief. They had moved through a rite of passage into young boyhood and were clearly proud of themselves. At least 40 or so people that afternoon had been stretched by the presence of dolphins in the water. The dolphins were the carrots that lured us into deeper water and rougher surf, coaxing us to swim farther from shore than we would have ever gone otherwise and all without flippers on.

DOLPHINS AS TRICKSTERS AND CLOWNS

Dolphins are clowns. I learned about this from my second roommate, Romni Cash, an older woman who has devoted her retirement years to clowning and storytelling. Clowns exaggerate our foibles and point out our shadow sides. They often play the contrary.

I asked Romni, "Where did you first connect with dolphins?"

She said, "At a marine park in Canada. I fell in love with them and it totally changed my life. Shortly after that I left my husband. They've been guiding my life ever since."

Eventually they led her to Hawaii where she took up clowning and more recently began to delve into the ancient art of storytelling. Intrigued by the dolphin/clown relationship, I asked Romni to tell me more about playing the fool.

"The Indian clown or fool is very much part of the ceremonies," she said. "He greets people as they leave. He rides his horse in backwards. If the shaman is sprinkling something sacred on the people then the clown or the fool will sprinkle dirt. The reason they do this is to make people aware of how sacred the occasion is and by mocking it and making fun of the occasion, he just makes them aware of how they are mocking their spirituality and not taking it seriously enough. They often deal with drunkenness, which of course, is such a problem in that community.

"If you study any religion you will find that in its beginnings there was usually a clown or a fool who was a part of this. For instance, in the Catholic Church, the Feast of Fools was celebrated in the church. That was a time when the people in the congregation donned costumes. They wore donkey's ears representing a donkey that Christ rode, also representing the devil so that you got the paradox. Then when the mass was read the response was 'Hee Haw! Hee Haw! Hee Haw!'

"This was very cathartic for the people and very useful. It was stamped out eventually. It wasn't very comfortable, of course, for the hierarchy in the church. If you go back and look at any religion you will find that there has been the need for the fool to tell the truth with impunity. The Yaqui Indians, for instance, would work with masks when they reenacted the crucifixion.

"Of course, somebody had to be the bad guys. So what they would do is hold a little cross between their teeth behind their masks, as if they were saying to spirit 'You know, I'm really one of the good guys."

"Can you talk about the symbolism?" I asked.

"The role of the clown is to support the mores in the society," said Romni. "And the way the clown does that is by exaggerating the frailties in the society. The clown focuses on what he sees people doing and then makes people laugh about their own frailties. That heals people very much to laugh at their own folly. For instance, the gymnastics that the clown does is about getting another perspective on your problem. The posture, the out of align-ment posture is denying your sexuality. When Emmett Kelly would crack open a peanut with a sledgehammer, that was about a disproportionate solution to a problem.

"I'm treating this as real head stuff, but of course, it gets to people in the audience at another level that is really so much more effective than a preachy approach, just as the story is. Symbols in story are such an effective way to get through to people's hearts, rather than their heads so that they really get the message and that's what happens with clowns. That's why clowns and fools are so very, very powerful.

"The clown has faith. The clown believes that he can overcome the odds against him so he's a risk symbol. The clown is naive. He doesn't have wisdom and knowledge and so forth but his faith is so enormous that he puts himself out there. He risks. He knows that if he falls that he'll get up again. He knows that if he gets in this tiny little car that he can get out again. So he's a powerful, powerful risk symbol. He's the zero card in the tarot. He's the one that takes the journey toward enlightenment.

"Anyone who has worked the dolphins knows they are tricksters. It is just a part of their personalities. The clown or the fool is the trickster. The fool can tell the truth with impunity. I like to think the dolphins are allowed to speak the truth, too; that dolphins are in the sea to play the comparable role to the clown or the fool on land. So it may be really important for us to listen to them and hear what they are saying. If they are saying the truth they may be just as important as a fool or a clown on earth.

"People feel such a joyful feeling when they see dolphins. To me that is an eloquent way of saying to people on earth 'Lighten up, be joyful, be happy. Play...laugh!' I don't think that we absolutely have to communicate with them in terms of language but I think we have to communicate heart-to-heart with them so that we get that message of the real truth. We get that in the Bible. The Bible tells us this all the time...we must become as little children. We must get back in touch with our imaginations, our spontaneity. What could be more spontaneous than the dolphin? What could be more childlike...not childish...but childlike than a dolphin?

"I think the truth they are trying to get through to us is for us to get out of all this head stuff, which is important too...but to get back to that authenticity that we had as a child." I couldn't help but think...that means allowing ourselves to grieve and cry like children also.

GIGI, JOE AND ROSIE

In her book "Beyond Boundaries," Gigi tells how her dolphin connection began in the desert, as it had with me. She sensed the still-present energy of an ancient ocean. During a time when she felt something missing in her life, the dolphin presence made itself known to her as an ally and messenger. Sometime later she found herself at Esalen, on the coast of California, spending a lot of time in the pool, swimming underwater. "One day in the pool I was swimming and moving and breathing deeply when I went into another state of consciousness," she wrote. "While I had never actually had a 'past life' experience (and wasn't sure what one even was), what happened to me was the closest to what I might envision one to be. Something came in and through my body, which is the way I experience these kinds of things...not visually. I had an experience of dolphin and whale. At this time, I had no interest in dolphins and whales, had never read any books on the subject, and didn't even know who John Lilly was. I wasn't attracted to dolphin paraphernalia, I could not even call myself a member of the New Age. Needless to say, I didn't know how to integrate this experience or even where to begin. I only knew that I had better find out a little more about this species called cetaceans." She ended up at Ojai, the land of the Chumash 'dolphin tribe,' "the spot where my introduction to 'real' dolphins was seeded," she said. There, she met John and Tony Lilly when they came to talk about their communication research with the dolphin. They invited her to come and swim with Joe and Rosie and learn more about their project. Said Gigi: "One look in Rosie's eye healed all the times in my life humans had looked past me; there was no distraction in their gaze or mine. The next moments Rosie took scanning my body, she rested her eye consistently on my left leg. It seemed no coincidence that this was the sole place of physical injury in my life—three leg breaks—and Rosie was taking the time to give it some attention. What the effects of those clicking noises were, I still am not certain, but the overall sensation was healing in nature.

"Duplicating one's experience of bliss is most often impossible—but practice helps. The moments after a complete physical expression, the moments after making love, the moments when breath replaces thought in meditation, these were the kind of moments I shared so easily, so naturally, so happily with Joe and Rosie. When I climbed out of the pool my cheeks smiled to the point of pain. I could not talk, much less fill out the log where swimmers recorded their experience. A rush of energy filled my body and I became aware of a real shift in my being."

Gigi wondered, "Was this a placebo effect? Had the dolphins done something to me or had I allowed something to occur?"

She returned to visit Joe and Rosie many times over the coming years. "During the days I met with Joe and Rosie, it had been a particularly difficult time for me to communicate on a social level with people. I felt such a distance from everyday life. When I met and touched the dolphin, there was a state of being, a state of exchange for which I had always longed and knew existed. So it was a confirmation of the existence and importance of that state of being and contact. It is similar to being in a sacred place with a spiritual teacher or having an incredible experience of nature. There is a very high state of being that each of us can touch. It involves a kind of full attention, an acute state of awareness exists; when you talk to someone or see a flower— you really see them. From my early days I remember being very conscious and careful of the fact that I saw people very quickly, and sometimes it could be intrusive or inappropriate for them. It could intimidate or threaten. I needed to learn to be careful with how I saw people because sometimes people weren't ready to be seen. With the dolphin, however, there were no restrictions or limitations. I knew the dolphin was seeing through me and I was able to be fully in my alertness, in my awareness, and in my openness."

It was this connection that eventually led Gigi to become director of the release program and to continue in her spiritual quest—a quest that led her to meet Peter Shenstone, an Australian storyteller who shares "The Legend of the Golden Dolphin" and whose acquaintance lured her to Australia, where she continues to visit as part of her "walkabout."

She introduced a brightly painted clack stick as a "talking stick" — which had been given to her during her visit to aboriginal settlements. In council sessions, the "talking stick" is passed from person to person. While an individual is holding it, no one else may speak. The stick is either rotated in the circle or placed in the center and may be picked up by someone who wishes to speak on a subject that is specified at the beginning of the session.

It is a powerful lesson in learning to listen and really absorb what is being said. The most profound communication may come forth from the silence of someone just sitting and holding the stick.

For five days at the Pacific Bridge Event we counciled, listening to one another's stories about our journeys and connections with a variety of species. "Dolphin," as Jim Nollman pointed out, was the word most often spoken among the group—Joe and Rosie came up frequently. John and Toni Lilly's names also popped up often as founders of The Human/Dolphin Foundation. It flourished in the late 1970s and is remembered as the first unofficial human/dolphin community. It was clear that all our lives had been profoundly touched and changed by our connection to dolphins and that they had led many of us along the path of spiritual development. No one challenged that concept, although some may have been more skeptical than others.

COUNCIL - COMMUNICATING FROM THE HEART

On the last day of council, Romni shared her clown presentation with us. She stirred up in me a lot of feelings that had been rising to the surface. This possibly was due to Linda's work on my back at the beach the day before. During the council session that followed I suddenly began to feel very emotional. I was sitting next to a young woman who had been expressing her anger and pain over the treatment of animals all week. As she sat talking next to me, I suddenly became overwhelmed by sadness, not for the animals she was talking about, but for us humans. The animals were well-represented in the circle. Humans weren't. It was to be our last council session, an opportunity to share what we were doing, the action we were taking in our lives to alleviate the abuse of the environment and the animal kingdom.

I felt too overwhelmed to speak when she handed me the stick. I almost passed it on. But that invisible child inside me pressed me to talk. I hesitated and then said, "What I have to share is an observation." The words came slowly. "I see people here projecting their personal pain onto the animals as a way of dissociating from it." As I spoke the tears poured down my face and for the first time in my life while among a group of people, I didn't bother to wipe them away. "For the past year, I haven't been able to disassociate." Every word that came out of my mouth felt like self-torture. Each word…each teardrop represented years of silent suffering. Not just my own, but the unexpressed pain of those who had died in my life without ever expressing their pain. I'd been carrying this inheritance around with me too long, holding it in trust until an appropriate time. My body simply couldn't hold anymore. It overflowed, spilling itself into the council circle and onto everyone there.

"Nothing is going to change", I told the group, "until we start to own our pain…to integrate it. It begins inside us." I pointed the talking stick at my heart.

What was missing in the group, came to me in that moment. "There is very little touching going on here. There is a lot of intellectualizing and I'm as guilty of that as anyone, but there is very little reaching out to others."

And then I shared with them how I intended to make a difference in the world. A man who had been staying at the retreat center all week but was not a participant had been trying to make contact with us. He seemed very sad about something and couldn't express what it was. Every time I probed what was going on in his life, he assured me everything was rosy, yet the air around him grew thicker. People avoided him. I'd been on the receiving end of that avoidance so many times in my life that I saw what was happening and decided to reach out.

I heard a couple of women in my group talking about him the night before with fear. He seemed a bit crazed to them at some level. "He's harmless," I assured them, "Just lonely." When the opportunity arose later that evening, I offered to do some energy work with him. I knew what he wanted was to be touched. He was very kinesetic and kinesetics need to be touched in order to feel loved and cared for. It was a risk for me to reach out to him. I was at a stage in my life when I truly wanted to separate sex from love and to break free of a pattern of attracting and being drawn to emotionally unavailable men like my father. He was very attractive and appealing but I didn't want a sexual relationship. I wanted to touch his heart and soul, and perhaps in touching his, touch my own. Reaching out to him symbolized my willingness not to run away from my own pain but as Stephen Levine says, to "touch it softly…just this much." By working with him on an energy level and using the techniques Linda had shown us, I absorbed his sadness, took it into my body, just as I had with my father, just as I do whenever I'm around unfelt, unexpressed feelings of other people. Their pain magnifies my own. It was this overflow that spilled forth in the council and could not be stopped. I'd been hanging out with bodyworkers too long, had learned too well the importance of touch, had spent too many years learning to experience my feelings to begin denying them again. I had offered up too much. My children. My marriage—everything to be in this moment.

I finished by telling the group, "Stopping the abuse of animals and the environment has to begin by owning our feelings and reaching out human-to-human to the people next to us." Before passing the talking stick on, I reached out to hold the hands of the women beside me.

What happened in the room after that was a revelation to watch. My willingness to touch a deeper level of pain inside myself, made it safe for others to do the same. Joan Ocean commented toward the end of the council about the elasticity of the group. "As each person shared, I felt myself moving in and out, up and down." In that last session, we became more dolphinlike, more fluid, more attuned with the movement of the ocean of emotion within us. We laughed and cried in equal proportion and in the process came into balance within ourselves and the world.

A man named Daniel, from an island named "Kansas," shared how he makes a difference in the world by stopping alongside the road to "turn over turtles," righting them to save their lives.

I wondered as he spoke if he turned over human turtles as well.

Two women with young children declared their contribution to stopping the pollution of the environment was to stop using synthetic diapers, a huge sacrifice as any mother of a young child well knows.

In closing the session that morning, Gigi spoke about the council process and how it had a way of continuing even after it had closed. People had a way of carrying it on in their lives and out into the world. Tossing a stone into the council circle I discovered was like tossing a pebble into a pond and watching the ripples spread out into infinity...out to the farthest star as Linda says. It was another way of touching people.

One of the people it touched deeply is Neil Westbrooke, a New Zealander who discovered himself in the presence of dolphins as a commercial fisherman. Some years earlier Neil took what he calls "wealthy, jaded businessmen" on fishing trips. One day on the way back to port, he stopped the boat in the middle of a pod of dolphins, got out his mask and snorkel and jumped in the water to swim with them. The businessmen called him a fool at first, but one by one as they watched, they too slid into the water to swim with the dolphins. "The transformation that happened with them was incredible" says Neil. "When we got back to shore, they stopped everybody they met to tell them 'we swam with the dolphins'. They were as excited as little kids." Seeing the impact their experience had on them, changed Neil's life as well. He opened to his psychic gifts, became a Rebirther and a student of the "Course in Miracles" and now finds himself being a support person to gay men with AIDS who have become close friends in the process of their dying. He is very tuned into the healing that springs forth in the dying process. The body may die, we agreed, but the spirit is healed by the experience, opening a door for the people surrounding the dying person to heal as well.

I was sitting by the swimming pool later that day, writing notes, when Neil came and sat down next to me. He acknowledged me again for speaking up and said, "You dumped your truth into that circle and when people speak a truth it can't be argued with. Once you spoke your truth, it shifted the energy in the room." We talked for a long time and then with reservation he asked, "How does it feel to be an invisible catalyst?"

I told him it was a role I'd been well-trained for and there was no point in resisting it anymore. It seems to be the role that my life experiences have set me up to play. I told him I'd observed a part of me in the circle that craved acknowledgment.

Having someone like Neil see who I was so clearly satiated that longing for recognition. He reminded me that "Maybe what you need is to
acknowledge yourself."

"I noticed something else," he said.

"What?"

"There was a part of you that was afraid to say what you said."

Of course, I denied it. "Who, me afraid?"

It wasn't until my last night on the Big Island, that I began to integrate
the week's experience. That night the dolphin spirits came to speak to me. At
first it was in images. A memory of my sister popped into consciousness.
She strangled herself in a mental hospital due to lack of attention and support. You might say she starved to death as a result of denial in the culture
and in her own family. And then an image of dolphins living out their lives
in dark tanks with not enough food and attention to keep them healthy and
happy arose. They, too, committed suicide. I got the message.

I remembered then what Helen and Romni told me about the dolphins
being clowns and tricksters, pointing out to us the frailties in society and in our
behavior, and how dolphins model man's behavior. Pretty powerful images.

It put me in touch with my pain again. That need people have to only
look on the light side and to never really explore their darkness...look what
it does to us. Look at how it destroys the very things we love the most in life.
Look at how it leads people, our brothers and sisters and parents and friends
to take their lives, if not through suicide then more slowly, through heart
disease, AIDS, cancer, accidents, drug addiction, overeating and in a host of
other ways. Look how it destroys the life inside us, paralyzes us, keeps us
from reaching out. That compulsive need to laugh, to escape, to deny that
pain and suffering are as much a part of our existence as the air we breathe.
It is the same need that causes us to imprison dolphins for entertainment
and then to banish them to darkness when they do not perform in accor-
dance with our wishes...when they refuse to support us in our denial. When
they refuse to smile when they are sad.

I had said to Neil, "I guess one of my roles in life is to flush out people's
darkness."

"Isn't that a way of helping them to lighten up?" he asked.

I hadn't thought of it. "Yeah, but it's a damned hard way."

"How do you cope with the pain of it?" he wondered.

I thought for a moment and then it came to me, "I guess my suffering is
my bliss."

"There really is no difference," he said. "The acceptance of suffering
gives fullness to our lives. It rounds out the joy."

I remembered then a process I'd done at the Gathering of Healers. I
was in a circle with a small group of women and Moon Dancer, the facilita-

tor, passed a stone around among us. She told us to plug the sound of our pain into the stone and hand it to the next woman. The sound of our howling nearly shattered the rafters in the old lodge. Moon Dancer cleansed the stone in water, then passed it again. This time she said "Place the sound of your joy in the stone." The walls vibrated. I noticed that the sound of my pain equaled and overlapped the sound of my joy. The experience blew open my chakras. A few days later one of the clairvoyant healers that had been at the gathering gave me a bodywork treatment and said, "You have this incredible purplish/blue healing energy rolling off you in waves." It's funny how the most subtle of all processes seem to have the greatest impact upon the body.

And so the spirits made it clear to me that night that some of us are here to help others get in touch with their suffering so they can experience their bliss—so we can all be more free, fluid and flowing like the dolphins. I also saw that some of us came to hold and mirror unexpressed anger and sadness so others can see themselves more clearly. That is, when they choose to see that the reflection they are looking at is their own. It's not a lot of fun holding all this pain until others are ready to own it. I'd just as soon be outside playing with the dolphins.

PLUTO FLUSHING UP THE DARKNESS

An astrologer came to spend a day and talked to us about the planet's entry into a new 12,000-year cycle and how the Pluto energy is flushing up our negativity and shadow sides in preparation for the New Age. He finished by telling us that the dolphins are from the outer galaxy...beyond the ego. Dolphins are like the energy of our high selves. They are able to astral travel to the farthest reaches of the Universe. Dolphin energy is present high in the sky when we see Sirius and the Pleiades beneath the image of the whale.

In his book "The Night Sky," Richard Grossinger refers to Pluto as the Lord of the Underworld. "The symbol of his invisible empire was the helmet that made men invisible," wrote Grossinger. The black hole is a perfect image for Pluto, but so is the frozen debris of solar system beginnings. Mythologically, Pluto is the source of wealth and grain, both of which come from the Earth. Grossinger calls Pluto "the appropriate agent of millennial and cataclysmic change."

According to astrologer William Lonsdale, Pluto draws us into the greater universe. "It's the last outpost that keeps reinstilling us with a cosmic perspective and keeps taking away our materialistic assumptions."

Pluto or Hades is the God of depths, the God of invisibles, says psychologist James Hillman. "Hades is not an absence, but a hidden presence—even an invisible fullness." No doubt about it. Pluto had been playing havoc with my life for a long time.

The night before the gathering ended a group of us walked out to the edge of the black lava field just before dusk. A bank of clouds blotted out the moon, making it invisible to the eye, but I knew it was there even though I couldn't see it. Molten lava spilled into the ocean. Steam billowed and merged with the clouds in the sky. Close by fiery cinders hissed and spit as they merged and melted and became one with the sea. They looked much like humans and snakes when they encounter one another with fear.

It seemed everywhere I went a message appeared, each one more profound than the last. The Big Island with its red hot energy seemed to be a place of purification and cleansing. A place where people are drawn when a shadow aspect of themselves is ready to merge and come into awareness…when the unihipili (low self) and the aumakua (high self) unite the force of their energy to lighten up the world around them. The Big Island, I was told, has the highest risk for a natural disaster than anywhere in the world. The activity of the volcanos, the high winds and heavy storm activity are a predilection to disaster. The island is a undermined by catacombs of red lava. After dark the fiery channels can be seen winding their way to the ocean across the black volcanic fields offering us a mute reflection of our own pent-up rage.

It was a relief to return to Moloka'i and the pure clean air and lighter energy.

17 *Dolphin Synchronicity*

A MONTH AFTER returning from the Pacific Bridge Event, I was on the move again. After three months of adapting to family life, I felt stuck and out of the flow, trading off too much of myself, too much freedom in exchange for occasional companionship. It felt like I'd moved back in time right into the issues I'd left behind in my own marriage. Life at the resort, though I loved the pristine white sand beaches, listening to the roar of the ocean and watching the rollers crash on the beach did not agree with me. I wanted to lead a simple life close to nature and yet here I was surrounded by material trappings, feeling disconnected and disheartened. It was time for a change but I couldn't bring myself to make the decision to leave. It meant I would have to let go of another attachment—the desire to be part of a family. Unable to make a conscious decision to leave, I regressed to an old childhood pattern of acting out and helped to create a drama to free myself.

As fate or St. Germain would have it, I happened to meet, Barbara a retired transpersonal counselor.

"How old are you?" she asked.

"Forty-nine. Why?"

"You're at the beginning of a new cycle in your life," said Barbara. "You've just come out of a time of crises when you were seeking your own identity. Now it's time to share what you've learned, to be a teacher and communicator."

She told me to count back 36 years and look at what was happening in my life then. There I would find the foundation for my current behavior and beliefs. At the age of 13, I was acting out unexpressed, unfelt feelings over the death of my mother and the loss of my natural family the previous year.

Very succinctly and directly she told me, "Stand in front of the mirror every morning and tell yourself 'I love you.' Practice Yoga an hour a day and get yourself away from other people. You need to live alone."

Naturally, I went into resistance. "Yoga every morning for an hour! Live alone! Talk to myself in the mirror! Yuk!"

"I know you don't want to do the Yoga, but you're missing the physical aspect, the grounding. You need it," said Barbara.

"OK," I meekly agreed.

"Have you ever had any psychotic episodes?" she asked.

"Well...not exactly."

"Well, you will. You're on the heroine's path," said Barbara. "Might as well get used to the idea. When your kundalini really begins to awaken and starts burning through blocks, you could get a little crazy. You're not to the top of the mountain yet. You've got a lot more valleys to go through and hills to climb."

"Gee, do I get a break for awhile?"

"Well, maybe for a few years," she said. "You're entering a new cycle, a time to share what you've learned with others. I see you doing grief work in a few years."

"I've known that was coming. I just keep putting it off."

"Have you ever heard of the "Course in Miracles?"'

"Oh yes, I've thrown it against the wall a few times when it tried to tell me there was no such thing as death, or illness and disease."

"I thought as much," said Barbara. "Well, get it out and study it again."

There was nothing left to do but to love myself, to go within and nurture the wounded child, to heal the schism. The surest way to effect the cure was to be willing to spend time alone, to be in relationship with myself in order to connect with the feelings that arise from the child level.

A week after meeting Barbara, I moved to the East End of Molokai and soon found myself caught up once more in the adventure of being alive, unfettered by family, tradition and the mores of living in "community."

ANSWERING THE CALL TO HAWAII

A series of synchronistic encounters ensued. A notice appeared on a bulletin board by a woman offering ukulele lessons. I'd given up all musical inclinations after my mother died and had at various times in my life longed for a reconnection. My favorite memory from early childhood was sitting beside her on the piano bench as the three of us children crowded around her to sing the latest pop songs of the 1940s. She played the piano each Sunday afternoon. I called and set up my first ukulele lesson for the next day. When the teacher mentioned that she had a recorder for sale, I bought it, remembering how often I'd been told that dolphins are often attracted to people on boats through the sounds of flute playing.

People who had obviously been called to Moloka'i, to Hawaii, by the dolphins, began to show up in my life almost daily. At a Hawaiian Culture class one evening I mentioned I was writing a book on dolphins and was given the name of a woman on the island who created a video for the Whale Museum at Kaunapali. Kate, it turned out, had her own boat and was looking for people to join her on expeditions in the ocean. She is a former swimming instructor and scuba diver who moved to Moloka'i 10 years earlier, not long after she was "killed" in an auto accident and came back to life. She moved to Moloka'i to escape the tourists and to live closer to nature.

Early one Sunday morning, we took her boat out to explore the reef and along the way, I took the opportunity to spread my father's ashes at the entrance to the harbor. He had told me to scatter his ashes on the ocean and I had resisted, thinking selfishly that if I planted them under a palm tree on the beach, I could visit the site and reconnect with him. But then I realized, he'd never allowed himself to go through his own water initiation or get in touch with the pain beneath his anger while he was alive. It was very appropriate that his ashes would now record the rhythms and cycles and flow of the ocean as a living being.

In the process of looking for someone to prepare my taxes, I spotted a notice on a bulletin board in town and called to connect with Barnie. He invited me to Sunday Brunch and in the course of conversing I learned he'd gone swimming with the dolphins in the Florida a year and a half earlier. It was at a time when he was going through a second divorce and everything in his life was in a state of flux. Several months later he visited a friend on Moloka'i. On impulse, he returned home to sell his belongings and resign his job and moved shortly thereafter to the island.

Barnie introduced me to Janie, a speech and language pathologist who had attended a seminar with Mary Caroline of the Dolphins-in-the Desert project, on Aqua Breathing. She soon found herself moving to Moloka'i hoping to connect with dolphins in the wild. She envisions that at some point in the future she will bring children who have speech and language difficulties together with the dolphins.

TRAINER BECOMES CARETAKER OF PLANET

The following weekend I was bored and looking for something to do when I saw a notice on a bulletin board again, this time for Spring Mud Baths. "Why not?" I thought. A.J., the proprietor, turned out to be a former dolphin trainer. In recent years he has been caretaking a powerful piece of land that was used in ancient times to prepare the bodies of Alii (chiefs or royalty) for burial. Born in Bohemia at the end of World War II, A.J. was smuggled through the Iron Curtain as an infant and later adopted by a Japanese-American family in Honolulu. Aside from dolphins and the loss of our parents in childhood, we shared an interest in Huna, Tantra and mysticism and spent an intriguing afternoon beside the spring-fed pond smearing mud all over one another, sun baking and 'talking story' under a warm tropical sun. For two weeks afterward, I tried to get his story on tape. He kept putting me off. I finally resorted to bribing him one afternoon with chicken sandwiches and a cold beer after receiving a strong telepathic message that he was very hungry.

In the late 1960s, the director of an ocean research organization asked A.J. to work for him and apply his horse training skills to dolphins in the research program. Part of his job was to train dolphins to jump from one tank to another and onto stretchers to be operated on. Researchers wanted to know how the dolphins' sonar worked, but said A.J. "They didn't even know what they were looking for.

"Some of the stuff I worked on was seeing if the dolphins could distinguish between density of materials. I set up tests to see how their sonar works and what they could distinguish, like the density of metal, wood, plastic and their various gauges. Basically I was a flunky who worked the animals."

"What happened to you during that period of time when you were working with the dolphins?" I asked A.J.

"It was kind of a high...something I looked forward to...it's kind of hard to explain...kind of a neat high. It's like having a relationship with a dog, but it seems a lot more. The animals were pumped up to be so extraordinary. You do feel a bonding. It's exciting. You kind of know who is who and how they feel like."

He worked with several dolphins at a time, depending on how many new dolphins were brought in. I asked him if dolphins died in the program and from what causes. He said they died from "Infections, mostly. That's what they put down, but I think it was more or less shock and depression — not being able to handle captivity. That's my personal opinion...and then, of course, they get sick. They pick up the nearest thing."

"In what ways did they die? I asked, "Was it mostly from sickness...or did they do things like batter their rostrums?" After talking with Helen I wondered whether other trainers shared the same view.

"That happened a couple of times," A.J. told me "but I think what happens is that they lost some of their senses and they just didn't know what they were doing. They were getting that bad off. Something got damaged in their minds so that they actually didn't see anymore, so to speak. Their sonar wouldn't work."

"From being in a cement tank?" I wondered.

"Yeah," he said. "Something got damaged and came through as an infection. It's not that they decided that they were going to bang themselves in the head. I don't think it's anything like that. I think something actually went wrong and they couldn't visualize or see."

I asked A.J. about the changes that occurred in his own life during the time he worked with dolphins. He became more aware, he said of "What is meant by 'ecology,' I became more aware of my place with nature. Before it just never really mattered that much. But then, all of a sudden, I could see more clearly how things were really...how we actually are. We're calling ourselves a great civilization and we're royally messing up our own environment. That time of my life is when I became aware of all that. Maybe it also had a lot to do with the people that you work with because people that were working with the dolphins were all inclined to be of a higher consciousness...outlook. Working with the dolphins influences everybody. We're kind of all in the same boat."

A.J. became disillusioned with the work after three years when he discovered that the money for the research programs was coming from the government. "A lot of the scientists that I worked with were arranging for grants. We were just making another workhorse out of the dolphins. All that money being spent on dolphins wasn't for man studying the dolphin to study the planet, the Earth, and then kind of reciprocating. It turned out that the grants and the money and all the work with the dolphins was being spent to capitalize on them—turn them into workhorses. It usually came from the Defense Department. The kind of work they wanted them to do was really gory stuff. In one experiment we designed backpacks for them to carry bombs."

"What were they going to blow up? Ships?" I asked naively.

"Whatever you blow up in war games," A.J. said. "Piers, ships."

"Were they ever used like kamikaze pilots?" I asked.

"We haven't been in a war since...who knows what they did in Vietnam. A lot of money was coming from the oil people. At the time they were just getting into or working on offshore oil exploration off the coast of California," A.J. said. "There was a lot of money coming in from Australia, too. Deals were being made because they had a lot of underwater work over there."

After he resigned as a trainer A.J. dropped out of conventional society and moved to Moloka'i. "I try to contribute as little as possible to the war machine...to the 'go get 'em and suck up the planet and turn it into money' kind of stuff. My trip is actually caring for the planet." On Moloka'i, he says, "I care for the planet...with my own little hands and my total time and my total way of thinking...just about."

The land he lives on is part of an ancient taro patch which he is slowly re-establishing. In the past 20 years, he has carved what he calls "a living sculpture" out of dense, overgrown jungle. Today, it looks like a park setting. Huge monkey pod trees shade an expansive lawn. Around the fringes, A.J. planted an assortment of bananas, papayas, ti plants and heliconia, which now provide him with an abundance of fruit. To hold the mosquito population down, he transplanted frogs to the spring-fed pond.

For several years, he lived in a cabin at the top of the hill, the perfect place to watch the weather patterns that shifted and swirled around.

"I live in the middle of the world...the center," he said. "All the weather, all the air moves right around here. It's like yin and yang, positive and negative. The two forces that oppose each other move right around this place..."

"Around Moloka'i?" I asked.

"The Hawaiian Islands, the middle of the Pacific and Moloka'i especially," he said. "The south side of the East End, this particular place, is where you can actually see the line when there's winter storms, and the two pressures come really close and increase. I'm living on the ragged edge of the two systems of weather. This is why we have the most ideal climate in the world right here and the most ideal growing conditions. You have a growing season all year round."

As a sailor, he is a keen observor of the weather and its effects on the land he caretakes. In the past three years he says the ocean level has begun to rise—washing away portions of the beach. It's also raining later into the spring. He believes these are the effects of the returning Ice Age, speeded up by the Greenhouse Effect, which is caused by pollution of the environment.

The ancient Polynesians had elaborate gardens that climbed up the steep rock cliffs and were watered by rivulets of water cascading from the top. A.J. senses that people will be returning to Moloka'i to once more lomilomi (massage) the land and regenerate the ancient taro patches and gardens that were once there. Meantime, he teaches people like me to tiptoe softly on the Earth and to take only what I need from the plants and no more.

I asked him if he still thought about dolphins and he told me, "Yes, when I see them when I go sailing, I get charged. It's a special charge for me like getting zapped with a bolt of energy."

Did you ever swim with them in the wild?" I asked.

"Yeah, a whole school one time," he said. "That was one of the neatest experiences with the dolphins that I've actually ever had. It was during the time I was working with them. I was on a sailboat race around Hanele Bay and up the Poli coast. We had light air, maybe four knots on an experimental trimaran built all out of epoxy. It didn't have an engine on it and it was really light and maybe that had something to do with the animals. There was nothing dense in it. I've never seen so many dolphins in one place in my whole life, maybe a hundred or more...a sea of bottlenose dolphins.

"I jumped in the water with them. We were only going four knots. We had a long ski rope with us, so I took goggles and fins and I went over the side and towed on the ski rope to see how it is to be in there with them. We were totally surrounded by them. These guys were clicking...there was all kinds of noise in the water. When I first went in, a road kind of opened up. Then they homed in on me, almost touching to check me out. As they were homing in it seemed like I could feel their sonar. I felt inside of me. It's hard to explain. I never felt that being in a tank with them. I could feel myself and it seemed because of their clicking or using their sonar on me. It was a really neat sensation. That's the first time I actually became aware of all the different pitches and speeds of clicks. It seems like when you're talking with them or you communicate with them when they're in a tank, the range is a lot less than it is when they are all together. When there's a hundred or more and they're all talking to each other...there is some incredible kind of clicking going on."

He stayed in the water with the dolphins until the wind picked up and he got cold. "I was dragging so fast behind the boat that I had a hard time keeping my goggles on. To me it seemed like a long time but it probably wasn't more than a half hour." They never touched him physically, A.J. said but they teased him a lot. "Whoosh! Kind of like they were trying to spook me a little bit...Ramboing me. I didn't touch them. I couldn't touch them, it was too hard just to hang on the ski rope. I couldn't mess around."

I was curious about what happened in his life after that. "My whole life changed right afterward. When I came back from that sail I broke up with the person I was going with." He finished building his sailboat and moved to Moloka'i. Since then he's led a more solitary life. "I was fortunate that once in a while somebody would come along, but I wouldn't give. Once I got over here, I wouldn't compromise my situation much. You always compromise with someone else but as far as lifestyle and what I was into, I wouldn't compromise. I was living in balance with nature."

He sailed around the islands for several years but kept being drawn back to the sacred taro patch on Moloka'i and for the past ten years has devoted himself to caring for it. "Moloka'i is very special," he said. If places have a consciousness or a power or an energy or a different vibration from other places then this place has a vibration that is stronger than I've ever experienced anywhere else."

"How is that different from other places?" I asked.

"It's hard to explain," he said. "It's powerful, it's moving and there's ways to interpret it. Personally, I could interpret it as a kind of a peace that comes over me...kind of a quiet place inside. I've always been able to do that...been able to manifest that quiet place at will, but here is where I discovered being able to communicate with someone that is further away from me than sight or sound using telepathy. Before I came to Moloka'i, I just thought of it being a coincidence. Like 'Oh, I was just thinking about you.' Like you today. Seriously, I was down pounding nails and I knew there wasn't any grinds in the house. I knew I had to go get some food....go to town or go pick taro. 'What I should do is go pick taro,' I thought, but I was so tired. So I go, 'Lana this is the time for you to make contact with me. If you're thinking about me, this is the time. You're my last resort. I wish you would come by.'"

I laughed when I realized what had happened earlier in the day. "I was having a difficult time deciding whether I should go to town to run an errand or come out here and write," I said. "So I finally decided to go to town, ran a few errands and bought some groceries. As soon as I got back, I called you. I had a feeling you were hungry. Of course, I thought it was totally unnatural for you to be inside this time of day, but there you were."

"I just got in," he said.

"Definitely telepathic," I said. "You were directing me like the dolphins."

A.J. shared his theory with me about splitting Adam and Eve as an allegory for 'splitting the atom.' When we split the atom we started moving backwards. "Growth" he said, "is growing out. It's blossoming. We're going backwards. We're splitting the stuff we're made of. We haven't learned." We believe we're great scientists but all we've learned to do is make things hotter—make the Earth hotter—learned how to spin things around a little faster and that's all, according to A.J. "We haven't grown. Radio, electricity, electronics is growing outward. It's an expansion. At least that's how it can be interpreted when we tune into the vibrations of this planet and of the universe."

"Duality is all about splitting or being separate," I told him. "That's what being born is about...being separate...being split-off. When you're talking about splitting the atom, you're talking about duality."

"The ancient polynesians believed that to die was to become One with themselves. You know the story about Adam and Eve has a real significance. You spend your life trying to find your other half and that usually happens when you die and you reunite again with Adam or Eve. If you're looking for your soulmate, you're trying to find Adam or Eve." Eve was split from Adam to make a female, and says A.J., "The polynesians believe that when you die, you become One again, you reunite with your soulmate or your male half or female half that got split. That's what dying is about. That's not death. That's growing. When you're together again, you're Universe again. People become angelic. You grow as part of the Universe. They say when you find your soulmate on Earth at this stage in life you can really swing off."

"What do you mean 'swing off'?" I asked laughing.

"You don't have to die, you become immortal, so to speak, in this life.

Maybe that explains why these 500 year old guys live so long. They've found their soulmates."

"Where are they?"

"Probably up in the Himalayas somewhere."

"Guess where I'm moving next?" I said.

DOLPHINS AS WAR WORKHORSES

My errand in town that day was to pick up a book and some copies of research articles I'd ordered through the library. The articles just happened to relate to the subject A.J. and I talked about...training dolphins for use as warfare workhorses.

According to an article in "Discover" magazine, the use of dolphins in warfare has escalated dramatically since the early 1970s and dolphins are now being used as "elite underwater sentinels" in a variety of Navy programs. Because they are able to achieve astonishing speeds in spurts up to 26 miles per hour and can dive deeper and faster than human frogmen, the dolphins have been enlisted into the Navy to help recover destroyer-launched unarmed antisubmarine rockets and to locate inert mines. During the Vietnam War dolphins were sent on surveillance missions in Cam Ranh Bay to identify enemy saboteurs floating down the river with mines attached. The dolphins identified the swimmers for Navy frogmen. Rumors persisted that the dolphins had been "trained to kill frogmen, attach limpet mines to ships and tag enemy subs with high-tech listening devices." Most recently dolphins are being used by the Navy to patrol the Persian Gulf and form an underwater perimeter around U.S. facilities to guard against infiltration by enemy frogmen."

An article in "Science" magazine says "Watch dolphins" are trained to sound alarms, attack intruders by disabling their breathing apparatus and prodding them to the surface."

Ethical and moral questions continually arise for the people involved in the training and research programs. Dolphin abuse is high on the list of issues that surface. Richard Trout, a 15-year veteran of various dolphin training programs, cites a variety of abuses. "Dolphins have been hit if they don't come up to the stretcher when they should, hit up side the head with fists and boots." Dolphins, according to Trout are also subjected to food deprivation. Often these incidents are a result of inexperienced trainers being used in programs where turnover of personnel is very high. "You can't cookie-cutter these animals," Trout says, "they will starve on occasions if they feel messed over. I've seen animals go into doldrums if they are handled negatively. I've never seen this before I came to the Navy, but I've seen dolphins come out of the water to bite at people's ankles." Like humans, dolphins become stressed. "Overtraining, working with a new trainer, or moving to a new environment" lowers their immune resistance making them more susceptible to disease.

Activists question the use of dolphins in human warfare.

Ben Deeble, an ocean ecology campaigner for Greenpeace in Seattle says, "One must question the ethics of harnessing these animals to carry out the violent activities of humans."

Between 1985 and 1989, the Navy budget allotted nearly $29 million on "advanced marine biological systems," which "Science"magazine calls the "euphemism for the program." The Navy, out of fear of arousing public animosity and opposition to its programs, is keeping them more secret than ever before.

THE DOLPHIN CALLER

A few weeks before I moved to the East End, I was shopping in Kaunakakai and came across a business card tacked to a bulletin board next to the bank. It read "Matt Sutcliffe, Outlaw Journalist." I dropped Matt a note to see if he had the inclination to read and critique the book for me. In his return letter, he expressed his metaphysical connections and a burning passion to connect with dolphins. He promised to come for a visit sometime soon and read some of the book. In late March he came to Moloka'i to visit his father and stopped by to see me. I asked him when he first began connecting with dolphins.

"Just after we moved to Florida when I was eight or nine, I was out in the water one day and a dolphin rubbed up against me. After that my mom and I would go out to the beach and she would play her flute to attract them.

"One day I was lying on a mat—like a little rubber floating mat—and I was visualizing a dolphin coming up. Thirty seconds later it happened. Just like that! I don't know if it was something that I put out that the dolphin picked up on or if it was the dolphin sending a message to me that was coming through.

"Another time, we'd been out fishing in the Gulf for three or four days. We hadn't really seen a lot of dolphins but suddenly a pod showed up. I was on the bow and they were riding the pressure wave in front. The captain stopped the boat and was kind of idling around. There was about six of them swimming and they all left except one and he was really big. It was just kind of swimming around sideways, kind of checking me out I guess, and I decided just for fun I'd see if I could send a thought and see what it would do. I got an image in my mind of it leaping up, just clearing the water totally and I concentrated on sending this thought. The dolphin stopped and was still looking at me and it released kind of like a ring of air. It was a bubble but it was in a ring form. Then in one just real fast motion—real fluid—it jumped way out and arced itself up. Amazing! I couldn't believe it—I could but I wasn't really expecting it to work that well."

"So was it just as you pictured it?" I asked.

"Yeah. Exactly. It was amazing."

"Have you had dolphins appear in your dreams?" I wondered.

"Sometimes I will wake up and remember I'd been swimming with them," he said." I would be on a beach and there would be dolphins. Sometimes I'd wake up and I'd know I dreamt about dolphins but I wouldn't remember exactly what had happened. Just a lot of interaction—or they would show up in a dream. If I was walking along the beach, they'd show up—just kind of making themselves known—their presence known. That was another thing that got me interested in them."

"What happened at college that made you want to quit?" I asked.

"I was splitting my interest between journalism and marine biology. The reason I left, is because I realized you could sit in a lecture hall with 350 other people, half of whom didn't want to be there, and listen to a guy talk. Or, worse yet, watch somebody on a video screen that he'd taped earlier in the morning, rather than doing what you actually needed to do. You're not going to get in a textbook course the kind of spiritual involvement I felt was crucial. So, I ended up leaving and moved to Hawaii. I haven't seen the dolphins yet, but I've felt them and I've been with the whales. That was worth the decision to leave college."

"Tell me about your whale experience?" I asked.

"The second time we were out, there were a lot of boats. It's kind of sad, every boat just heads right toward them. We shut the engine down and just kind of hung out and were catching rays and talking. No more than 25 yards away, two whales surfaced. At first we were really startled. They were loud. The blow hole is noisy when it shoots up. They went back down and we got out of the boat and went underwater. You could hear the whale song. We couldn't actually see them. We weren't actually close enough to see details but we were surrounded by clicks and echoes. It was really incredible. You don't know which way is up and you're just surrounded by whale song. It's really intense."

"Did you feel any sensations in your body?" I asked.

"Just a real lightness of being. Not really a physical sensation but something else—a lifting kind of. It was definitely there and it overcame the fear. You're thinking, 'God, these things are huge. They could do anything they wanted to.' We'd heard all these stories about one flap of the tail can send you straight to the bottom. We didn't really want to dwell on that. Once we got underwater with them it was great."

"Did you get any messages from the whales?" I asked.

"No...no."

"Did they look you in the eye at all?" I asked.

"Yeah, they were kind of spy-hopping, coming out a bit. They didn't do it a whole lot.

"Yesterday when we were crossing the Channel from Lahaina to Moloka'i in a 14-foot Zodiac I was asking for serious help. The wind picked up out of nowhere and we decided to keep going. About 45 minutes after we left the swells started picking up really big...about 10-foot swells. Every other wave swamped the boat. Water would just crash over the side. I had this cat and I was trying to keep it in the boat. I really thought we were going to lose it. We tried to turn around and almost got swamped. I asked for protection. I said,'You guys gotta do something, because I do NOT want to go out this way. I've got too much to live for.' I don't know if it was the dolphins that responded but I was definitely getting messages to, 'Don't worry about it, just hang in there and you'll be all right."

"How did you know you got it?" I asked.

"Just picked it up," he said. "I'll do that a lot. I'll ask for something—sometimes I'll even ask questions and I'll get answers that way."

"Can you give me an example?" I asked.

"Well, I try not to overdue it. A few weeks ago I was lying on the beach and I got this message: 'Tell your dad not to forward any mail.' I didn't think much of it. I got over here to Molokai and he had received a letter from this girl I knew in Florida who I really want to hear from. He'd gotten this message that he should hold onto it for me but he said, 'Aw no, that's crazy. The mail's real quick and he'll get it before he comes over' but I didn't. And I've moved. And it may be a little tricky getting my mail."

"Telepathic?" I asked.

"Yeah, for lack of a better word. My mom and I also have a good telepathic connection. It helps. The trick is being able to rely on it instead of just hearing it, getting the message and not acting on it. The trick is having enough faith to just go with it."

"Is it the initial voice you don't listen to?" I wondered.

"Sometimes I do and sometimes I don't. If it's a big inconvenience I'll just brush it aside. That hooks in with the dolphins a lot, too. When I'd go out into the water, I'd know where to go and that's where the dolphins would come up. They'd be right there. Or I'd be sitting on the beach picking a spot and the voice would say, 'Go a little more this way' so I'd sit and look straight out and they'd come up. I'm sure you've experienced it too...they'll do almost anything to give you some kind of sign. Just before I came out here I was at Madera Beach and I was wading in the water and there was some dolphins far out near a sandbar. I was standing there watching and all of a sudden this little fish started jumping out of the water and this dolphin chased it right up in front of me. It chased this fish and jumped up and got it right in mid-air and took off with it and that's the shallowest water I've seen them come into. It was only about two and a half feet deep. It was like a display. I'm just curious about what it's all about—why I'm here."

"Do you have any idea?" I asked.

"I think to help facilitate," he said. "What I've always wanted to do is work with dolphins. One way or another I think it will happen. I don't know how. That's what I fancy myself doing."

"Calling the dolphins in?"

"Yeah, in the wild, I think would be the best option. I think it would be the purest choice," Matt concluded.

Matt introduced me to his father, Claud, a former professor. He had resigned his position to move to Moloka'i so his wife Bonnie could give birth to their first child underwater, hopefully with dolphins present. I would have to wait another week or so to hear her story.

MASS PLANETARY INITIATION

Meantime, I asked Claud if he happened to have a copy of The "Sirius Mystery" by Robert K. Temple that I could borrow. When he brought it to me the following week, I found a folded page in the front of the book. It was a brief promotional article by Vincent Sellick of the Shekinah Foundation of New South Wales, Australia. The article mentioned his upcoming book "The Path of the Dragon" —which contains an outline of a plan for the mass initiation of humanity.

Sellick believes that the dolphins are drawn to humans to learn how to individuate their consciousness while humans are drawn to dolphins to learn to live more in the heart center. He attributes mass-stranding phenomenon of cetaceans to the fact that dolphins share a unified consciousness. "The fear, distress and panic engendered by an individual's (cetacean) experience is powerfully transferred to the mass consciousness of the herd, resulting in the total identification with the stranded individual's experience by each member of the herd, as if they were one unit of consciousness. This precipitates in the subsequent stranding by the others who are compelled by the mass experience to identify fully with the stranded individual's, mind, heart and body."

Sellick adds "It is the complete symbiotic exchange that is possible between humans and dolphins that has led to the unprecedented, world-wide interest in dolphins that is evident in the world today."

In "The Sirius Mystery" Robert Temple suggests that we must consider the possibility that Sirius, being a watery planet, is the home for amphibious beings like mermaids and mermen who "might in some way resemble our intelligent friends the dolphins."

This doorway leads us to another glimpse, yet another possibility. "The consciousness evolution of life-species on this planet (Earth) is governed from Sirius by way of a planetary Bio-Magnetic Grid...." Sellick believes. It is through this grid that the mass initiation of humanity will take place. "All over the planet humans will instantaneously experience "an inductive pulse of Love energy, bringing their heart centers into full and vibrant activity. This can only occur, however, if a certain key number of human lives unite in their efforts to create a consciousness bridge to key the Sirian energy fields into the planetary consciousness. A worldwide network is currently being established to complete this vital work."

A high frequency of dolphin activity along major biomagnetic grid lines such as Monkey Mia in Western Australia and Byron Bay in New South Wales, leads Sellick to think that dolphins serve as bridging agents to the Sirian "love pulse" energy. Telepathically sensitive human beings are helping to form a consciousness link with dolphins to complete this united land and sea network of consciousness.

ST. GERMAIN AND THE WHITE BROTHERHOOD

One Saturday afternoon following ukulele lessons, my teacher and her husband invited me to look through some boxes that were part of the estate of an elderly neighbor. The neighbor just happened to be a Theosophist. Among the boxes I found a virtual treasure of out-of-print books by Madame Blavatsky, Krishnamurti, C.W. Leadbetter and A.P. Sinnett, all students and teachers of ancient wisdom and The Mysteries. There were so many books, I couldn't decide which ones I wanted. The inner voice kept nudging me to buy the whole lot. "I don't want any more stuff," I kept insisting. I was close to getting down to little more than a carload of possessions and I didn't want to start accumulating again.

The mosquitos started driving me crazy, along with the inner voice, however, and I relented. It was late when I arrived home so I decided to leave the three boxes of books in the car overnight. Around four in the morning I woke up and had a strong impulse to go out haul them in and sort through them. I had definitely stumbled into a storehouse of ancient wisdom here. Along with Blavatsky's "Secret Doctrines" there were books on Egypt, occult Chemistry, an assortment of books on Eastern traditions such as Zen Buddhism, Yoga and Tantra, as well as on the subjects of world religions, immortality, astrology, kundalini and western philosophy and psychology. I was awed at having the first opportunity to purchase it.

Several days later I began to wonder if my music teacher's husband was another of St. Germain's messengers. Sure enough, the next time I visited him, without knowing of my connection, he asked, "Are you interested in St. Germain?"

"Yes, he's my spirit guide and the motivator behind the book I'm writing. Why do you ask?"

He walked to a sideboard, picked up a silver-colored pouch and pulled out a handful of old photographs and snapshots mostly of Krishnamurti. Among them were two unmistakable images of St. Germain. Along with them in a frayed leather-bound frame were two photos of Indian masters. Inside was a smaller folder containing a picture of Jesus and five masters, one of whom looked very much like the image of Merlin that had flashed through my mind a year and a half earlier and then appeared in poster form the following day. For some reason, I had the impulse a few days later to thumb through a Summit University catalog that I'd had for months and hadn't looked at. Inside I discovered images of three of the masters. They included El Morya, Kuthumi (St. Francis) and The Maha Choan, all members of the White Brotherhood who gather at Mount Shasta in the inner sanctum. I took it as a sign that a host of new "teachers" were making their presence known in my life.

Among these treasures were some comments from a Krishnamurti lecture on living spontaneously and fearlessly in a desireless state. Funny how it showed up just as I was beginning to ponder desirelessness and fear, looking at how my longing to be part of a traditional family system consistently set me up to experience pain.

He spoke about spontaneity or living in the moment. Spontaneity happens when the mind is unprepared and undefended. It comes out of the unknown and is an incalculable, creative aspect of ourselves. Krishnamurti advises us to watch our emotional states and "you will see the moments of great ecstasy, great joy, are unpremeditated; they happen mysteriously, darkly, unknowingly…"

Planning, expecting, hoping for an anticipated outcome is a sure way to inflict pain and suffering on oneself for it is in direct conflict and resistance to what is. And what is, is simply not changeable in the moment, it just "is." When we desire, we set ourselves up for disappointment. "Pleasure" reminds Krishnamurti, "is a spontaneous thing…unsought, uninvited; whereas fear is the common result of a series of mechanical habits." When we resist fear and attempt to rid ourselves of it, it will not leave. When we embrace it, become one with it, then in the "midst of that flame of suffering, in the midst of that fear itself, when there is not any desire to escape, to analyze, to dissect it, find out its cause…" a process will arise that will dispel it.

Fear is a function of the mind, says Krishnamurti. It is not an emotion. Fear is aroused when our survival feels somehow threatened. As is commonly the case with dolphins who are stranded or separated from their pods, I had a fear that I couldn't survive without a family or relationship even though I'd been living alone for the better part of seven years and overall have been happier than ever before in life. Still my desire to be part of a traditional family, to be in relationship with others persists. It is an instinctual ego fear, not something I or any of us can will away. Humans, and all forms of life are united through consciousness. Consciousness enables us to experience the joy and suffering of others. It is our desire to avoid suffering, however, that gets humans in trouble.

Desire is not an emotion from Krishnamurti's point of view but grows out of a mind that is forever seeking satisfaction. Without desire, there is no dependency, no need to search for satisfaction. Instead when you see something beautiful, you appreciate it in the moment and are stirred by it at a deep level. In a state of desirelessness there is no need or yearning to recreate the spontaneous beauty of this moment in the future but simply a willingness to enjoy the adventure of the unknown aspect of becoming which is available to us every second. There is no need to worry about the future for it is unknowable.

It is not the unknown we need fear but the known. We know what human greed and unconsciousness is doing to the planet. We know the weather patterns worldwide are shifting. The ice floes are melting causing the ocean levels to rise. This is due to cutting of the rain forests. There are gaps in the ozone layer from high levels of hydrocarbons in the atmosphere from burning plastics, driving automobiles and using fluorocarbons in spray cans. Cities are choking on smog. Forests are dying from acid rain. We are contaminating the ocean with oil spills and garbage and threatening massive disturbance of the ocean floor and ecology with offshore mining. These pollutants and destroyers of the environment all stem from human desire for satisfaction, a craving for something we believe we must have to be happy only to discover too late that happiness exists in the now and cannot be stored up or planned or saved...as in a savings account.

Just as I was pondering all this, a letter arrived from Neil. He offered a few more insights on the nature of suffering to expand on our last conversation.

According to the Buddha, "Life is suffering," Neil wrote. "I think of it more than a 'part of the whole of life is pain.' Joy and pain are not pieces of life or opposites, but 'Life is Joy' and that contained within that whole Life/Joy is pain. The pain is contained within it and yet that very pain itself is joyful. To me the concept/realization of the truth of this is such a vast relief. Thank God I no longer need struggle against pain. I can just embrace it and move through it and on."

Neil continued. "People don't give a shit what you say as long as it comes from the heart/from your truth. And when that happens there is no place for anyone else to go except their own heart/truth/experience.The suffering itself does nothing, it is the willingness to embrace all of life, the suffering included, that gives us GRACE. Graceful birth, graceful death, graceful life. I truly believe that Grace—Divine Grace—comes with acceptance."

A quote from Da Free John ended the letter. It was: "You think to be enlightened is to be free of pain. It is not. It is to feel the pain more keenly. To feel not only your own pain, but the pain of all those around you and yet all the time, you are in Bliss."

UNDERWATER BIRTHING LEADS TO ALTERNATIVE LIVING

I encountered Claud and Bonnie the following week heading toward town in their little red jeep. I was driving out to swim in A.J.'s pond. Instead, we drove back to my place and sat in the lanai beside the pool to escape the wind whistling through the palm fronds. Bonnie told me the story of Kukui and Lelani's births and their connection with the dolphin energy.

They were living in Florida when Bonnie became pregnant with Kukui and decided she wanted to give birth underwater. Right away Claud said "Yeah, with the dolphins."

Joe and Rosie were living at Dolphins Plus in Key Largo at the time, awaiting the start of their release process. Claud explained how they had been used in the Janus communication project under John Lilly's direction. "They were using a computer to synthesize speech back to the dolphins so there could be two-way communication. Then they discovered, like everybody else does, that it's just easier to do it telepathically. The computer just kind of gets in the way."

Bonnie called the Lillys to explore the possibility of giving birth with Rosie present. Toni agreed. "I started going over there and spending a lot of time around them" says Bonnie, "but they had problems." They were not happy and they (Joe and Rosie) didn't get along with each other. Joe was very aggressive. Bonnie began swimming with other dolphins in the compound who sensed that she was pregnant and frequently nudged her in the tummy. "I was doing a lot of work with dolphins. Everyday I would come home from work and take my snorkel and go to the Gulf. I was in the water with them a lot." Bonnie said, "but it was not meant to be."

Toni Lilly told her about a man named Daryl who had spent a lot of time in Russia with Igor Charkovsky. He knew a lot about underwater birthing, was coming to Miami and Bonnie was urged to see him. He intended to create an underwater birthing center on Moloka'i and had gathered several pregnant women from around the world to begin the project. Daryl appeared in St. Petersburg a day or so later, met with Bonnie and Claud and convinced them to come to Moloka'i to have their baby. "I sold my business and Claud resigned his professorship. We gave up everything to do this," says Bonnie.

"By the time I arrived on Moloka'i, I was already nine months pregnant and nothing had been organized. Daryl just sort of disappeared for a period of time. "I felt really bonded and close to him in Florida but once we arrived on Moloka'i, the energy was totally different. He was like Dr. Jekyll and Mr. Hyde. I'm a very trusting person and I kept giving him the benefit of the doubt and denying my own feelings. What I decided was that I was just going to have to give up the idea of giving birth with the dolphins. There just wasn't anywhere here where I could give birth with the dolphins."

Instead, she said, "I borrowed the bottom of an isolation tank and had it set up on the property, overlooking the Pacific, under the stars but the water was muddy. Nobody had checked the water, so it was pure mud. The thought of giving birth in this mudbath was too much. When I went into labor, I went into the tub, it was just gross. I tried to rise above that and say 'OK, God, I don't know why this is happening, but lets just get on with it.'

"All these people from the 'ohana who I didn't really have a heart connection with were around and Daryl was right there while I was in labor, standing over my head meditating. Hours and hours later, I said, 'I just can't let go in this muddy water' so they found a kiddy pool and they had to boil the water on the stove and bring it into this pool. I got in and it wasn't deep enough. Finally, my midwife who was a naturopathic doctor, said 'Let's get out. It's been a long labor. Things aren't flowing well. I think you better go over to Maui and just get checked out so you can come back here. Kukui ended up being born in the hospital with massive meconium aspiration."

Claud interjected: "Meconium is fecal matter. So here you have this Being of Light being born full of shit. Whoa!"

Bonnie added, "Here I was trying to create an ideal birth and everything that could have gone wrong did. I had retained placenta so we both almost died. We were in a hospital. So I had to overcome my resistance to the whole medical thing…to seeing my baby stuck with tubes. My whole idea of bonding…every idea that I had I had to give up and surrender. I had to surrender her and say 'Well, if she's not supposed to incarnate now, then I'll have to give her up.' It was really hard, especially in the New Age Movement with all this emphasis on ideal births. If you don't have an ideal birth, a woman has to deal with tremendous guilt feelings, as well as feelings of failure."

"Well, it's another lesson" I agreed lamely.

"Well, yeah it is and it's a lot of pressure if you go for that but if you don't…there weren't any dolphins, it wasn't underwater…"

"Yes, but she's still beautiful," I interjected.

"Yeah…she's still a free spirit." Claud added, "She chose to deal with some real heavy karma. Anyway, the whole center fell apart and we knew we couldn't stay on the ranch anymore. I got to watch the forces of good and evil at work in Daryl's life and how that related to me. It's like Elizabeth Kubler-Ross says, 'We all have a Mother Theresa and a Hitler in us. It's just a question of which one we choose."

"One of the messages in the New Age movement, is that there are people who will take advantage of you," added Bonnie.

I agreed, "One of the lessons is to learn discernment."

"Yeah," Claud said. "Daryl was very tuned into the importance of the underwater birthing movement and he took every advantage of that...but basically it was our spiritual greed that got us into trouble and that's a very important lesson to learn."

"Well, whatever it was it got you here..." I reminded him.

"Yeah...it got us here and just two valleys over from where we are now," added Claud. For the past four years they have lived in a small self-sufficient community high in the mountains, in a cabin that "breathes", alongside a roaring stream. Bonnie bathes in the waterfall a few feet below the cabin every morning. "The day we finally decided to stay on the island, we went to the little church in Halawa. That day the dolphins showed up in Halawa Bay to let us know we made the right choice. Choosing light and life," Claude said. They spend their days caring for the girls and working three hours a day to maintain the garden and grounds, living as close to nature as one can get and still have a roof over your head.

"My feeling is that the dolphins may lead you one place thinking that you are going to do one thing and then you end up doing something totally different," I said.

"Your experience is very typical," said Claud. "I think they aren't into being with us physically as much as kind of setting an example, you know, living lives of joy. And they teach awareness. The whales are really that way with their 'Can you see me now?' Tim Wyllie's experiences are similar. He swims out, they go away. He swims back in—there they are. They play games with us. The stuff you wrote about lightening up is very well taken, too. Like I said they play games. You think, 'here's the whole ocean-...where's the whales?' But after a while you can tune in and feel where they are. Yeah, they're teaching us Oneness."

I'm told all true spiritual teachers test your committment to the path by being elusive. You must pursue them. The dolphins and whales are no different.

It was getting late and Kukui was due in town for a dental appoint-ment. "Is there anything you want to add," I asked Bonnie?

"Just my own personal triumph over fear. When I was pregnant with Leilani, we lived in a very isolated situation and it was like the same situa-tion again, except it would have been even harder to evacuate me. There was all this history I had of a birth. I felt I'd done everything possible to create a beautiful, perfect ideal birth and it turned out the exact opposite. So I thought, 'Do I succumb to my fear and try and set up all these alternatives?' Or do I just go for a home birth and try and do it in a bathtub, depending on whether or not the streams are dirty. I just had to do a lot of rebirthing and working through all the stuff and I finally got the message, 'Yeah...just do it…go for it.' So I did and it was a beautiful birth and everything was right. I really had to take a risk."

The two girls were growing restless with grown-up talk. Kukui's plea brought the interview to an end. "Mommy, I'm hungry." she cried.

"Do you have a banana or something," Claud asked.

"Fresh off the tree," I assured him.

On the way to the car the conversation drifted to whales. "When Kukui was two months old, we swam with the whales. We both just jumped in and swam with them. I had absolutely no fear," Bonnie said.

"Oh, Kukui swam with them?" I asked.

"No, she slept in the boat…the only time when she was ever asleep for that long. It was like she gave us a gift. We kept swimming toward them and they wouldn't come. Finally, we just stopped and I just started getting into my breathing and snorkeling…your breath is kind of amplified. All of a sudden I looked out and about 25 yards away, there was this beautiful huge whale just floating on the water."

Claud said, "I have this image of this huge eye. I was looking at the whales underwater and all of a sudden there was this big eye looking back at me from 20 feet away. Big eye! Wise old eye! Beautiful eye! They're such great beings, so powerful, and so graceful…And have you ever heard them sing? It's so amazing, so awe-inspiring! Talk about your ecstatic experiences! Yeah, they're our teachers for sure. Majesty! The Kingship/Queenship principle…That we're all Beings of Light. Now is the time for the conscious evolution of our species. We owe it to Earth and to ourselves."

Claud sends out a newsletter on occasion to friends and calls it "Center for Peace." The point he makes is that each of us must "center" before we can create peace in the world.

One afternoon a week or so later, I hiked up to the community and spent the night. Claud read the Shakertown Pledge to me out of a book called "Taking Charge," written by the Simple Living Collective of the Friends Service Committee. It resonated deeply with what I'd been striving for in life and hadn't quite grasped. In essence, it calls for humans to honor the Earth as a gift from God and to lovingly care for and steward its resources; to recognize that all life is a gift and a call for joy and celebration. The pledge itself is an opportunity for individuals to consciously commit themselves to act as world citizens, to lead an ecologically sound life of creative simplicity. It calls for sharing personal wealth with the poor and joining others to reshape institutions so that they reflect a global society in which everyone can access resources needed for physical, mental, emotional, spiritual and intellectual growth. The pledge calls upon individuals to commit themselves to be accountable for products that they create and avoid producing those which harm others; to properly nourish and care for their own physical well-being; to constantly examine relationships in an effort to communicate more honestly, morally and lovingly; to pray, meditate and study as a way of refreshing and renewing oneself; and to participate in a community of faith.

As an adult I've avoided being involved in any form of organized religion whose dogmatic and rigid belief systems impinge on individuality and freedom. However, in these words, I found a covenant that I could live with and be in harmony.

The next morning Kukui (Claud and Bonnie's three-year-old Master Teacher) and I strolled through the mango forest along the stream looking for the circle where the fairies dance. We never found the exact spot Kukui had in mind but we sensed their presence all around us and stopped for a moment to visualize them. While I couldn't see the fairies, I did see and smell signs of wild pigs. Fresh tracks and the familiar smell of manure wafting to my nostrils, worried me. Kukui, however, was unconcerned. "My guardian angel is watching over us," she affirmed while stopping every few feet to gather seeds for her mother to make earrings or a bracelet. "I want to take her a gift." As she held my hand and stuffed my pocket with the seeds, I was shifted back in time to the Michigan farm and the long walks through the woods that I took with my daughter when she was Kukui's age. Then I was in so much emotional pain, I couldn't savor the experience. The gift of Kukui's lighthearted company in this moment replaced the memory of that old pain. I paused for a moment to give thanks for the gift of her presence.

Later, Claud and I talked about the process of lightening up. "Hanging out around kids and dolphins is the easiest way I know of," I told him. He agreed. That night after the girls fell asleep, we climbed to the loft to talk. Claud asked me, "If you could talk to the dolphins, what would you ask them?"

Nothing came to mind. "I don't have any burning questions," I told him. For me, it's the journey of the Initiate, the mystery of unfolding that intrigues me. I'm satisfied now with the knowledge that they are leading us to live more authentic lives, to be more in the moment."

Later, as I pondered this, a question did arise. I told Claud, "I'm curious as to why they are guiding people to the islands. Is it to create a survival community, or is it more personal?" My wonder is fleeting, however. I have no compelling need to 'know' the future. There is a vision implanted in my mind of how I would like my life to be but I am content to allow it to unfold, to live in the moment and acknowledge and give thanks for the joy that is here right now. I am thankful for the Clauds and Bonnies and Kukuis and Matts and the endless flow of dolphin people who are appearing to enrich and enhance the experience of being alive. Wherever I go I seem to connect with dolphin conscious people. They have become my 'new' universal family.

That afternoon, Claud saw me wandering around the garden and suggested I climb the old jeep trail to a ridge that overlooked the community. I hiked up the steep trail and around a curve and there was the Western shore of Maui—its condos and high rises protruding skyward. Maui appeared to be floating like a dab of whipped cream in a cup created by the Moloka'i's mountain peaks that curved around it in the foreground.

I sat on a smooth slab of gray rock to meditate and ponder the two worlds that existed within a matter of a few miles from one another and yet seemed like they were on different planets. Maui's overdeveloped shoreline represented the material world. The community that lay behind and below me around a bend in the jeep trail, represented a more spiritual lifestyle. Sitting on a rock, atop a mountain between these two worlds, I got clear on which one I was choosing. Until that moment, I seemed always to have a foot planted in each world and couldn't quite let go of the material world, as Bonnie and Claud had done. "It's hard to give up old habits," A.J. had said to me. Yet I knew I was approaching the time of the final letting go, a time of absolute surrender to Higher Wisdom, Power and Love.

18 *The Artist/Warrior*

ONE MORNING I called A.J. to ask if I could come out and write under the monkey pod trees. In the course of conversing he said, "Hey, an artist friend of mine just sailed in this morning with his girlfriend. He's going to stay a few days and paint the banana trees." I didn't think much about it until later that day when A.J. said, "You should talk to Stewart about his experiences with dolphins and whales. He's been sailing all over the Northwest and South Pacific and has lots of stories.

"Not another story," I thought. "I'm never going to finish this book." Still I couldn't resist talking to him. The next morning, tape recorder in hand, I found Stewart in front of his easel beside the banana grove, busily brushing bright greens and fuchsias onto the canvas. In the midst of it, a banana tree was coming to life. We made arrangements to talk after the morning light had faded.

He found me a few hours later and we walked out to the floating lanai beside the spring-fed pond. To the sound of the wind rustling through the reeds near the shoreline and the croaking of frogs, we talked about whales and dolphins and the nature of life and consciousness. Stewart asked me what the book was about and when it was clear I wasn't on a crusade to save the dolphins and whales he said, "I think people's desire to save mammals in the sea is related to their wish to correct so many things that are going wrong with themselves or with humanity. They choose or find one particular fascination, which could be dolphins or it could be the Universe or it could be bumblebee life or whatever. Through that they find a particular channel for themselves to touch with whatever universal truth or process might allow them to relieve themselves of problems they may be experiencing.

"In all things that are on the island or the Universe, there seems to be the sum and total truth of all there is. If you could find a way of knowing, a process that creates a great form of meaning for you in any particular facet of nature, then you've got a trail for yourself to evolve to better understanding. People do choose that when they find themselves in trouble."

"The dolphins are just one totem," I suggested.

"I would say one of the media, one totem, but especially available to the human race because people seem to be able to communicate with them on a very sensitive level that really gives them those marking points, those way signs that say, 'Yes, you did say 'Hello' to me. You did respond. We are in communication'. You could look at the stars forever and never be certain whether this is or isn't a truth. The same with bees. Did it sit on you and love you or did it just forget to sting you, or what? But the response, the rapport that is set up with these more intelligent mammals is a great confirmation."

I asked him about his dolphin and whale experiences and he told me "I've lived on the northwest coast of British Columbia for more than 15 years and traveled around in a kayak, painting and living in solitude. I would quite often spend more than two or three months completely without contacting any human forms and I would often be in rapport with dolphins, especially Orca or Killer Whales. To me they are very powerful in their communication ability. There were eagles and there were seals and there was every other life-form. I saw that they are all as important. They were always sensitive, if you became receptive enough. All this hoo ra ra about 'Save the whales', well save everything—communicate with everything. Whatever people choose, whatever way they find to evolve and become more sensitive and cooperative and supportive, is good.

"In the kayak and in the sailboat, I had a lot of experiences. Schools of dolphins would come around the boat and I'd jump over and trail on a rope behind the boat. The first time it happened, I jumped in the water and called out with a sort of plaintive cry to see what would happen and immediately, out of a school of about a 100, two appeared on either side of me. One shouldered me over toward the other. They both touched me. Their skin was really, really soft and very lovely to feel."

"That's unusual for them in the wild to come up and touch you," I said.

"I don't know," Stewart replied. "I know that they help each other if one gets shot. One will support the other in the water. I guess I was doing about six knots."

"They may have thought you were in danger," I said.

"Oh yeah, because I made a plaintive cry," said Stewart. "I'm so used to their sounds. Up north there was a research station and I got used to hearing their sounds underwater and responding through a hydrophone. I got to understand the more urgent sounds and the more loving sounds or just the clicks and knocks and rattles that they make, whatever it might be. I knew that I'd sort of called for help."

"How did you happen to spend time in the kayak?" I asked.

"I moved to the west coast of Canada from Montreal. I left behind the cultural paraphernalia that exists out east for the artist. At the time, I found there was much greater liberty. The artist doesn't have to fit into certain frameworks of culture. I wanted to be free of that and live a more natural life and get away from the city. I came out west and eventually saw that in order for me to do my watercolors and painting without always having this crippling financial problem, I had to relieve myself of food costs, clothing costs and rent. After seeing the west coast and adventuring around —always with a paint box—I decided that I could build a kayak that would be big enough to handle easily and put all my watercolor equipment on board and travel. I'd grown up around the St. Lawrence River with a canoe so I knew the water very well.

"Without having any other resources I would learn to live off the land and camp on beaches. I'd be assured of privacy and I'd be assured of all the time I needed without interruption to paint. That's how it all began. I loved the life. It was pretty difficult. In fact, when I first started, I was a vegetarian, basically because I didn't like killing things. I lived for the first two years without even eating clams—and there are so many of them on the west coast. Finally I killed my first fish. I had a lot harder time with death than the fish did. We both had a hard time. From then on I became more and more of a west coast native, living off the land as it supplied seafood and lots of forms of life.

"Through that, and as a young person I was always interested in wildlife, biology and how things worked, but it wasn't until I was on the west coast that I started to realize how much communication really goes on. I saw how complete it is by learning that I could talk to a raven."

"You could talk to a raven?" I asked.

"I could talk to a raven. I could let him know verbally whether or not I was friend or foe and he would go back ashore and tell all the crows in all the trees—there are hundreds—to 'shut up' and they would. It would just take a word. If you were paddling to an area where there are hundreds of crows and they didn't find you to be a friend, they would drive you out with their cawing and whooping and racket. A raven would fly out to the middle of the little area that I might be paddling in and make a noise to me and I would make a corresponding noise and he would come down, swoop in closer and make another noise and I would say, 'Yeah, yeah, that's right' through intoned sound. He'd go flapping back to shore and if the crows started to caw at me when I came in, he would make a loud noise and they would shut up and that would be the end of it. This process is a regular occurrence in the wilds, whether with wolves or deer; all is communicated.

"I've talked to other people and they say 'How can you go there? The crows will drive you nuts'. I say 'Oh, no problem'. That is a form of communication that's so sensitive. It's all true. If you leave yourself open, it will occur on almost any level. There can be a tremendous amount of trust built in a short time between two beings of what we call different levels of intelligence. They will just open to communication...."

"If you're willing to be in silence..." I said.

"Yeah, silence, peaceful, loving feeling. I feel you can transmit a thought and, of course, you can throw a feeling out from you and so can they. This is how I feel the whales and the dolphins communicate. My own little theory is that, if you listen to the sounds of whales, you can hear them going audibly off the very top of our audible scale. It seems fairly obvious to me, or I presume from what I heard, that it also goes to a lot higher range than I can hear. I just apply that to vibration.

I feel that they transmit sounds on vibration that we don't hear always. I also consider that thought is vibration and that if one should refine the ability to use those vibrations properly, one might be able to throw a thought from one point to another, whether it's close or far."

"As in telepathy?" I asked.

"As in telepathy. I also believe that this is a very probable skill that not very many people develop to a very refined state. I do believe that there are people that are fairly adept. It's difficult to define whether they perceive on a very fine level or they actually hear manifested thoughtforms. When you get down to that level of sensitivity it's difficult to say whether you think in words or you think in perceptions."

I told him, "It seems to be different for people. Some people will get empathic feelings of communication from dolphins or seals or whatever. Other people get images. Other people come straight through with thoughts. I think it goes back to our dominant mode of taking in and expressing information."

"I've always just felt, perceived." Stewart said. "As you say, you have an empathy with the situation. One time in particular when I was sitting with a pod of whales, I suddenly started to feel this restlessness that was sort of churning inside me. I realized that it was coming from the whales and they were telling me that, 'We are hunting and have to go with this inflow of tide'. I was exhausted that evening. I had to make a decision to say good-bye now; we were having a tremendously powerful communication. We were resting all together on the top of the water. It was in Johnson Straits and I knew that there was a good coho run. The whales were going toward their mating grounds and I thought, 'Oh, that must be what they are doing.'

"It was full moon and I thought, 'Oh, they want to run up with the moon and they want to catch their food. Is that right?' I sent that thought out and suddenly, Ka BOOM! This tail smashed on the water. It was about 40 feet from me and I thought, 'Well, this is right on.' Then I said 'Well, OK, I'll see you later.' I knew I had to head for the tallest rock and camp on it for the night but then BOOM!. The same whale's tail smacked on the water and they sounded and left. I had the definite perception that we had mutually agreed to part company. I'd spent about two hours with them traveling down Queen Charlotte Sound passing into this area. That was one of my first really powerful experiences. That really told me this is really a very close communication of actual patterns and thoughts, rather than the 'Hello! Are you there?' of the whale coming to me and passing on. This was done with a mental call, without any sort of banging on the kayak, or mechanical communication."

"Several people have mentioned that during their whale experiences there was something like a bubble of knowledge being passed from the whale to the human." I said.

"Well, I would think that what you said depends on the person's level of understanding and how prepared they are. Let me put it another way. When a person is purifying themselves or coming upon knowledge of that level, sometimes you go through very slow steps and gain small amounts of knowledge. Other people might be prepared enough by being really calm in their bodies but they're not experienced. These people, because they are capable, may get a very large amount at once. Other persons of less experience when confronted at this level will often be unable to receive and will shut doors due to fear. When I say 'shut doors' I say that they are thinking in symbols and saying, 'What is happening? Shut the door.' Another person might be able to leave that door open and never put up bars. That's what thoughtforms do; doubt, fear being thoughtforms. Whereas, if a person is prepared, it's there—the door is open. I've lived outside in the wild enough to know this. Especially when you are in the water with a two- ton mammal that is totally equipped to devour you at any moment and it's dark outside, that whatever you might suppose can happen, may. Fear brings the object. If you are afraid you might get eaten, you just might."

"You were already tuned into being in nature when you started kayaking," I interjected.

"Well, living outdoors a lot and camping you do become attuned to that. I actually became very sensitive to communication prior to that because I'd been involved in Yoga and I'd been through some solitary hikes in the

Rockies and in the Stein Valley of British Columbia. These hikes introduced me to the Indian shamanistic side of things. I was fairly adept and very open to these possibilities and occurrences. And I loved to be outdoors. I loved living things. There is nothing in me that ever wants to hurt life and animals feel that. It's very easy for me to walk along the beach and walk by a bear and the bear will walk by me."

"And you never have any fear?" I asked.

"Well, you see that's it. If you have fear it shows on your body. As you know, if you meet a dog in the yard, they sense what you are; whether you are aggressive; whether you're fearful. They even say that they can scent it. Scientifically that's very possible given their sense of smell. Also, I might spend six months or more of the year in bare feet and never contact anything that is not familiar to those animals, except fire. All my scents are the same as they have on them. I'm living the same way as they are except for fire. I think that brings you closer to them too. When you travel slowly by kayak or by bare feet in the woods, animals quickly get to know you're in the vicinity — in their neighborhood. If you camp there for a week, they get to know you."

"Did it affect your art?" I asked.

"Everything affects my art. Every moment. Everything I think and that surrounds me. Yeah! My art is really a media for me to evolve and learn through and express what I experience."

"What brought you to the Hawaiian Islands?" I wondered.

"Probably the warmth. A friend of mine was here. I came to visit. I hurt myself in the kayak so I could no longer kayak. I had to give up the kayak and eventually ended up with this 36-foot sailboat. Originally, in order to cure this torn abdominal muscle from the kayaking, I decided to go down to Southern California and get on a bicycle. I bicycled up to Joshua Tree National Monument to paint for the summer and in the fall I did a little bit of carpentry for a friend there. They had $99 tickets from Los Angeles to Hawaii, so I bought one. I realized I couldn't go back to the kayaking. What I left up north was very cold weather and a kayak. That's all I had waiting. It meant sawing wood for the winter. It was a pretty austere life. So I came here and I swam and I bicycled and studied the ocean.

"I thought, 'Now what do I do with my life? I have to change somewhat. What about a larger boat?' So I changed the scale of traveling on coastlines to traveling on the planet, from continent to continent, and do the same thing on a larger scale. I could work on maybe larger watercolors, maybe pastels, maybe oils eventually. And that's what I'm doing now. I studied the ocean and what kind of a boat I would have to build to do this. Watching from the north shore of Maui for a winter I cast off many ideas. Originally, I was going to make a very fast sailing trimaran kayak — a very large kayak with two outriggers that I designed and refined. Eventually, though I bought this boat."

"Sounds like a very idyllic life," I said.

"Well, some people think of it that way and in truth it is a pretty nice way for me. I'm sure a lot of people wouldn't find it very pleasant."

"So you've traveled to Tahiti, Tonga." I said.

"To the Marquesas actually. As an artist I don't often have a lot of money. I left the Hawaiian Islands here with $300 and spent four months in the Marquesas. I came back to the Hawaiian Islands and after a winter here went to Samoa, then to Tonga. I spent as long as I could in Tonga and then left there in November of that year to get out of the hurricane season. I spent what was summertime in New Zealand and then I had to decide whether I was going to carry on around the world or go back to Canada. I decided to sail back to Canada which I did in 76 days."

"You're always painting something different," I said.

"I like to always challenge myself. I feel that art is a calling, rather like a warrior's calling. You have to constantly break your own barriers of knowledge; challenge yourself with the unknown; refine the creative intellect. I never repeat myself.

"If I find a certain type of artwork or a mode that people really might love to buy let's say, I am at that point usually ready to drop it because it's so easy to repeat yourself or create something that is marketable. That is not the job of the artist; to make commodity items for people. I think the job of the artist is to ask people to confront themselves; ask people to question reality and to have the bravery to surge forward for the reason of evolution of man's mentality…"

"Go beyond the known…" I said.

"Yeah, go beyond the known. I think it's one of the tasks of the artist. In order to carry on that, he has to do it himself."

"Keep reaching out—searching," I offered.

"Right."

"Have you ever painted dolphins and whales?" I asked.

"No there are enough people painting dolphins and whales. I tend to paint some of those completely untouchable sensations or perceptions that have occurred through life experience. Sometimes you think you might be even communicating with more than something on this planet. I'm a very visual person. I get some incredible, almost not recordable visual patterns. I often thought that with electronics now it would be grand if we could have a set-up that would be a big screen that would record your dreams and your thoughts or these visions.

"Dolphins have a very sensitive media in the water. Vibrations really travel there. That's a large part of it. To me, I don't assume that dolphins are more intelligent than man. That's not the point. I think they are probably much more sensitively oriented, especially since they don't have all these toys to play with. They don't have all the options. They'd love to, though." Stewart laughed.

"You mentioned that you have experiences that take you into other realms?" I asked.

"Well, when I was first becoming involved with the mentality of Intelligence, I questioned. That was when I was young. My original background was as a Protestant but when I was 10-years-old my father came home and said, 'Forget the church.' He was a very good baritone singer and we were an impoverished family. The church wanted him to give 10 percent of his income, which was almost nil. We couldn't possibly do that and he was angry and said, 'It's just a big money trip. You don't have to go to Sunday school.'"

At 10 years of age, I had to have something to replace that. If all that wasn't true…this God idea…then what was true? A good friend of mine was a Catholic and I spent a lot of time when I was young discussing this matter with friends. As I grew older I had a couple of psychic experiences that made me delve further. I had a situation once where my heart stopped…my breathing stopped and yet I was conscious. In fact I was super phenomenally conscious beyond anything I could dream. When I came back, as it were, into my body self, I realized my heart was beating and I was still here. During that time, there was nobody there. I was just conscious. I'd forgotten during that time that I'd had a body.

"I thought, 'Those Yogis in India don't stop their breath and do all those positions just to show off. They do that in order to be where I was and they must have it down to a science. They must have been doing this for thousands of years and they must know a helluva lot about the universe of communication. I was living on the west coast of Vancouver Island in a shack that I'd built for the winter at that time and I went back to Vancouver where I knew this Maharishi. I stayed there for three years and ended up teaching Yoga and meditation. At the same time I was able to spend approximately a six month period where I was just basically fasting and never slept. I would meditate and sometimes it would be eight hours a day. I was capable of meditating as long as I wanted and being very calm. At those times a lot of powerful experiences came upon me that I was able to receive and process. I refined my psychic machine to the point that I was open to experiences. So now, you might say, I'm rather fearless mentally. I don't care what I see or feel. I know that it's a movie screen."

I told Stewart, "I had an experience the other day where it was like once you surrender to the knowledge or feeling that there is a much higher power, it's perfectly safe to let go of all your fears and just allow yourself to be guided by that higher source of Intelligence."

"That's what I meant that I've had what you might call extraterrestrial, extrasensory, extraknowledge experiences that make you wonder,' Where does this information come from?'" he said.

"Yeah, I got into questioning, 'What is the source of knowing?' Do you know?" I asked him.

"I don't know," he said. "In fact, I was just reading an article the other day where quantum physicists were asking, 'What does God think?' Now that's totally ridiculous compared to what you would have heard from them 20 years ago. ' That energy is there. ' They're acknowledging psychic energy. They're acknowledging the link between thought and vibration and the physical universe. When we are completely empty, we are totally part of all that there is. I feel that to presume any particular thoughtform to be the truth or the untruth is rather confining. We are a part of all. When we empty ourselves of everything—all that there is, is. We are only a vehicle.

"The mentality of the human race right now can only think within certain perimeters of thought," said Stewart. "We are, when we are perfectly refined, open, intelligent, I would say, people with a much expanded, mentality. Intelligence refined has a greater source of knowing than the more minute one because the vehicle is much more expansive. But here is the thing that is really amazing.

"I once was reading with this fellow from India who was a sixth-generation Yogi and has all these ancient holy books. He had them with him in Canada, when I was there. At one point, myself and another fellow, we were his closest students—the ones who had stayed with him the longest and could understand the deepest points—were listening to the Yogi read from the Upanishad. He was translating it because it's not yet in English. He stopped at a certain place and I thought, 'My mind is getting too tired, I can't pick up on this process of almost mystical logic that is creating meaning for me at a level that meaning hardly exists.' If someone asked me to tell them what he had just said, I couldn't explain it. So, he was reading this and I said, 'Hold on, hold on'.

"He said, 'One minute please,' and he kept on reading because my other friend right beside me was still totally concentrating. I looked at his eyes and I could see he was really enthralled and I was completely blank. These words were going by but they meant nothing. About two minutes later, the same thing began occurring with my friend. So he said, 'OK, I want you to see this again.' And he read it all again and the same thing occurred. There was a point at which I could no longer understand what he had said and my friend couldn't either.

"The Yogi said, 'OK, this is the point. In this book there is a place that I can read to and understand, but there is another 10 volumes that have come out of Tibet which do not yet apply to the human race because they are not evolved to the point psychically where it has anything to do with them.' Not only does it not have any pertinence to life right now, but it's not translatable because there is no basis for it. There is no framework of mental process for these thoughts to be cohesive."

Are these the ancient records the dolphins are telling us we must lighten up in order to access, I wondered. "Where did that knowledge come from?" I asked Stewart.

"That's exactly it. Where did it come from? How ancient is knowledge? And where does it come from? There was this book where they had these sort of giant tattoos entrenched in the Andes Mountains and all these things that make you go, 'My God, why are they there? Who did them? It leaves a lot of questions?'"

"Chariots of the Gods?"

"Yeah, exactly. It's easy to say, 'I don't believe in that' or 'Pooh! Pooh!' But there's too many unanswered questions."

As usual the conversation became so intriguing, I didn't want to bring it to an end. I stopped the tape recorder for several minutes and turned it on again when the subject of Kundalini experience came up. Meantime the birds twittered happily in the treetops, the frogs had long since given up croaking and the sun was drifting toward mid-afternoon. Time disappeared from consciousness as we talked. A slight mist began to fall. The wind swept through the lanai but it only faintly registered on my awareness.

"The rising of the Kundalini," said Stewart, "is really what we were talking about before where a person takes on a tremendous knowledge in one shot. Either you block it off or you're ready to receive it and let it pass through. There's two types of Yoga that are involved with the rising of the Kundalini. One is the Patanjali's Yoga, which is Hatha Yoga. It's brought up slowly through relaxation, meditation and culturing of energy and awareness of its movement. The other is Kundalini Yoga where the power of Kundalini is actually forcefully built up and then shoots through the spine into the head creating a more phenomenal experience."

"Is that Shakti?" I wondered.

"Exactly. There's a lot of power there. I look at it from the physical level. The same thing occurs when a person takes a rapid overdose of some drug probably. The Kundalini type of Yoga is a bit more dangerous for a person unless they are coached very carefully. I've heard of people being thrown half way across rooms and going unconscious and breaking out in tremendous sweats and perspiring due to improper training. Whereas, the Hatha Yoga where it is brought up slowly, there is an opening of all the forms of the mentality to the point where the Kundalini has risen. In other words, the thousand petaled lotus has opened because you have opened it petal by petal by petal and then it just blooms and there you are."

"That's the more natural way," I stated.

"Well, my discipline was that—Hatha Yoga—which was a very healthful, physical, relaxing sort of thing and slow culturing through meditation and the opening of the chakras and the opening of the mind to greater possibilities. Personally now I don't lean more towards Yoga than to anything. The quest for knowledge is really the ultimate, and personal process," Stewart said.

"Is painting a meditation?" I asked him.

"Actually it is in practice. I never really thought of it that way but they say that painters live to a quite old age because they spend so much time in what might be called the 'theta state' when you're working. You leave most of your thoughts elsewhere and are involved mostly in that. As a painter and a liver I'm a person that is mostly involved in life. I'm very much involved in all forms. I care for people and care about the ecology of the planet and all these things. I don't live in a state of meditation all the time. You need your mind to do the things that require the mind to be acute—action and reaction. Generally, meditation sort of leaves off to the side—you sort of let it all drift by and you are just there."

"Do you feel like you're able to be in a place of observation, where part of you is observing life instead of being caught up in it?" I wondered.

"Much more so. When I originally started looking at meditation or becoming involved in it, it was because I had no recourse. I was so tossed about in the storms of life that the confusion of it all was driving me crazy. The more I knew the more I became confused until I saw that through meditation I realized that I was given enough presence and peace of mind that I could sit back and say, 'Not only are you confused, but you could be a million times more confused because you are also every other mind on this planet. There is just no end to the multiplicity of beings. They're not you. Like we we're saying, you are the sum total of knowledge. You are the calmness of the Universe. You are. This is simply that. Now I can go and say 'So what.' Should I become involved in an argument on an ecological level, let's say with some corporate leader who wants to dump 5,000 pounds of some chemical into the creek beside my house, I, at least have the ability to calm myself down and to realize that my thoughts are my thoughts. They are not me." He laughed.

"Blowing through you," I offered.

"Hopefully."

"So what do you do about the corporate executive?" I asked.

"Well, that's what I say. We are on this planet and we can sit back and meditate and we can pray that they don't dump that water in the creek. I think, for myself, that it's a rather more noble way to go to actually confront people with the things that they do, and how they affect other people. I think that's a duty, I feel I want to take upon myself. But I don't have to sit back and meditate and pretend that someone else is going to do it. We are bound to some activity."

We talked at some length about the mind and the nature of consciousness and knowing and how we often trick ourselves into beliefs and behaviors. "The mind is so subtle and so devious in so many ways that we have to be diligent always to keep it clear, not to delude ourselves. Be very acutely aware what you are thinking. Don't assume that because something came in meditation while you were quiet, that it's right. Don't use it as a power and say, 'Well I had this vision today that I should do this and therefore it's right and all of you should do it.' That's what happens. 'Sure I hear that. I'm aware of that but is it really my mind? Or is it possibly, just on a more subtle level manipulating me?'"

"Your ego or your fears?" I asked.

"Yeah. I take in as much information as I can from as many sources as I can muster and even then I allow one step in front of the other and should something come in the path, I'm ready to make a move on that too."

"You practice discernment." I offered.

"Right, and what you call that kind of a ballet dancer's attitude of stepping forward in life. It's like the martial arts of the Japanese. That to me has a lovely understanding. 'When a force comes to you, better to take that force and move with it and utilize it.'"

"Like Akido," I said.

The mist in the air finally grabbed our attention. Stewart had left a fresh painting on an easel beside the banana grove and needed to rescue it from the moisture. And my mind was going on overload.

19 *Joe and Rosie Calling*

WHEN THE WHITE Brotherhood made their presence known to me, I said in response, "OK. I surrender my life even more deeply to your wisdom and intelligence. Show me the way." It didn't take them long. After talking with Stewart, I was sure the book was finished. I had written down the very last story. I couldn't imagine that there was anything else that needed to be said although I'd been thinking I needed to balance the book out with some scientific or research oriented information. For three months I'd been telling people, "No more stories. I'm not talking to anyone else about dolphins. The book will never get done. It just keeps growing and growing," but, of course, when you're in the flow it's difficult to come to a dead stop.

The morning after I surrendered to the guidance of the White Brotherhood, I was driving down the road to a brunch and encountered Claud driving in the opposite direction. We stopped and he shouted across the road, "Well, you did it again. Roberta is coming in tomorrow." Roberta Quist Goodman was the trainer/trainee for Joe and Rosie during the last year or so before they were turned over to ORCA to be released into the wild. How could I resist? I opened myself to the flow once more. "Joe and Rosie had certainly been popping up a lot," I thought. I'd never even heard of them until I started collecting dolphin lore for the book. "Is it possible," I wondered, "that they planted a seed in the collective mind of cetaceans around the world? Is it possible that Joe and Rosie instigated the Call of the Dolphins?" If so, they obviously had a few more words to say and who better to say them than their good friend and pal, 'Bertie.'

A few days later on a misty mid-afternoon, I hiked up the jeep trail to the community to interview her. We sat around the table beside the outdoor kitchen talking, as Bonnie prepared pumpkin pie for dinner. Roberta left her husband David behind. She came to Hawaii on the spur of the moment and without a penny to find her task/meaning/gift in life—something that eluded her in Nashville. David is cutting his first record album there.

Roberta told me, "The first new people I met on Maui were Moonjay and Kutera who are taking people out on dolphin swims. Then I come to Moloka'i and the first person I meet is you—seeker of dolphin lore—and then A.J., an ex-trainer of dolphins. I'm wondering, 'Should I listen to the message here? Or isn't there one?' Ha! Those dolphins are so enticing and elusive in turns," Roberta said.

"How did you get involved with working with dolphins? I asked."

"I was on Maui in '78. I read "Communication Between Man and Dolphin" by John Lilly and knew the truth in it. One of the things Lilly said is, "In the province of the mind, what we believe to be true either is true or becomes true within limits to be found experimentally and experientially. These limits are then beliefs to be further transcended." Scientifically what he had to say about dolphins sounded right, them having larger, more convoluted brains than ours and living in an environment that opens up the mind. I wanted to meet them. I was filled with respect and willingness for dolphins to be my teachers. First I called to them in my mind and asked them to come to me and to show other people that I was special because I figured I'd have to have a Ph.D. to be able to even touch a dolphin. Right?

"So I thought, 'OK, maybe if the dolphins show the people that I'm special somehow, then I can work with them.' I'd call them at night even before I'd met them." She moved back to the San Francisco Bay area and found that Dr. John Lilly was just setting up his operation at Marine World/ Africa USA in Redwood City. "I wrote him a letter that was never responded to. Maybe another year went by and I went out there finally, just to check it out. I had resistance about going to a marine park, but I did it. I found out they had a petting pool and I went out there and the dolphins in the pool immediately came over and were all over me. I fell in love with them. They were so wonderful."

Eventually, after several weeks of visiting the park, one of the researchers in charge of the Circe project noticed that Roberta did indeed have a special rapport with the dolphins and asked her to become her assistant. "That's how I began to work with the dolphins. John Lilly was working at the same park." About nine months later, Roberta became a diver in the park.

"I was free to go into the water with them anytime I wanted. There were about a dozen dolphins and two orcas and a pilot whale. This was wonderful because the research had a lot of restrictions on it. They deprived the dolphins of human contact in both training and research in order to get the dolphins' attention. Calling themselves a bilateral communication study, they were supposedly studying a context in which the dolphins were able to tell the researchers what they wanted. But, in fact, the dolphins were deprived of everything they wanted in order to have the dolphins tell the researchers what they wanted. So they went on a sort of 'strike.'

"When I could freely interact with them I'd play with them for hours a day and they'd never get enough at certain times. As their research went on, they didn't want to come over at all. The dolphins didn't want human inter-action at all because we were asking them in sessions what they wanted and then depriving them when they weren't in session. Not believing in the research at all, but knowing that was what I was going to have to do to be around dolphins, I continued going along with the project while sneaking time with the dolphins." She would come in early and leave late to be with them.

"Did they limit their food also?" I asked.

"No they gave them as much as they wanted. By the end of the day the dolphins were given as much food as they needed. Anyway, I went to work as a diver and for a year cleaned the underwater tanks. One of the exercises that you had to go through, a kind of initiation, was wrestling the head diver in order to prove yourself. So I wrestled with the head diver. Threw him in the tank. My purpose in being in the dolphin tank was to soothe the dol-phins and to mediate between them and the divers and keep up a playful atmosphere in the tank. The divers being in the dolphins' world enabled the dolphins to take out any aggressions they wanted to on the divers and they did. For no apparent reason, they would start beating the divers up, knock-ing them on the head, butting them or taking their flukes and slapping them.

"These were show dolphins. Five dolphins and a 20-foot pilot whale were in there. Four dolphins most of the time (after one died). Having to be in the tank for three to four hours at a time to completely scrub the bottom of their tank, the dolphins interfered constantly and it was our job to get it done. The head diver wanted to get it done and all in one piece, so we wanted to stay in as long as possible. I found, that indeed, I did help calm the waters and keep us in the tank longer to get our job done. Part of that job that I laid out for myself was playing with the dolphins. I got to go around play-ing with them more often than working and scrubbing the bottom of the tank which helped out the entire operation.

"Sometime during that period, I decided to search for wild dolphins— free dolphins. I had an opportunity to come to Hawaii again. I came to live on Maui and tried to get out with humpback whales and dolphins. They were very elusive. I went over to Lanai and spent weeks over there camping at the harbor, waiting for them and waiting for them. They never came into the beach for us. Everybody else went over there and they told wonderful stories about how the dolphins played for hours with them. Finally when I was living on a 92-foot charter boat I had one great interaction with wild dolphins. That was the only one in a year.

"I missed my babies. My dolphins had had babies themselves and I was anxious to go home and see my own. I say 'my dolphins' but it's just the love that I have for them, it's not possessive. I hope they are here for all people. The bunch in captivity were calling me back to them, so I came back to work with John Lilly's group. At that time, everybody else was quitting. Some of them had worked there for four years and were very dedicated and wonderful people with the dolphins. They were all quitting for one reason or another.

"Since nobody else came to work with them, I eventually went ahead and took over the operation. I brought work-scholars to Marine World to work with the dolphins all that winter and summer and we had a wonderful time un-training them from their previous lessons. I ran a series of experiments on them that was creative and exciting to me."

"What were they?" I asked.

"Well, one of them was one that Karen Pryor had done with the dolphins at the very beginning at Sea Life Park, asking them to do some novel behavior. I made up my own rules for the game but it was basically based on her idea. They come to the side and they expect a command that comes through a computer in the form of a whistle and they'll perform it and then they get a fish. When I didn't give them any commands and I just stood there and did a shrug like, 'Well guys, what are you gonna do?' They kind of looked at me funny and they did a bow, a perfect bow. Well, that's not something new, so I didn't give them a fish. And they did another bow, and another bow and then they got frustrated and Rosie flipped over backwards splashing water and I gave her a fish and said, 'Great Rosie. Here's a fish!' And she looks at me with a kind of 'Huh?' and they started doing the most remarkable and wonderful things!"

"Like what?" I asked.

"One thing Joe did was swim around the tank really fast to get a good wave going. Then he surfed on the wave with his tail held up out of the water but horizontal to the water just a couple of inches out of the water, just zippp! And then surf. He glided. Like an airplane. Zoom!

"Rosie would just go over to the other side of the tank and just hang motionless and then come back asking for a fish with a face that said, 'Did I do a good job?' Then it kind of turned into, 'Make me laugh. OK, guys, make me laugh. What can you do to make me laugh?' They would do all sorts of funny things and they would have to put variations on each thing they came up with because I wouldn't reward them again for the same thing. It was always something new. They usually made me laugh."

"What were some of the things they did?" I asked.

"They might keep their fish from the last time and throw it across the tank or go pick up a dead fish from the bottom of the tank and throw it at me, or jump up and snap at a seagull that was flying over. Spontaneous things. Whatever they thought of. I was asking them to think, rather than just to respond. And letting what they did be right. In another experiment, I decided to undo what four years of training had expected them to do. Every year for four years they were expected to do the same thing everyday, three to five times a day, a hundred trials a day. I came in one morning, went to the side of the tank and asked the computer operator to put in 'wave peck' which was not the first thing they usually do. They usually right off do 'bow.' Well I put in 'wave peck.' Well, they expected to do a bow so they went ahead and did a bow and came back and really didn't expect a fish because by then it had registered, 'That wasn't bow, that was wave peck.' And I said, 'Great!' and I threw them a fish. They were intelligent enough and aware enough to know that I'd given them a fish for doing the wrong behavior to a whistle. And it only took that one trial—one time—and they knew that I was doing something different and I expected something different from them. The very next time when I asked them to do something, it was through a square. They were expected to go through a PVC square. They did a bow over through the square instead of sliding through the square like they normally did. Again they did something different. When I asked them to 'jump touch ball,' they both jumped at the same time and bumped into each other in mid-air. I'd never seen that before. What I wanted was for them to make up their own behaviors to the whistles and see what they would come up with and see if they would assign meanings and stick to those meanings, but they didn't do that. They didn't stick to any meanings. I'd put in the same tone twice in a row and they'd do two different things. So that was something I trained them to do in one trial.

"We did that for several weeks and then a French television crew came in to film us doing our regular sessions. Two days before the film crew came in, I had them do maybe one-half of a session one day of the real stuff and when the crew came in, the dolphins did it 100 percent correct.

Trainers tend to have superstitions about training and what not to do. They believe, 'That's what we're training them to do and you can't mess with that.'"

"So you blew all their belief systems?"

"Well, I didn't because nobody knew about it. I haven't published it or said anything about it to anyone."

"Was this documented on the film?"

"Well, the film showed them doing it right. We didn't take video tapes.

We only took notes. There were some work scholars with me at the time. I had each work scholar think up an experiment. Only one really thought of an experiment. He wanted to teach the dolphins 'yes' and 'no'. That was something I'd been thinking about but hadn't really formulated. The dolphins had also been mimicking underwater sounds for 'fish, innertube, ring, Joe, Rose'; mimicking the underwater tones and also our voice put through what we call a digi-talker, a digitalized human voice. Every time we gave them a fish they heard the word 'fish.'

"I went to the side of the tank and held up a tennis shoe, something they'd never seen me hold up before, and I had the computer operator put in the word for 'fish?' as a question. With a pointer stick, I would point up and down, because they could follow a target up and down. I'd hold up a tennis shoe and point no side-to-side. When they shook their heads 'No', they got a fish. And then I'd hold up a fish and have them shake their heads 'Yes' and then give them a fish. This was not following their training. It was completely different. It took 25 trials and Rosie was doing it perfectly.

"They weren't doing it perfectly for the first seven trials, so we thought of putting a string on each one of the objects and throwing it to them if they said 'Yes'. That was great, because here's a basket say and I'd ask, 'Is this a fish?' If they said 'yes' I'd throw it to them just like it was a fish. And here comes this basket and they'd duck down.

"It didn't take them long to realize they didn't want all these things in the water. They weren't going to eat them. In 25 trials, Rosie was getting them correct. A work-scholar's grandmother came that session and was very astounded that the dolphins were answering 'yes' and 'no'.

"We started doing other things, too. We only had so many whistles in the computer. Unfortunately, we didn't have a programmer that would put in anymore. I would ask the dolphins, 'Is this a ring? An innertube?'

"The process had been going on all summer to move them out of there. Marine World was due to close in September and relocate to Vallejo. There was a group of investors that came and had a wonderful swim with the dolphins and they decided to help us get them out of there. We moved Joe and Rosie to Flipper's Sea School at the Dolphin Research Center in Florida, hoping to release them."

"They were ideal candidates to be released back into the wild because you had spent a lot of time un-conditioning their behavior," I said.

"Yeah. I didn't really believe in being a trainer and I resisted it all the way through. I think my dolphin in Project Circe, the first project I worked on, didn't do so well because I just laughed and laughed whenever she'd make mistakes. Whenever she'd do 20 wrong things in a row, I would just be laughing and thought it was great. I thought she was saying something. So she didn't perform as well as the other dolphin did who was under strict training."

"What was the purpose of Project Circe?" I asked.

"Bilateral communications. Being able to set up a system where the dolphins could tell us what they wanted and when. Like I said, in the process of doing that for the last eight years the researchers have not let the dolphins have anything they wanted when they wanted it. They deprived them."

"They used the information they gathered and turned it against the dolphins?" I asked.

"No, I believe they could see the information just by getting to know the dolphins, as I did. In the first couple of days I knew what they wanted. They were wondering when the dolphins wanted fish, toys and human interaction. Just those three things. When I first started observing them and playing with them, I could tell they wanted fish about twice a day, usually in the morning and at night. They loved human interaction, especially during those times, and lots of it with people they loved. Toys, they could play with off and on all day. In the middle of the day, they kind of relaxed. When they were sexual or playing with each other, they didn't want to have anything to do with people. Those things were easily observable in a couple of days. I believe the head of the project also knew this and could see it for herself and yet they spent eight years depriving them of those things, not totally, but it was a deprivation in order to find out when the dolphins wanted those things. And what sense is that? It seemed totally silly to me.

"It was the start of a larger communication system, of course. They didn't know it was going to take eight years to get the symbols and the board that was properly submersible and to build upon it. Hopefully they would have an entire vocabulary, but they haven't."

"The Janus project, was that what you did at Marine World?" I asked.

"Janus? Yeah. That was John Lilly's project with Joe and Rosie. Janus is the God of portals, looking in both directions."

"What was the purpose of the Janus project?" I asked.

"Well, Janus One, John Lilly's original creation, was to take each letter of the alphabet and assign it a small band of frequencies. By playing a keyboard, a regular computer keyboard, you could make tones that would spell out words. Therefore, it was a creative language. You could spell any word you wanted in any language you wanted and teach them whatever language you wanted because the letters had direct associations to tones. From what I heard there were a couple of strong characters in the project and they evolved it into Janus Two and then eventually Janus Three which was not at all what John Lilly wanted. Janus Three, which was the project that they worked on for four years, was taking arbitrary whistles and assigning them meaning and they only had about 40 whistles on their keyboard. They were just arbitrary whistles with meanings for nouns and a few verbs— things that trainers had taught their dolphins. 'Jump, touch ball. Go through the hoop. Go through either a square hoop or a circle hoop. Wave pec. Bow.' They tried teaching them some nouns like football and ring and things like that. 'Fetch ring, fetch ball'."

I wondered if the research was being done to train show animals.

"I'm not sure what they were trying to do," Roberta said. "It ended up they were trying to see if dolphins could respond to acoustic signals for performing behaviors. That wasn't the purpose, but that's what it ended up being and they've done that very well with much better trainers and much better dolphins response at regular marine parks. Trainers have done that.

"Dr. Lilly and I would argue about what our study should be. He wanted to teach dolphins English and I wanted to learn dolphinese. I would like to bring their modes of communication and understanding of one another into humanity, to upgrade our system. The completion of either method would be fabulous! There was a spin off experiment that involved the digi-talker and the dolphins trying to imitate human voice digitalized. It squared off the rounds in our voice so they could use their clicks to simulate it."

I asked Roberta for more details about Joe and Rosie's release program. She told me, "When I brought them to Florida, to Dolphins Plus, I was trying to un-train them. I never was a trainer. I was un-training what they learned and yet training them in another thing, but it was mixing up the rules. Sort of, 'Whatever goes, let's make up new rules…'"

"Allowing them to express themselves…" I said.

"Trying to allow more expression into their sessions. They liked having fun with their food. They liked having some kind of stimulation. Mostly, I just liked being in the water with them. When we got to Dolphins Plus, I started feeding them off my windsurfer, just the board, in order to get them used to a boat. I thought we would eventually have a boat they could follow around and we could keep track of them out in the sea personally. I was also rather intermittent with them and unpredictable as far as feeding schedules. We didn't always feed them at the same exact time because out in the wild they are not going to eat at the same times of day. They couldn't depend on me. I was the person who always came and swam with Joe and Rosie for a little while and left and then came back and swam with them for a little while and left. So I was already the kind of a person that a dolphin out in the wild might see once in a while or not be so attached to…lessening their attachment to us. "I read in Rick O'Barry's book, 'Behind The Dolphin Smile,' that what he tried to do was an un-training program. So he continued with the flow of the work. Project ORCA didn't want anybody that had been involved with Joe and Rosie to see them again until after they had been released or forever. So I stayed away from them as they went through their release program. They were released in July of 1987. They spent about a year and a half at Dolphins Research."

"You spoke to me earlier about the transformation that happened in your life as a result of working with the dolphins. Tell me more."

"Well, one transformation occurred when I read John Lilly's book 'Communication Between Man and Dolphin' and completely accepted that, yes, there was a species on this very Earth that was equal to and greater than us in those qualities we deem human. I sincerely believe, knew, that their abilities in the world and their modes of communication and their lifestyle was better than ours. I believe they are more truthful with each other; that they can understand each other on a deeper level; that they cared for one another more; were closer to one another; that they lived a more stress-free life in the wild and had better control of their bodies. What we don't have conscious control of, like our breathing, they had to have conscious control of."

"Do they ever sleep?" I asked.

"I don't know. It's been theorized that they sleep half their brain at a time, but I don't know. I draw the analogy to when we have to be conscious to drive a car—and yet we can kind of sleep when we drive a car. We can go into a state of meditation. Just imagine going down a long stretch of straight highway, you can get there without knowing how you got there, or even through red lights and city streets, you don't remember."

"Sort of astral travel," I said.

"Yeah, and I think that the pod consciousness is strong enough, perhaps if one member of the group were awake, that he/she could control the others' breathing." Roberta thinks it's possible that the dolphins breathing could be controlled through their group mind.

"Did you ever test colors with them? Do you have any sense that they were able to see auras?" I asked.

"I have a sense that they are able to see or experience what we call auras. It may not be a 'seeing' of that field, but they can sense that field some- how. I've been at the edge of the petting pool with 30 hands in the water and they came right to mine whether they could see my face or not. I would duck down over the side or hide behind another person or whatever. Very quickly they would recognize my hands and come shooting across the tank. Perhaps it's sonar and they've got it down, but on the edge of the tank you've got a concrete sounding board right behind it that's going to reflect everything. I haven't devised an experiment to see whether they can see auras. My feeling is that they sense that field. It's a real field and I think they have a conscious sense of it."

"Through sound vibration with their sonar?" I asked.

"Yeah, because of their acute hearing, that could be a whole other sense than what we think of it as. It is a visual sense.

You've probably heard the hypothesis that they can send pictures into each other's brain just by sending the echo that they've received from the picture itself. Their hearing is a visual sense."

"Using sonar, they are seeing something and transmitting what they see through the sound of it? Is that what you are saying?" I asked.

"The sonar waves they put out are bounced back to them and then they hear them and through that hearing, they form a picture. Their hearing is actually in pictures of the object."

"Then they transmit the picture," I said.

"If they turned around and instead of sonar, did clicks that exactly matched the echo they heard from something, then they can send that picture to the other dolphin exactly."

"Because Joe and Rosie have popped up in this book so many times, I'm beginning to wonder if they may have put out a message that it's time for us to start releasing—because they were successfully released. Do you think that's possible?" I asked.

"Definitely I'd love to see dolphins released, especially those that aren't being used or are being mishandled. I'd definitely like to see them released. Of course, the fantasy of the New Age is that there will be no more zoos and no more captivity of any species."

"But do you think it's possible that Joe and Rosie are sending out a message?" I wondered.

"They contacted a lot of people's hearts. It's possible that they could now expect those people to take that heart connection and do something with it. There's conflict in my personal desire. I want to release a dolphin that right now is participating in designing tuna nets that dolphins can see and escape. I've always had my heart set on releasing her, but I wonder if it isn't important for her to finish that project first."

"Somebody said that Rosie volunteered to be a teacher," I interjected.

"From reports, she seemed to have just jumped onto the boat almost ...jumped into the arms of people. She's always been people oriented."

"Joe wasn't that way?" I asked.

"Not from reports. He seemed to have put up a fight. They were only two to three years old. They were undersized when they were caught, under the legal limit of six feet three inches, as far as I hear. They were young, very young. They were caught in the Gulf of Mexico off Gulfport, Mississippi. We thought about releasing them there which is their normal home, but it is such a dirty place, so full of boats and traffic, that it didn't seem a desirable home for them. They could have been caught again, too."

"Joe was always basically aggressive around humans?" I asked.

"He's a real sweetheart. I think he was more psychic. He picked up more of my psychic communications than Rosie. I've had other people say this too. Rosie is just a playful lady, but it's Joe that really has the deep, meaningful little moments. I've had interactions with him that really connected."

"But if he didn't like you, he wouldn't let you in the tank?" I asked.

"Well, they went through stages. When they were first caught, they were wonderfully friendly and loved people. They were put in, for example, with maybe 20 schoolchildren from the Esalen Children's School at a time, and people that had paralysis. Kids swam with them. Invalids swam with them; old, young, lots of people swam with them, lots of hours a day. At first they were very willing to do that. John Lilly had told them, agreed with them, that they would be held for a year's captivity and then they would be released back to their same pod."

"He made this agreement with Joe and Rosie?" I asked.

"Right, when he caught them. A year went by and at about two years, they started getting quite aggressive and it would be out of the blue. Somebody they normally loved would suddenly get beat up for very little apparent reason. They couldn't figure out 'Why did I get beaten up?' I was one of the few people still getting into the tanks with them. I was a diver at the time and had the balls to get in with them. I also had the respect while in with them to leave the possibility open that I could be attacked at any time. A lot of other people weren't respectful or weren't trusting enough. It's not to say I wasn't knocked around by them, or knocked around or kicked out of the tank. But not as much."

"You really connected with what John Lilly said in his book. What else happened in your life." I wondered.

"Well, that's like a whole religious uprising right in itself. Imagine what it would do to conventional religions to find out that, 'Yes, indeed there is another species on this planet that is spiritually higher, more evolved than you are.' Tell that to the pope! Even though I wasn't conventionally religious, there was still that threshold to go through and the realization and the hope that gave me. I always thought, 'Perhaps there is someone I can communicate with better than people.' I had a difficult time with people; communicating and being with people. They weren't as deep as I would like them to be. Their interests were not my interests. I was not interested in fancy clothes, fancy cars, more money and boyfriends, per se. So there wasn't much to talk about if I wasn't interested in the things everybody else was."

"What were your interests?" I asked Roberta.

"Oh, travel and exploration, before dolphins. Easy living in out of the way places. My mother always had a library of metaphysical books and I very much enjoyed reading those since I was 10 or 11 years old…Ruth Montgomery…the easier stuff and fun stuff like "Journeys Out of the Body"

"That brings us to spirit guides. Have you ever had a spirit guide? Or did the dolphins become your spirit guides?" I asked.

"I've never had a conscious conversation with a spirit guide that was separate from myself. The dolphins wouldn't talk to me either. I never heard a conversation in my head until after I stopped working with captive dolphins. They wouldn't be a spirit guide in that way but the whole essence of them and the realizations are messages similar to those others experience with their guides."

"Did you get images from them?" I asked.

"No. I didn't know where my ideas came from. When I first began working with them I wrote a story about having a baby in the water with the dolphins and that was before I heard that it was happening and people like Estelle Myers were interested in it. Those images could have come from the dolphins, but I didn't attribute them to the dolphins. I tried two dozen different experiments on how to communicate with them to get a response I could depend on. I didn't know what psychic imagery was. I didn't know what thought transference was. I knew about it but I couldn't recognize it in myself. I was always listening in my head trying to figure out, 'Could that be the dolphins?' I didn't have the spiritual connection as much as a really heartfelt love and admiration and 'knowingness' that they were a superior being to me and to those people I knew. I considered them of the level of Masters. Anything I've heard that Masters can do, I believe that dolphins could do. I'm mixed up now. I'm not sure what I believe now, but at the time it was, 'Whatever you can believe Masters doing, dolphins could.' I would sit in a pool and try to have the dolphins come and materialize at the pool for me, believing that they could take their body with them. I don't know if they can do that, but it was an experiment I would try. I was open to that belief anyway.

"That was a transformation of thought systems and application. I could look at any animal in the world and now see it as more than I thought it was before. On my way through Marine World to the dolphin tanks everyday, I passed the elephants and the giraffes, and the zebras and the llamas and in each of them I saw a new being because of my work with dolphins."

"Did looking in their eyes, did that have a particular impact on you? People say that llamas are very wise also and you really see who they are through their eyes," I said.

"I couldn't get that. I couldn't tell when the dolphins were looking at me especially because their eyes are very dark. Dark pools without light. I spent a lot of time just looking at their eyes, both underwater laying side-by-side, staring into their eyes and at the side of the pool holding them in my arms, staring into their eyes. Their eyes didn't hold as much communication for me as a lot of people have reported. They've reported seeing their eyes over the edge of a boat or from a tank from afar and instantly knowing the animal and being able to tell so much from their eyes. That wasn't so true for me."

"Sounds like you already had the heart connection," I said.

"The heart connection, yeah. I'd always swam like a dolphin and people associated me with dolphins. But I never knew a dolphin and never really reached out until I read John Lilly's book. Then there was an immediate opening."

"Since Joe and Rosie, what have you been doing?" I asked

"Having my child, Harmony, and raising her."

"Harmony was born with the dolphins?"

"No, my husband David and I, we tried to birth her with the dolphins. It was almost an accident to suddenly find ourselves at Monkey Mia, Australia. I was eight months pregnant and we camped out for a month, until our funds were out and our rent was up on the truck we had. We decided to go back after I was two weeks overdue to a town a little closer to hospital facilities. I ended up having her in a hospital. But for my eighth and ninth month, I was in the water with the dolphins at Monkey Mia everyday."

"How was the interaction at Monkey Mia?" I asked.

"I loved living beside them, but it was like being with captive dolphins in many ways. They were brought there by the fish and they expected fish from people. We never did feed them—so we had a different sort of relationship with them from the people that fed them. If a dolphin came up to a person they expected fish from and they didn't have fish, they just swam to the next person, whereas, when we separated ourselves from the people feeding them fish and they came over to us, they didn't expect fish. It was to play with us and interact with us and then they would go back to the people that had fish. Or they would come to us when nobody was out or they didn't want to eat. They acted a lot like captive dolphins. Their mind was on the fish and they would come right into ankle-deep water just to get a fish."

"That's not normal for them, to come into ankle-deep water?" I asked.

"No."

"How did they happen to start coming into Monkey Mia? They've been coming in there a long time," I said.

"About 20 years ago, one male dolphin started following a fisherman in and getting their scrap fish and came right along the pier. Eventually the dolphin came all the way up to the beach and pretty soon brought friends of his. Now there's a family of them that's been coming for 15 years. There's about four to six of them that come in everyday, twice a day and perhaps another 10 that stay out and once in a while a few of those come in."

"People swim with them there and interact with them, but not at the level you were doing," I said.

"No. The dolphins wouldn't trust most people coming out into the water with them. They wouldn't do much more than come in to check them out and zoom around and go out. There were a few people that had wonderful swims with them. The 18-month-old baby dolphin, Holly, once laid on my lap, her belly pressed up to my pregnant belly. They developed a trust after living there over a period of time."

Roberta and David attended the Homo Delphinus conference in New Zealand with Estelle Myers at the Maori center. Through the connections she made while there she and David were invited by a woman named Fai Hast to come to Australia to work on a dolphin film. It never materialized but Fai provided them with a place to stay. From Sydney, they drifted to Monkey Mia. I asked her what she got out of the conference.

"I got a feeling for the Maoris who invited us to their marae which is their sacred temple or church. This was one of the first times that white people had been invited to sleep at, not a tourist marae, but a regular marae."

"Timothy had said that what came out of the group meditations was this image of an evolved species on the planet that was part human, part dolphin," I said.

"There was a man named Jacques Mahol who was there and he had written a book, unfortunately not in English, called 'Homo Delphinus'" By the name of it, you can imagine it's a new species, half human/half dolphin or watery human, whatever. He'd written that quite some time ago and had a television series in Italy—also called 'Homo Delphinus.' He brought that with him. And David, my husband, and I with our dolphin connection had a real feeling of Harmony's connection to dolphins. We wouldn't have been surprised if she came out with flukes. I was kind of planning on having a tank in the living room where that would be her playpen," she laughed, "so we were kind of open-minded to a new species coming about. Jacques started us on our way to Monkey Mia. He said that Holey Fin, the main female dolphin, was waiting for something and he thought we and the birth of Harmony might be it, an important link in the transition to homo delphinus." Roberta read a book entitled "Aquatic Ape" and it sounded right to her, so she had no problem adjusting to the idea of an aquatic human.

"Do you have any past life associations with Atlantis or Lemuria or coming from another planet?" I asked.

"I've been regressed once and from that regression I went back into a baby whale body next to this immense, comforting mother. What a feeling of protection and comfort that was! And back into Greek times around the time of the 'Boy on the Dolphin.' I don't have much of a feeling for Atlantis, more of a feeling of Lemuria. Lemuria feels more like home and, of course, Hawaii feels like home."

"Hawaii is supposedly part of Lemuria. Do you have a different sense of the energy of say being in Florida, versus being over here?" I asked.

"Yeah. Florida. People go there to die. Which brings up another thing. A friend of ours accessed to a big computer bank and asked it to correlate the places where dolphins go with the places that old people go to retire. He found that there is a very close correlation of the population. It's not only tropical places, but other places of the world as well where they are very closely tied to places where people go to die and dolphins come in.

"That's interesting. Do you have any idea of what that is about? Are they helping people make the transition?" I wondered.

"Yes. In Maori legend the dead spirit, newly alive spirit, goes to the farthest north point and then the dolphins come and help bring the spirit to an island offshore, 50 miles or so offshore. It's kind of like a purgatory- type place where they await their ascension. The dolphins guide their spirits from this life into the next life.

"I also have a strong remembrance of being an African in the hull of a slave ship, dying there with many others and feeling and hearing the whales call to us. They infused us with the will to live and be in peace in our hearts."

"So they really are intermediaries and sentinels?" I asked.

"Yeah, in legend. One of the aborigine beliefs is that when we transition we become dolphins. As we grow, evolve, then we can go into dolphin bodies. They have the calling of the dolphins with dolphin sticks and so forth. There are some references to dying and dolphins in myths in their culture as well. Talking about spirituality, I was thinking about our view of God. Our view of God is Oneness. That's an apt description, don't you agree?"

"Yes," I said.

"As we become more God-like we become more One."

"Heal the rift; the separateness," I said.

"I think that perhaps dolphins may have the other view. That right now in the physical bodies they are One. That's what they are trying to become, more individuated Gods. Godheads. Sources of power that are unto their own, rather than coming together and being creative as one, separating and becoming distinct creative beings."

"Is that something they are learning from humans?" I wondered.

"We're both learning what we need from each other."

"What would be their purpose then in becoming more individuated?" I asked.

"Well, I think that we each see God as something that we're not. And here in the human world, we are very much individuals."

"We talk about the split or the separation that is causing us to harm the environment, to harm other species, so I don't understand why the dolphins would want to become more individuated."

"It's not our individuality that is harming. A person unto himself can take to being a conservationist all in its own power. He/she doesn't have to band with other people to be a conservationist or an ecologist."

"So it's individual identities," I said.

"I think we see God as something we're not instead of giving power to what we are and so we see God as being Oneness. Dolphins have become the symbol of Godlike characteristics to us. Well, dolphins see us as power-ful individual creators. One person can pick up a dolphin and take them to a tank and sit there and work with them everyday on their very own. One single person has a lot of power of creation, of whatever the creation dream is. So it's a matter of, 'What do we have for them? What do they have for us?'

"This isn't a fully evolved thought. I felt from Rosie, an asking for help with the male sexuality issue; that their male sexuality is too overpowering in their life's goals and so gets in the way of creating other things, other than sexual relationships or power-type bonds."

"Can you be more explicit?" I asked.

"I think that females think that a lot of human male energy is involved in sexuality and that there is a lot of conflict between males and females around that issue. It branches out into other things without our knowing it, but it comes back around to sexuality and identity as a human sexual being. I go on that kind of assumption. Maybe all females don't think that—maybe not even a majority, but that's kind of how I feel. I feel that female dolphins have a similar feeling; that their male dolphin friends are just too involved with sexuality and it's grounding them way too much and it's making issues where there don't need to be issues if the sexuality was just smoothed over a bit. We don't need to procreate for babies anymore. We've got this planet populated enough and now it's time to go onto something else."

"To use the sexual energy to be creative in other ways?" I asked.

"Yeah, turn it into another energy or use it some other way. Now it's time for a revision and not just purely sex drive."

"Have you ever been involved in Tantra?" I asked.

"No, not in this life, as such."

"Well," I said, "the Tantra philosophy of sexuality is to take that energy and transform it, for the man to hold his seed and to use it to generate more creative energy. They don't give up being sexual but they transmute the energy."

"I think lovemaking is wonderful and I think there are wonderful highs you can go to in it, but I don't think it has to be an issue in every relationship. I think some relationships are appropriate with sexuality and some aren't. When you're a sexually attractive female, it's difficult to go through a number of males thinking they are the one; that he is appropriate for you sexually."

"Dolphins don't mate for life," I said.

"No. They have different partners."

"Is that something they are trying to teach humans, that it's OK not to have just one mate?" I asked.

"I'm not sure. I think perhaps our families are getting more loosely defined, not necessarily as in open marriage as it's been defined in the past, but that perhaps families are not the best answer to doing our best here on the Earth and being the most creative. Dolphins may have that to teach us. The issue I was bringing up is that the female dolphin energy is asking female human energy to help transform male sexual energy."

"Not just for humans, but dolphins also?" I asked.

"Not just for humans. It may be for every species."

"Well, we talk about male humans being abusive, but in every other species I've seen, living on a farm, for instance, the sexual act is an act of aggression and there's nothing gentle or nurturing about it," I said. "Yet, we expect male humans to be gentle and nurturing and supportive when that's not a natural facet of sexuality. For the animal species, it's 'Let's do it and get it over with' unless, of course, they practice Tantra."

"Well, among the whales and dolphins, especially the whales, I do feel there is more tenderness about it," said Roberta. "And it's not to say that we don't ask for it, or any of the females. You see the females ask. It's not to put down either of the species' sexuality per se, but it's just a thought that came through from Rosie."

"Are female dolphins as sensuous or sensual as far as touching...?" I asked.

"Well, you were asking what I got from the dolphin's eye. Well, I love that physical, in the water contact with dolphins. That's where the communication for me lies."

"It's a kinesetic experience..." I said.

"It's a moving, flowing, graceful interaction between two beings, each person doing what they feel like doing in the moment in response to the other's response to your response, back and forth in a dance that is just wonderfully intuitive. They've really taught me intuition of the moment, 'right now' intuition.

"It's something without words. It's not psychic because there aren't any words, there's this feeling of what's graceful and what's not graceful and they love grace. They love grace!

"I think they create an artform of it and for some dolphins that is their creativity. Their artform is grace. They'll express grace so beautifully. That's how they are born to express themselves."

Roberta added that she spent hours with dolphins in what might be considered Tantric rituals: caressing, holding, touching, making eye contact. The dolphins responded by being very gentle and nurturing, brushing their pecs against her skin and stroking her legs with their rostrums. Touch is a very important part of the human/dolphin contact.

"Where does all this energy that they have come from? Why are they so much more energetic, for instance, than humans? Where do they get that power to thrust themselves out of the water?" I asked Roberta.

"I believe they have control of ki. I've been hit by a dolphin and the power of the rostrum actually hitting my arm was not strong enough to create the sensation of hurt all the way up my arm. Other people have reported this too, that they have the power of ki, using it like a whip...the crack of the whip, where there's the power that shoots out."

"Almost a transference of energy then, versus physical contact," I said.

"Yeah. I think they have an emotional ki and a physical ki. They can zap positive or negative; love or rejection at you. ZAP! It hits you. People can be emotionally devastated by it."

"Do you think they can use that ki power to kill people if they wanted?" I asked.

"Yeah, they could kill people if they wanted to. I've seen results of angry dolphins and people being in operations for hours having their livers sewn up and patching up broken rib cages."

"That's from actual physical contact," I said. Cetaceans are known to zap fish and stun them? Can they do that with humans?"

"I haven't seen it happen but I wouldn't put it past them. I would say they may be capable of it," Roberta said. They have respect for us. They are very controlled around us and having so much respect for us, they are not going to kill us when they can or even hurt us as much as they can. They are very controlled beings. Humans who are very cruel to them can get in the water with them and be safe. And then again, I've heard of dolphins leaping out of the water to bite a trainer or knock them off a ladder. I find them teaching me both a control of movement and trust of intuition. Control goes together with intuition."

"Tell me about this vision that you have of creating retirement homes for dolphins? Releasing them," I asked Roberta.

"For me, I imagine myself living side-by-side with a dolphin and eventually with a pod of dolphins, quietly and accessibly, where people can come and learn what dolphins are like, but not as a 'center' or something that is exploiting the dolphins or charging for learning from the dolphins. But it would be a place that would support itself. A place were there is the opportunity for people that truly just want to live around dolphins, to come and live around dolphins."

"A human/dolphin community," I said.

"In the Human/Dolphin Foundation, I was the director of Project Communion which was in-water tank work leading to a human/dolphin community release program. I don't see setting up some sort of spiritual center. At first, I had ideas of a dolphin retirement home, but then I don't want to label it so that it becomes only that. If some people are not into dolphins only, they could do their art there if they wanted to. It would be a place where dolphins can form a pod and go out to sea together—previously captive dolphins. They may not be accepted by the wild dolphins and they'll have a better chance of survival together in a pod. They can come back and receive fish or nourishment or human interaction when they choose and go out when they choose. It would always be there."

"You're looking for a place in the Hawaiian Islands to do that?" I asked.

"I've been looking at different places in Florida, New Zealand, Australia and always perking my ears up when people mention different islands in the Caribbean or South Seas. Right now I find myself in the Hawaiian Islands, so I'm looking around here. I'm not sure where or when, or if it will happen. It's a personal longing and you can only go by your own personal feelings. My personal feeling is I want to live with dolphins. I LOVE dolphins and that's my motivation. I want to be in the water with dolphins and I love them and I can't take any more of living with them in a tank. I want to bring them out of the tank. It's a very personal, you can call it selfish motivation, but at the same time I have a great sense of wanting to provide other people with that experience as well who are truly drawn to that."

"What happened with the people who swam with the dolphins? You mentioned handicapped, children, the elderly?" I asked.

"Handicapped people and also groups of children."

"Was there any follow-up on what happened with those people?" I asked.

"No, but we all hear reports now. Now it comes back. You said you keep running into people who swam with Joe and Rosie. We had the only swim program in the world for a long time and people weren't charged to come and swim with Joe and Rosie. They only had to have a connection with one of the people that worked there and that person could bring them in to swim. John and Toni brought in stars and scientists, Baba Ram Dass, Susan Sarandon, Rupert Sheldrake, Olivia Newton-John, Robin Williams and Kris Kristoferson and others. I have a book of reports from people that have swam with Joe and Rosie during one year."

Just as with Stewart Marshall, I kept drawing the interview to a close, thanking Roberta and turning the recorder off, only to find we were still talking dolphins.

Roberta continued. "I found a language I wanted to teach the dolphins and I began by teaching them four symbols which when put together meant dolphin. Each of the symbols in the language is one whole word in our language. The word for 'dolphin' that I made up was the composite 'feeling, water, life, thing'. The four symbols were a half a heart, a square with an equal sign below, a leaf and a large black dot, all strung together. In a state of meditation I'd say in my head, 'Feeling-water-life-thing, feeling-water-life-thing, feeling-water-life-thing.'"

"Then you flashed the image—a visual image," I said.

"I had cards in front of me that I printed on and each symbol was on a different card. The next morning I went to the tank and Joe came up to me and I went, 'Well, what's new? What went on?' Let's get some confirmation here. The tank is perfectly circular and from the point where I was standing he went down and cut straight across, tangent to the other end of the tank and then came in a swooping circle and around—right in the shape of a half a heart. Then he looks up at me and squirts water at me. He never does this! Just squirted water at me. Whoosh! Whoosh! Then he turns over very slowly, still concentrating on me, and lifts up his pec. What does his pec look like? A leaf. He kind of puts it up there and wiggles it a little bit, not a wave or anything—just kind of hangs it up there and then down he went and came up underneath a black innertube and played with it on the end of his rostrum real slowly, again with eye contact. Then he came over to me and did a tail slap right in front of me. BAM! And swam off."

"Amazing," I said. "Is there any doubt they understand what we tell them?" We laughed.

"Unfortunately, I didn't continue it, but I had my confirmation for myself. It's not something I can publish, but it's confirmation for myself. I played remarkable games with Joe. In one of them, we would charge toward each other spontaneously and I would just go full force underwater, flippers on, as fast as I could. I also had a scuba hooka hose on so I could stay underwater for as long as I wanted. I went right for him 'cause I knew he could veer off if he wanted to, and at the last minute he would veer off and we'd keep eye contact and as we passed each other, I would wink and he would wink and then we would charge again and just go zooming by. If for some reason he couldn't wink because we went by too fast, as soon as he saw me again and made eye contact, he'd wink. We did this 11 times."

"Without any former training?" I asked.

"Just a spontaneous, once-in-a-lifetime experiment. It just happened. I never tried to do it again. I winked a lot to say, 'I love you' to Terry, the dolphin in the Circe project. That was my thing. I would wink at her when I'd really feel emotionally connected to her. This is my sweetheart. In a special tender moment, I would wink at her and she started winking back at me and then at the end of the day, I'd say good-bye, leaving the tank at last. 'I'm freezing. I gotta go home,' I'd say. She'd wink at me and I'd have to come back and hold her one more time. There were a lot of special moment. Swimming side-by-side with Joe we had a bubble around us where water didn't flow and time didn't exist."

We turned the recorder off to take the pumpkin pie out of the oven and check on kids. Then Roberta continued.

"I'm not a channeler. I'm not a psychic. I came in from a scientific factual approach, and believing dolphins were our Masters and were to be listened to. Suddenly, all around me as the years went on, people started worshipping them and receiving channeled messages through them. I didn't have that happen. I had few encounters in the wild while these people were having amazing experiences in the wild.

There was one day when I could hear them. There was a group of us on a boat. A group of people that are like-minded can form a group mind if they are directed enough and focused enough. I was in the water and they were on the boat and I received questions and gave the dolphins answers. They asked things like, 'What are these boats? Where do they come from? What are the cars? What is all this stuff you're doing and building and where does it come from?' I said, 'We can do anything. What do you want us to do? We're absolutely capable of any technology. They said, 'We want to go to the stars."

Laughing I asked, "Which star?"

"They looked up and said, 'We want to go to the stars. 'They asked me how I swam and I swam all different strokes. They asked me who I was and what people were? I had a conversation with them, but that was the only time. It was brought about by a group mind. There is a group in San Francisco headed by Dr. Richard Gierack that formulated a group mind and went down to Baja and met with a dolphin group mind who were very startled to learn that, 'Here are humans in group mind. What are they doing in group mind?' He planned out a week's activities in a month and when the group went physically down to Baja they met with the dolphins in the places they had planned the month before with the dolphins. That group, through their experimentation, felt that three people could transfer emotional-type information and five people could transfer images of time and place and more concrete information. Some people, channelers, accept that they can do that themselves. They may tap into a collective group mind or have enough power of themselves. If 'normal' people want to create a kind of out-of-body group mind, they can do it."

"Do you think when you're communicating with dolphins, it's generally through the heart?" I asked.

"Yes, mine is. I've stood at the edge of the tank on a perfectly calm beautiful day with the dolphins sleeping in the tank. With no body language give away that I could tell, they would excite themselves into a frenzy, where they would be chasing each other around the tank and jumping clear just by giving energy and loving them so much. Just saying, 'Oh Boy!' They'd be racing around the tank after being calm and peaceful.

"And trust. Communication is developed through trust. I trusted the dolphins. Terry is a dolphin who was notorious for biting people and I trusted her completely. She opened up to me and let me play in her mouth. One of the researchers working with her said, 'Boy, that would be the day when I got to play in Terry's mouth. I dream of that level of trust.' Here I'd already done it and wasn't able to tell them about it because I was private about my developing a relationship with her. She had carefully led me. My hand was about a half a foot in front of her rostrum and she opened her mouth a couple of inches. Then she put her rostrum right on my hand and then backed up and opened it again a little bit more. Then she put it where I could see that she couldn't possibly get her mouth around my hand. My hand was straight up and down and her rostrum was open against my fingers and palm. Then she backed up and came again and slowly mouthed my hand, a tiny bit at a time. The development of trust was so controlled and so cognizant. Pretty soon she was mouthing my arm all over without hurting me. Here was a dolphin that people greatly feared—had a lot of fear of her hurting them by snapping at them. She would snap at them. The remarkable thing wasn't that she missed them, it was that she MISSED them. She was perfectly capable of biting them if she wanted to."

"How long had she been in captivity?" I asked.

"She was probably in captivity about 10 or 15 years when I first met her. Now it's about 20 years. She's about a 30-year-old dolphin."

Just then Claud came up with Leilani on his back. We'd been brainstorming earlier in the day for the name of a non-profit organization that would provide seed money out of the proceeds of this book for release programs and other projects that would ensure greater freedom for all species on the planet, including humans.

"I've got it," he said. "We'll call it 'SAVE THE HUMANS FOUNDATION'"

Roberta laughed, "How presumptuous."

"Maybe they don't want to save us," I chuckled.

"Sister, have you been Saved?" Claud asked jokingly.

"No, but I've been reborn many times," I laughed. "The dolphins will love it," I assured him.

Roberta went on, "At the bottom of the tank, scrubbing away, the dolphins demanded trust. A female dolphin that was seen as the more powerful of the group would come skimming right over my head, very slowly and would let her flukes just brush past my head. If I flinched at all, she would whack me with her flukes. So I had to be very controlled and open and trusting to make sure she wouldn't whack me with her flukes. Then she would pass right over. If I flinched. Boom!"

"It's like somebody shooting an apple off the top of your head or having somebody throw knives around your body," I said.

"Yeah. With their mouths too, they would insist on me putting my hand across their teeth and brushing along their teeth all the way to the back of their mouths. If I flinched anytime during that or didn't have a completely relaxed trusting hand in their mouths, they would bite me."

"It was like, 'OK, lady, if you're going to hang around you have to get over your fear,'" I said.

"Yeah, and most of the time, the little fear that I did have had been developed by hearing people's stories, telling me, 'Terry bites. Terry bites.' Or, 'They're going to beat you up.' The male divers were much more frightened of them than I was. I'd go on scrubbing and they'd be fencing with the dolphins. They'd all get up against a wall fending them off and I'd be down on the bottom scrubbing away. There was a 20-foot pilot whale that had a crush on me. He would come up and again, do things of trust. He would lay on top of me. This is 2,000 potential pounds on land, laying on top of your legs or biting on your flippers."

"I would say he had a 'crush' on you," I told her.

"Right. I've had him come with his huge black hulk and just come right up to my head and infuse me with all this sound and information. I knew it was information of some sort. Several different levels at once, several different kinds of information all at once like...Whoosh! Stories of the ages. I know I have them in here. I have no idea what the information is yet but it's in there. All I could do was say to myself, 'Hold this. Hold this. Keep this here somewhere,' and try to be as receptive as possible. I'd say, 'Oh, this is great. Wait till I decipher this.'"

"That's probably the next book—maybe your own book—it will just come pouring out," I said.

"All that I can write is fantasy because the 'facts' that I write would not be considered non-fiction."

We stopped talking to eat dinner fresh from the garden and hot pumpkin pie, fresh from the oven. And for at least the tenth time I said, "This is it. The book is finished. No more stories."

Just then a chiropractor and his girlfriend who were visiting the community for a few days appeared for dinner and as we sat chatting and getting acquainted, I couldn't resist asking, "Do you have any dolphin stories?"

"Oh, yeah. I swam with them in Florida...at the place where Joe and Rosie were..."

20 *Living the Dolphin Lifestyle*

PEOPLE HAVE A habit of showing up spontaneously around Jim "the dolphin man's" pastoral paradise and I was no exception. One afternoon I dropped by and found him wrapped in a pareau, napping in a hammock beside the stream. Next thing I knew, we were up to our pecs in a dialogue on dolphins and humans in community, room temperature fusion, the pyramid structure of palladium and the measurement of time, which I learned doesn't exist. I'd given up getting his story months earlier, but he just happened to be in a talkative mood and I just happened to have my tape recorder along in my backpack. Long after the sun had set, the stars had fallen into the sea and the mosquitos had been lulled to sleep, Jim was still expounding. We ran out of tape before he ran out of talk. Jim speaks the language of a mathematician/scientist and I am basically a mystic. A vast mental schism lay between us, but the subject of dolphins has a way of bringing people together at the heart level. As time passed the communication gap became unimportant. Hanging out with Jim is like entering a mind warp. We zoomed from the bottom of the ocean depths to black holes in space and beyond, back into present time and out again. It was like spending six hours on a carnival ride that turns you upside down and inside out. When you finally get back to Earth, you can't walk straight. My mind was stretched beyond recovery.

As founder of the Cetacean Relation Society, Jim assumes the role of inspiring people to "stop the bad impressions" we humans are making in the watery world of the dolphins and whales and put our "best fin forward." The dolphins called him to Hawaii in the late 1960s when he took a sabbatical from teaching high school math. He spent his time free diving, surfing and connecting with cetaceans in deep water. For several years he'd been hanging out with Olympic divers off Catalina Island meeting and greeting dolphins in their living room at around 70 to 100 feet and taking part with them in a natural underwater ballet. He became so enamored of the "dolphin lifestyle" that he decided to try it for himself.

"It's wonderful," he says. "No worries. Being happy. Daily naps in hammocks by the quiet stream or laughing rapids or roaring waterfall. No bills." He retired from teaching formally and for the past 18 years has become the informal teacher of hundreds of people who drop by to visit him on his land.

His philosophy is to live simply, cause harm to no living thing and to not contribute to the pollution of the planet by driving cars, or consuming and collecting material goods. "I help rather than hinder Gaia to recover from the enormous burden of unnatural wastes we have expected her to absorb." He's lived without a car for years because he says, "A gallon of gas costs a million dollars in cosmic costing and takes out 18 pounds of oxygen to convert to CO_2. Bad exchange." He sees the issues of industrialized society and its pollution of the environment as overwhelming if you look at them all at once, but believes humankind is sufficiently ethical and realistic enough to change its ways, given workable options.

One of the workable options he is helping to create is to show people how to live self-sufficiently from the food grown on a 21-bed biodynamic mini-farm. "Four billion people are going to have only 2,100 square feet of arable land by the year 2000." We humans, he senses, won't have a future, unless we stop squandering and wasting resources. "I am a little pilot (whale) project for humanity," he adds, "honestly reporting the headway we make toward leaving as little trash on the path behind us as the dolphins do."

He's been closely following the developments of cool temperature fusion and has had a long-time fascination and revulsion for a picture of the palladium crystal—which he found in his daughter's chemistry textbook. "It's almost pornographic," he insists. "The news is crackling with chemist Pon's claim of room temperature fusion in a palladium core wrapped within a platinum helix and energized to draw deuterium into the palladium matrix. Deuterium is a common constituent of sea water so there is plenty of it. We could have energy in wild places without destroying the wild places to get the energy there." Instead of dangerous poles marching down the road, we would have solar panels on rooftops. "If we are addicted to grid electricity and we are a growing population," says Jim, "well, goodbye to all the remaining wild places." Palladium, on the other hand, holds out the promise of clean energy but Jim sees a danger. "Its availability holds the possibilities of the hydrogen bomb being in the hands of defective individuals rather than defective governments. These are dangerous enough without these million new wild cards (individuals fooling around) which would create an enormous up-scaling of instability. Total change of game! Change is already almost catastrophic, so the dream of clean energy for individual utopian humans might be here but it might also have brought with it the possibility of enormous destructive power to individual anti-utopian humans. That could be our doom. Chaos! The drowned temples of Atlantis!"

Speaking about humans he said, "We're sure an explosive thing. To think after all the other beings living millions and millions of years—that much time—that humans have come on in such a short time and threatened the end of the Earth. It's amazing what a virulent form of life humanity is. Watching that Earth through billions of years developing, and then having some form of life that could come on so quickly in technology and go beyond their little muscles and discover the secrets of the sun—one could be horrified by that. But" says Jim, "I'm glorified that we have been adequate to the understanding of the fundamental laws of the universe."

Enter the dolphins: Are they coming into the act to teach us how to survive our own brillance? As archetypes of cosmic consciousness, they could show us how to manage, moderate and balance our intellectual power and hi-tech knowledge through the wisdom and compassion of the heart.

Jim plans to experiment with the cool temperature fusion idea by creating an undersea temple where humans and dolphins can come together and learn from one another. The undersea temple will be secreted upon chicken wire with about 500 watts being put into it. It secretes the minerals of the ocean, mainly magnesium. "You can make organic shapes very rapidly, hard as coral, harder than concrete." He envisions the shapes looking like the palladium crystal in the chemistry textbook. "I'm going to use this technology so that we can swim through these undersea temples with dolphins. These are the Atlantean shapes. Perhaps this recent knowledge of the transmuting of elements in the palladium matrix was discovered earlier and destroyed civilization and this sources my revulsion to the picture of the palladium crystal. Dolphins swimming in the temple before signified a drowned civilization. This time it will signify man's readiness to become more dolphin-like to avert a catastrophe," says Jim.

"We're returning to the knowledge of the sun, when we talk about fusion," Jim relates. "We're really talking about the knowledge of how the sun works and bringing it to ourselves rather than a thing that is out in the distance 93 million miles away. You only get one-sixth billionth of its total energy output. It's almost insignificant. I think one day of that hitting the Earth is more energy than we've used in the history of Man, but we just haven't harnessed it. It has been harnessed for millions of years through photosynthesis and biological transmutations (fusion) then through decay and through dinosaurs eating the photosynthetic creations—the plants — and running higher energy. We're moving toward higher order and we're coming into a new range of higher order, and knowledge is what it is the order of. This knowledge has immense power, but it has immense danger."

Jim teaches and models pod consciousness and feels that to live in harmony on the planet we must all become "podners." He sees himself as a sort of a "Catcher in the Rye." The catcher stands out in the rye field and catches the children before they run off the cliff which they can't see. In another realm, he says, "I'm a scout that looks at ideas and lives myself into them and programs myself through them to see how we humans are going to handle it."

Embodying, not with his mind, but with his body, he attempts to live the theory of relativity and be in n-dimensional space. "I don't want to believe a truth is too abstract to be lived in the body/mind. I'm trying to have the knowledge of it in my mind and find out, discover by meditating, and the other ways—swimming with dolphins—what it means when our mind has so far outstripped our body. Our mind has out-evolved our body in three crucial ways that can be reunited in an underwater kinesthetic restructuring which I've developed and call 3-D, G-free, automobility. I find our body/mind adequate to the understanding of the unity of cognition of being in the Universe."

Having brought himself into unity with the dolphins under water, he wants to share that experience with others by establishing a school of humans who will "experience ourselves not just as solitary human beings but as podners. How do we do that?" Jim asks and then answers, "By shaping our gladiatorial energy like the dolphins. The dolphin lives in that full-on beingness and they're not in danger because of it. They live in a full-on presence of timelessness because there is no time to protect." In this state, he says, "You are so richly yourself that the conservative aspect is out-to-lunch for a while." The conservative aspect is that part of ourselves that lives in fear of the future and fails to enjoy the moment. "The custodian of the moment takes a vacation," Jim says. "Everything is right here, all at once. The image of ourself sitting in a body thinking about the external world is wrong. Time is what keeps everything from happening at once, a condition of our cognition," he insists.

We humans lose our sense of timelessness when we incarnate in the human body. "If you want to have knowledge about the world, then you're going to lose the unity—you're going to lose the pure experiencing, the pure being. Rather than a human being, you're going to be a human doing. Well, dolphins are humans," he explains. "They are the true humans. We haven't reached full humanity yet." Jim's hope is that we humans can recover our beingness. "Dolphins are the cue—not just dolphins, but the proper thought about what dolphins are—the proper relation to dolphins. We're way down the line in bad impressions but the proper approach is coming to the dolphin. What do the dolphins think of us who capture them from their free, unbounded, untrammeled existence and place them in a tank with concrete walls creating a nightmare of reverberatory echoes? What is being communicated to dolphins and ourselves by these, our actions?" Pondering the Alaskan oil spill, he says, "The humpbacks, our friends, are going back to the Bering Straits to all that oil. Right now, if we could electro-magnetically tune into them, we could turn them around and say, 'Don't go home for a while. We messed up your home. We haven't learned how to make love, we've only learned how to have sex. Excuse us. We're sketchy at this point. We're teetering on the edge.'"

He relates to dolphins as advanced beings and sees that they are way beyond us in their "dimensions of joy and bodily energy, a divine comedy realization, with humor and togetherness." During one of his dolphin engagements, he says, "I was singing to the dolphins a song about their divinity and one appeared and was photographed with a full-on historical halo," which he believes is the first photo of an enlightened being. "This is their idea of a good joke after we had eight telepathic together connections within 20 minutes."

To Jim, "Dolphins represent total perfection of embodiment of beingness—not doing. When people think, they go right to comfort and wealth and protection from the world. My place takes people out of that need to be human and not do all those things of comfort. Because we're so weak, we fall right into the trap of wanting more…doing more." Dolphins, on the other hand are into 'beingness.' "While humans are doing, doing, dolphins are being, being. "We're coming up to this ancient knowledge of how to live on the planet, peacefully and successfully and without fear. We're spiritually coming home. We've never been there in this form. So all these metaphors of what actual freedom in the moment is and how you can live it—they can be lived but they can't be lived out of a world that has denied its own future."

Jim says our minds create metaphors because we are the realities within the metaphor. "We are Gaia awakening. We are Gaia who has a heartbeat of 7.85 hertz, our alpha rhythm. We are that thing waking up. We are a spherical shell of being living the life-forms within a little bit of a depth of the Earth and atmosphere. We are a hologram—expanding light—expanding Universe. We're a hologram that has its major existence as a magnetic form living within the resonant cavity of the Earth."

He has hope for humans in the midst our awakening. "Thank God, we are topophilics. We have the ability to love place. We have the ability to create a beautiful place on the planet and live in the Garden of Eden. We're born in miracles. We live in miracles to the extent that if we truly want to embody that and not hide, we get to. We get to live in miracles and they're ever present. And if we are willing to live them and not record them or have knowledge of them, you can dip into the realms of the unknown and then to the unknowable where you'll not return with anything that you can speak of. Its the unknown, the unknowable realm, out of which, great masters teach, all true wisdom arises.

He suggests that we "Loose the bonds that now strangle us at the noonday of our understanding of survival's laws. Copy the dolphin that lived eons beyond us—with big brains—harmoniously. Regard your imminent death. Adjust your scale of necessities. Get together, but get together simply naked. Out of your garden. Don't get together out of technology with a fast boat. Get together naked as an animal that walks down the mountain to the sea and gets in. What's the least we can hurt it? Can we make fins out of bamboo? Can we scar the Earth not at all with our toxic path? Leave no toxic path, is what we have to do. Ahimsa. Cause harm to no thing. If we have this be our goal of living in this state of dolphin harmlessness and yet full-on knowledge and power to create anything that we can imagine, then we shall have become gods, non-amnesiac gods. Our spiritual birthright will have been fulfilled. History will end. Our story will begin."

Jim calls himself a "black hole scout," someone who likes to explore the outer fringes of agreed-upon reality and beyond. One of the holes he likes to scout is the idea that we may be computers. "How do you know you're not a computer?" he asks. Another is the idea that in the future, it may be normal to have dolphin friends who want to get together and play. "They might come up on land. They will want to windsurf or skydive." It doesn't seem too farfetched when you remember the legend of the Dogons—which depicts our descending from Sirius B as half fish, half human.

In a flight of fancy, he imagines going down to the pools below the waterfall on his land at night, building a roaring fire, turning on underwater lights and swimming to dolphin vocalizations that were recorded earlier in the day out in the ocean. "We don't use cars, we only walk on green paths to friends' homes and to the sea. We go to the garden for food and we live like dolphins. We catch fish out of the ocean, share time with the dolphins and bring food to them. "Maybe they're going to like Thai basil in a special sauce on top of tofu."

I imagine them waddling up the road to eat linguine and pesto with us and Jim becomes inspired. "Maybe they're going to come up and swim some laps in the pool. Maybe they're going to go off the waterfall when the water in the stream is on full force." When the dam gates above Jim's land are opened, the stream turns into a raging river. "I'm afraid—but they might want to. They might want to swim up the waterfall when it's heavy—play salmon. We'll show them some films of salmon and they'll probably just try it right away. We'll meet them down there in the video room and swim around with them and play them some Rachmaninoff. We'll give them instruments so that with their minds they can sing their song. Anything humans do with their hands, dolphins can do 'cause they've got all the ability to choose what button to push with their sonar. Their singing turns into their choosing new levels of time—manipulation played backwards—'finipulation.'"

"Civilization," says Jim, "is just beginning to arrive. It just begins to arrive when you have context and we haven't had context until we had dolphins coming into consciousness. The end of the long loneliness."

In his book "Dolphin Dolphin," author Wade Doak refers to Jim as "homo delphinus," but says Jim, "as the Victorians classified us as homo sapiens sapiens—man thinking about thinking—homo hobo delphinus might be more appropriate for me. I am unwilling to support the idea of working for a living when dolphins don't and they have better lives than most of ours.

"How can we stand for a thing like that? To the hammock!"

He advises all humans to retreat "to your most wonderful place to exhale your own fragrance, tea bag that you are, hanging in the cosmos." As for himself, he says "Hammocks for me, by waterfalls, in trees, by the kitten box, in the garden, beneath my favorite fruit-dropping tree."

PM Magazine featured Jim training a pod of people to join him in his attempt to hold the interest of dolphins by being interesting. "The 11th commandment" Jim says, is "'Thou shalt not bore God.' It's my motto with 'dolphin' standing in for God while she is on vacation. It's good practice for them," says the wizard of timeless being.

After nearly six hours of talk and six weeks of pondering what he told me, I concluded his main message to be *"Consume less. Do less. Be more."* Maybe mystics and mathematicians have more in common than they realize.

His last words were "Live in harmony with the Earth to be worthy of communication from the dolphins. Live as free as the dolphins."

21 *Dolphins: Open Heart Therapists*

THREE YEARS TO the weekend after my first connection with what had seemed to be dolphin spirits on the open ocean, I found myself crossing the rugged channel between Moloka'i and Maui on my way to Lanai on A.J.'s trimaran. Roberta, Claud, A.J. and I hoped to swim with the spinner dolphins in the wild outside the harbor. The sea was the color of lapis, deep blue and brilliant under the afternoon sun. A.J. stood at the helm, his hair flowing behind him, looking victorious and confident like a conqueror, as if he'd been a Polynesian chief or sea captain in past lives who had maneuvered this passage many times and knew exactly how the boat and waves would dance together in harmony. The challenge for A.J. was to slice through the white crests of 10 foot swells without getting us wet.

We picked up Roberta near the wharf and the next morning motored to Lanai. Just as we were coming to the entrance to the harbor, we spotted the dolphins in the distance, near the rocks. It had been a long hot afternoon. I'd fallen off the boat, but managed to catch a sheet on the side and found myself being drug through the water some distance before A.J. could reach the engine to turn it off. We took it as an opportunity to stop for a swim. Claud floated on his back and spewed water, like a spouting whale. We were all played out and decided to wait until the later in the day to take the Zodiac out to greet the dolphins.

They didn't disappoint us. An hour or so later, as we surfed through the waves, veering toward the rocks, we spotted them come up alongside a small yellow fishing boat moving toward the harbor. They leaped and frolicked and spun around in the air several times as we clapped and cheered them on, just as I had pictured them during a meditation in Jim's pool a few weeks earlier. Hearing us, they apparently decided to swim over and check us out. We got so excited, we forgot what we knew to be the appropriate way to meet them—enter the water one at a time, slowly, so as not to frighten them. Instead, three of us plunged in at once. A pod of 50 or so swept by beneath us and zoomed on before we knew what was happening.

The next morning we decided to hang around the marine preserve hoping to swim with them in the bay. We spotted them searching for their breakfast, but they decided to by-pass the bay and head toward the rocks around the corner. As Claud and I hiked down the cliff a few minutes later, I looked out to see two human forms swimming out of the bay on the trail of the dolphins. By then they were long gone, but the human dolphins persisted. One of them undulated in the water mimicking the motions of the dolphin. "She's got to know Starheart and Jim," I thought to myself. We watched her swim through the surf and waited until she climbed the cliff to talk with her. Sure enough, Jim and Starheart were friends and had shown her how to undulate and swim like a dolphin.

"The last time I was at Jim's place we colored together," she told me laughing. Her name was Toy and she was raised on an island off the Florida coast where many dolphins are captured for marine parks. No doubt she had many stories to tell. With a name like Toy, I'm sure the dolphins love her.

The other swimmer turned around and swam back into the bay whence he had come. We connected with him later. He was from South America and first came into communion with dolphins through a channel who had taught him to mimic their clicking sounds. He imitated them perfectly and used the sounds as a tool for healing. "The dolphins transformed my life," he insisted.

We talked with him briefly as he waited for the ferry to take him back to Maui. He was anxious to meet people who could show him how to connect with dolphins at will, at his convenience rather than their's. "That's not how it works," I told him. "You're in their world here and they don't keep schedules or make appointments." When it comes to connecting with dolphins in the wild, we humans are definitely not in control. The dolphins, however, lured him to venture farther out into deep, rough water in their pursuit than he would have otherwise and had stretched him, as they have a habit of doing, beyond his usual limitations.

That afternoon, we took the Zodiac out once more and skirted the rocks, waiting for the dolphins to appear. They didn't oblige, so we entertained ourselves by acting like dolphins in the deep, deep water, hoping the sounds of our laughter and frolicking might attract them. It didn't.

It became clear to me once more that we do not need to swim with dolphins to be more dolphin-like, to be spontaneous, playful, lighthearted, energetic, and free—to swim with the dolphin inside ourselves.

As Helen, the captive dolphin advocate said, it's time for us to go to an underwater context, to learn what it's like to live as a dolphin in the ocean—to think like a dolphin and to discover what it's like to be deprived of and to miss the sound of the ocean, the rhythm of the waves, the interaction with other forms of sea life. It's time for we human dolphins to daily feel the sun on our skin and the experience of traveling in vast open spaces while enjoying the energy of freedom and play. When we "crawl into the skin of the dolphin," we will have a greater sense of responsibility toward them—toward all life-forms on the planet, including ourselves.

Two days before the manuscript was due at the typesetters, one last big piece of the puzzle came to me in an article entitled "The Healing Power of Dolphins" by Janet Colli, a transformational counselor. In 1987, Janet was dying of cancer when she had a dream. In the dream she wandered up to a bulletin board and saw a notice. It said she was to dedicate her life to facilitating dolphin encounters with cancer patients. "My life?" she asked.

She'd had no dreams of dolphins nor any desire to connect with them until then.

Her cancer healed that year and she decided to explore the idea of whether or not "close-encounters" with dolphins could indeed spark a cellular change and healing in other cancer patients. It wasn't until a year later that she had an opportunity to swim with the dolphins in Florida. Janet wore a life jacket to keep her afloat which made maneuvering difficult. A dolphin surfaced next to her. Janet grabbed its dorsal fin and was taken for a spin around the lagoon. It struck her later, that her dolphin encounter mirrored a basic pattern in her life. She had difficulty trusting her own strength and believing her environment would keep her "afloat." She often struggled to maintain control. "I had always kicked and pushed people away, when what I wanted most was to be close. But closeness demands at least one open heart. Since my diagnosis of cancer four years ago, I have made many faltering attempts to get close to other people. When I reached out and grabbed that dolphin's fin, the effort of all those years was transformed."

Janet's story is similar to many others I'd been hearing in the previous two years. The dolphins *are* open heart therapists. There is no doubt they are leading many people to heal old wounds. But my curiosity was still unsatisfied. I wanted to know why dolphins are appearing in human consciousness at an accelerating rate. The phenomena behind 'dolphinmania' and 'delphic bliss deficiency syndrome' was still a mystery to me. That is, it was—-until I read something Janet wrote. "Dr. Stephen Jozsef, a biofeedback researcher who was formerly with the Drake Institute for Behavioral

Medicine," she said, "believes that dolphins exist predominately in the alpha state." He hypothesizes that because they live in alpha state themselves, they facilitate that state in humans.

"Aha!" Suddenly the mystery was solved. **ALL** the people I had met and interviewed were involved in processes, careers or lifestyles that took them into alpha state. Meditation, deep breathing, listening to soft music or to the methodical beat of drums and chants, shifts us into alpha state, as does living a contemplative life. And, as Stewart said, painting is a form of meditation as well. The people who shared their dolphin stories with me were rebirthers, artists, musicians, meditators, former dolphin trainers or like Jim Loomis, live simply and quietly and spend a great deal of time around and in the water, living close to nature. They have been routinely shifting into alpha state for many years and connecting with 'pod' consciousness. Many had journeyed and spent time at vortex sites, ancient ruins or in the wilderness where the veil between dimensions is thin and creates what an artist friend calls "bleed through."

Since more people are participating today in these alpha state processes through personal growth seminars, support groups, and various forms of therapy, it follows that more and more people are tuning into cetacean consciousness, which Aldo Aulucino described as a "communal collective consciousness." The language of this consciousness is non-verbal and comes through as a "felt" sense that is then translatable through symbols, images, movement, music and art. Children are in an alpha state, according to Janet's article, until they are around six years old, which explains why the dolphins are so drawn to them at petting tanks and in the wild. They are on the same wave length. Clearly, dolphins and children have a lot to teach adults about the process of 'lightening up' which is what the Earth itself is doing— shifting to a higher vibration rate as it is magnetically drawn toward the sun by the movement of massive planets that are in orbit around us.

There is after all, a logical explanation for even the most mystical phenomena, if we open our hearts and minds to realities that can only be perceived, sensed and felt from within at this time in evolution.

In alpha state, we are very relaxed and we sense the interconnectedness of all life-forms at a much deeper level. Our awareness is heightened. Some of that heightened consciousness is retained as we come back into the waking state. It is that "awareness" of interconnectedness that changes us and causes us to pause and think about the effect we are having on the environment and in our personal lives. As we and the planet move closer to alpha state and stay there longer, it becomes more and more difficult to act irresponsibly—and get away with it. It seems we are evolving as a species and as a culture, in spite of our old, bad habits.

Rebirther Bob Mandel has written a wonderful book called "Open

Heart Therapy" in which he talks about Primal Laws which are, in essence, the operating codes that run our computer-like bodies and our lives. These unconscious, automatic beliefs dictate how we react and behave toward ourselves and one another. In reading the book, I realized that my Primal Law *was* "I don't want to be here. I'm unwanted." Born to parents who filed bankruptcy at the end of the Depression, lost their home and didn't want another child, I arrived sensing that "I don't belong here." Studies have shown that babies pick up non-verbal feelings of rejection and unhappiness while still in the mother's womb. My reaction to being born into and raised in a hostile and unhappy environment was to assume the cloak of invisibility and to freeze emotionally to protect myself from overwhelming feelings that, as an infant and child, were threatening to survival.

It was easy for me to "hide-out" and at the same time "fit-in" in a culture where varying degrees of emotional paralysis may well be commonplace but are as yet unrecognized. "Denial of feelings" is a major symptom of dysfunctional family systems. Once I got through my teenage years, I didn't "act-out" again until I decided it was time to thaw out in my late 30s. The traditionally trained psychotherapist and psychologist I went to for help were baffled by me. After a certain amount of time, they ran out of skills and didn't know how to treat someone who was frozen at the core, but beginning to thaw around the edges. At that point, I began to fall through the cracks of agreed upon reality and had to find my own way out through alternative methods of therapy and self-help processes. It was writing autobiographically about the past that literally blasted the block of ice inside me to pieces. It was a metaphor for my suppressed rage, pain and fear. I experienced a major shamanic breakthrough which looked to the people around me as though it were a "breakdown." It was a harsh way to be reborn but I was determined to be free.

Like Janet Colli, I wanted to be close to people, and at the same time I kept pushing them away. It was the dolphins who finally released me. In allowing myself to pursue them, to let go of my attachments to people, places and things and follow the callings of the heart—I experienced what it was like to be free, fluid and flowing.

Just as the dolphins called me, I now call for the 'loners' of the world to unite. It is time to let go of our fears of being intimate, of feeling dependent and helpless and powerless, to go "beyond boundaries" as Gigi Coyle says, and open ourselves to the reality of the New Aquarian Age. This New Age is one in which cooperation and unity are the by-words. 'Getting close' is an overwhelming emotional risk for someone whose experiences have taught and reinforced a belief that "everyone I 'get close to' dies or leaves," and yet, I'm unwilling to pay the consequences of a closed heart. I prefer to keep 'pushing myself off the plank' as Stewart says—into relationships—into the writing of books—into workshops, adventures and experiences that will stretch me beyond the limits of my ego-fears.

I see the dolphins as the Open Heart Therapists of the Aquarian Age, come to teach us about fluidity and flow, about opening the heart to other dimensions—to the invisible realms—out of which our souls chose to incarnate in physical form. As we join them in alpha state and become more 'childlike' in our behavior and beliefs, it is easier to let go of rigid mind-sets and no-longer-workable institutional structures and attitudes that have led to the pollution of the planet, the devastation of its natural resources and to war, conflict and the abuse of ourselves and one another.

Splitting the atom and using nuclear force destructively, without the wisdom of the heart, we have brought the Garden of Eden, to the brink of disaster. Splitting Adam into Eve in myth and metaphor, as well as in reality, created a polar planet on which we could come to know ourselves but now it's time to reunite in consciousness, to experience that there is no separation between man and woman, between human and animal, between higher and lower forms of life. We are all sons and daughters of 'God'—of universal consciousness. Earth **can** be a Garden of Eden once again—a "New Atlantis," a place where unity and cooperation and abundance provide every human and every life-form the sustenance it needs to evolve spiritually, mentally, emotionally and physically.

Jane, my friend who died of cancer, had given me a ring following a visualization she had led during a joint workshop we facilitated. She beckoned us into a treasure cave above a white sand beach. The cave was filled with every treasure imaginable and we were to choose one to bring back with us. I came out of the visualization empty-handed, so Jane pulled a ring of lapis, as blue as the ocean deep, from her finger and gave it to me. It was set in gold and fringed with tiny diamonds. The ring, she told me, had been styled as a symbol of Janus, the Roman god of portals, of endings and beginnings, which usually depicts two faces looking in opposite directions. I wore it every day for nearly two years following her death until a stone fell out and I took it as a sign to put the ring away.

The stone fell out a few days after I had thrown away a manuscript I'd been working on for seven years. It was entitled "In Search of the Nourishing Lifestyle" and dealt with resolving issues around feelings of powerlessness and abandonment that stemmed from the death and loss of caretakers and loved ones. Writing about the past and thinking about the past trapped me in suffering and pain, in the unresolved pain of those who had died, as well as my own. A year or so earlier the voice of inner guidance had come through one morning as I lay in bed meditating and said, "As long as you are searching, you will never find."

"OK, I replied, "I'll call it 'Creating the Nourishing Lifestyle.'"

The voice retorted, "As long as you are creating...."

"OK, OK. I got the message. I'll call it "Living the Nourishing Lifestyle.""

Throwing the manuscript away symbolized my willingness to BE the nourishing lifestyle and get on with the rest of my life. It represented a psychic death, an ending, that made way for a new beginning, the start of this book and my water initiation into the world of dolphins and whales. Jane's transformation out of the physical world coincided and in many ways facilitated my emotional transformation. Her dying helped me to free myself from the frozen past, to make choices that would lead me to follow my bliss, to embrace the unknown, to be the writer I'd known I was meant to be since I was young.

As the Huna group prepares to journey to the pyramids of Egypt, I look forward to learning to dive into the depths of the ocean and swim with cetaceans in the "dolphin man's" underwater pyramid, an undersea temple of transformation—to be 'born again' out of the Great Mother. Suffering, I learned is the pain of being separated from the Source—from the safe, life-giving umbilical cord of the mother—and having to face our fears while feeling helpless in an unknown realm of existence. The dolphins are acting as midwives to humankind as we give birth to our New Selves and the New Age. They are guiding us to dive deep into the areas in our psyche where our greatest fears of separation lurk so that we may embrace and integrate them and free their control over our behavior, our bodies, and our lives.

As Jim pointed out to me, 'consciousness' or 'God' cannot come to know itself until it separates from itself. We humans incarnate in physical form so that consciousness can expand its knowledge of itself. Expansion and contraction are the labor pains of the birth process that expel the baby from the womb, but as Athena said "birth is not meant to be painful." Neither is death. It's time, not only for a transformation of the birth process on the planet, but for a transformation of our views around death and the way in which we live our lives. Life, death and birth. They are all occasions to celebrate for they are all rites of passage in the soul's progress toward Enlightenment—-all part of a natural cycle of evolution that enables us to grow into higher consciousness.

I gave up trying to write the last chapter. There is no ending to this book, just a constant, continuous unfolding, one moment flowing into the next, doorways opening and closing, one story ending so that another may begin, one life dying so that another can be born. One wave in the ocean giving way to the next. The Old Age ending as the New Age begins. It's all a matter of tuning into the rhythm. What I learned from the dolphins, from the merry chase they've led me on for two years, is that when my heart is blown open, teachers and teaching experiences flood in, other dimensions of reality reveal themselves. Each time I allow myself to feel the pain in me and in the world more deeply, each time I let go of my resistance and take a flying leap into the unknown, I grow and expand, get more in touch with my fear of reaching out and reach out more. Each time I allow more of myself to be seen in the world, I get more of what I need and want, more love, more touching, more fun, more joy, more adventure, more freedom.

And what about the threatened polar shift and reclaiming ancient records you ask? Well, the mystery of it all is still unfolding. The dolphins call—maybe Joe and Rosie's call—grows louder. "Trust in the unknown. Believe in your own immortality. Surrender your fear. C'mon! Jump in! The water's fine!"

Bibliography

Beckley, Timothy Green *Kahuna Power* New Brunswick, N.J.: Inner Light 1987

Colli, Janet E., MA *The Healing Power of Dolphins* Common Ground of Puget Sound: Vol. IV, No. 1 Summer 1989

Campbell, Joseph w/ Moyers, Bill *The Power of Myth* New York:Doubleday, 1988

Dolphins San Francisco: Marine Mammal Research Fund 1980

Friends Service Committee *Taking Charge* Simple Living Collective

Cayce, Edgar *Edgar Cayce on Atlantis* New York: Warner Books 1968

Gibran, Kahlil *The Wisdom of Gibran edited by Joseph Sheban* New York: The Philosophical Society 1966

Grossinger, Richard *The Night Sky, The Science and Anthropology of the Stars and Planets* Los Angeles: Jeremy P. Tarcher, Inc. 1988

Hoffman, Enid *Huna, A Beginner's Guide.* Gloucester, Massachusetts: Para Research 1976

Holing, Dwight *Dolphin Defense* Discover: Oct. '88, Vol 9:68-72

Jung, Carl, et. al. *Man & His Symbols* New York: Dell Books 1964

Krishnamurti, Notes: Holland Star Camp 1939

Levine, Stephen *Healing Into Life and Death* Garden City, New York: Anchor Press/Doubleday 1987

Long, Max Freedom *The Huna Code in Religions* Marina Del Rey,California: Devorss & Company 1965

Marine Mammals Join The Navy Science: Dec. 16 '88 Vol. 242:1503-1504

Nayman, Jacqueline *Whales, Dolphins & Man* London: Hamlyn Publishing Group 1973

Nollman, Jim *Animal Dreaming* New York: Bantam Books 1987

Nollman, Jim *Interspecies Newsletter* Friday, Harbor Washington Summer 1988

Prophet, *Mark L. & Elizabeth Clare Saint Germain on Alchemy.* Summit University Press 1985

Reichenberg-Ullman, Dr. Judyth *Underwater Birthing* Spiritual Women's Times, Summer 1988 Seattle, Washington

Sannella, M.D. *The Kundalini Experience* Lower Lake, California: Integral Publishing 1987

Stark, Sherie *The Cetacean Mystery: Communicating with Higher Intelligences Here on Earth* UFO Magazine Vol. 2, No. 2 1987

Stewart, R. J. *The Prophetic Vision of Merlin.* London:Arkana,1986

Temple, Robert K. *The Sirius Mystery* Rochester, Vermont: Destiny Books 1976-87

Willis, Koko; Lee, Pali *Tales From the Night Rainbow* Honolulu: Night Rainbow Publishing 1984

Wyllie, Timothy Waterbirthing: *Where the New Masters Come In* Metapsychology Magazine Summer 1987 Volume 3, Number 2 New Zealand

Zambucka, Kristin *Ano Ano The Seed* Honolulu: Mana Publishing Co. 1978.

CALL OF THE DOLPHINS

AUTHOR
Lana Miller

& Jim Loomis, "The Dolphin Man"
Present techniques for -

- **Dolphin Dreaming**
- **Interspecies Communication**
- **Underwater Birthing**
- **Pod Consciousness**
- **Waterspace Ballet** ™

(A Key body-mind underwater integration system
that develops and refines human aquatic skills).

Lana Miller, a former owner of a wellness center and Jim Loomis,
a "nature boy" from Maui, Hawaii who has been skin diving with
wild dolphins for 40 years share their stories and
philosophy of graceful living.

" Follow your heart and live as free as the dolphins,"   they advise.

DATES, TIMES & LOCATIONS

Rainbow Publishing Company
P.O. Box 19730-616
Portland, Oregon 97219

Cetacean Relations Society
and
Rainbow Bridge Newsletter

Let's become "podners" in planetary evolution
by healing the past and surrendering to a "lighter" future
through more enlightened living in the present.

Lana Miller and Jim Loomis

invite you to liberate the dolphin spirit inside you
through a connection to "dolphin conscious" people and
cetaceans around the world.
Upcoming events and worldwide dolphin encounters
are featured in a quarterly newsletter.
Profits will be used to free captive
dolphins and humans and release them back into the "wild."

Annual Membership Fee: $25.00

Supporting Membership Fee: $50.00

Contributing Members: Whatever your heart tells you.

Send to: Rainbow Bridge Publishing
P.O. Box 19730-616
Portland, Oregon 97219

POSTER

FULL COLOR 24 x 30 LITHOGRAPH

$25.00   plus 2.50 Shipping

Send check or money order to:

Rainbow Publishing Company
P.O. Box 19730-616
Portland, Oregon 97219